Labor relations
for school leaders:

A practical guide to labor contracts, negotiations, strikes and grievances

 Richard W. Perhacs

ISBN 978-1-4675-6522-6

Published by the Pennsylvania School Boards Association

DEDICATION

This guide is dedicated to school superintendents...
the hardest working people I know.

Acknowledgments

This guide is the result of over 35 years of practicing law, most of it spent in the service of local government employers. It has been a long journey and many people have helped me along the way – far too many to mention by name. Still, a few stand out.

My partner and mentor, Richard Zamboldi, guided me through my early years and taught me so much about the practical side of labor relations. Without him I never would have made it. My partners Mark Wassell and Mark Kuhar have backed me up when I needed it and shared their insight when my clients' problems required collaboration. I am immensely proud of my association with both of them. And, of course, I am grateful to my firm, Knox McLaughlin Gornall and Sennett, for providing me with an environment in which I could reach my professional potential.

My secretary and assistant of many years, Sharon Byers, deserves special mention for the effort she put into this project. No lawyer could have better support. Without her, I would be lost.

I also am very grateful to those who graciously agreed to review the manuscript prior to publication and who offered both encouragement and constructive criticism. This helpful group included two of my firm's associates, Julia Herzing and Carsen Ruperto, as well as a number of school superintendents and board members whom I have the privilege of working with on a regular basis. It also included many other clients and professional acquaintances. Thanks to all of you.

A special word of gratitude also is due to Stuart Knade, Esq., Tom Templeton, Steve Robinson, Dave Davare, and the rest of the folks at the Pennsylvania School Boards Association both for supporting the work of professionals like me and for making the publication of this guide possible. I am especially grateful to Stuart for contributing the foreword and for his kind words.

Finally, and most importantly, I owe my family the greatest debt of all. It can't be easy having a husband and father who works dreadful hours, late into the night. In a real sense they share me with my clients, and they always do so with good humor and understanding. They have always appreciated the importance of the work that keeps me away from home so often, and they understand that my time away from them has been spent helping to keep schools working.

Richard W. Perhacs
Erie, Pennsylvania
January 2013

Foreword

It is a privilege for me to help introduce "Labor Relations for School Leaders," a guide that the education community has sorely needed for a long time. More than 40 years have passed since it became lawful for public school employees in Pennsylvania to unionize and collectively bargain, and much has been learned over those decades about the applicable law, procedures, players and practicalities involved. But until now, most of the accumulated wisdom about this crucial aspect of school system management has been stored only in the heads of the many veteran labor law practitioners representing public school systems across our state, who constantly must educate new school board members and administrators about the basics they need to understand and the pitfalls they must guard against. And since the faces on school boards and in the administration building tend to change fairly frequently, the need to educate our school leaders about these things never ends.

In this guide, one of Pennsylvania's most experienced labor attorneys gives us benefit of his more than 35 years of labor law experience, packed into an enjoyable and easy-to-read crash course on the essentials, filled with practical observations and plain English explanations. In devoting the time necessary to get this all down on paper despite his incredibly busy law practice, Rich Perhacs has done a great service for all of us involved in public education management. I have no doubt the result soon will become required reading for school administrators and school directors, substantially shortening the labor relations learning curve and strengthening our school leadership.

Stuart L. Knade Esq.
Chief Counsel
Pennsylvania School Boards Association

TABLE OF CONTENTS

Introduction xi

Chapter One: The Labor Relations Environment And Its Participants 1

    The Adversarial Nature of the Labor Relations Environment 1

    Union Representatives 5

    Board Members 6

    Labor Counsel 7

    Superintendents 10

    Bargaining Units and Organizational Activity 10

Chapter Two: The Statutory Framework 13

    Act 88 and Act 195 13

    Unfair Practices Defined 15

    Procedure 17

    Remedies 18

    Deferral 19

Chapter Three: The Negotiations Process 21

    Preparing for Negotiations 21

    Ground Rules for Negotiations 23

    Common Errors of District Negotiators 24

    Going Public 28

    Increments, Jumps and Bumps 30

    Binding Arbitration of Contract Terms 33

    Can We Learn Anything from the Private Sector? 35

    "We Just Want What All the Other Teachers Have" 36

    Changing Arbitration Outcomes Through Negotiations 37

    The Consequences of Unsuccessful Proposals 38

    Ethics Issues and the Negotiating Team 38

    Negotiation and Past Practice 39

    The Union's Back Room Committee 40

    Fact Finding and Non-Binding Arbitration 40

    "Early Bird" Negotiations 42

Final Offers and Union Committee Recommendations 43

Retroactivity, Contract Extensions and the Status Quo 45

Tentative Agreements and Documentation 46

Ratification Votes 47

Mediators 48

Mandatory v. Permissive Subjects of Bargaining; Impact Bargaining 50

Negotiating Subcontracting and Unilaterally Implementing Proposals 52

The Siege 57

Communicating Directly with Employees 57

Union Information Requests 58

Act 93 Plans 59

Concessionary Bargaining 61

Leverage 61

"Meet and Discuss" 62

Chapter Four: Specific Contract Terms **63**

Union Security Clauses 63

Recognition Clauses 65

Insurance 65

Early Retirement Incentives 67

Probation and Trial Periods 69

Employee Evaluation Clauses 70

Seniority Clauses 73

Transfers 74

Sick Leave Provisions 74

Workers' Compensation Provider Panels 76

"For the Life of this Contract" 76

Statutory Savings Clauses 77

Safe Conditions Clauses 78

Discipline Clauses 78

Maintenance of Standards/Past Practice and Zipper Clauses 79

Miscellaneous Monetary Provisions 81

Criticism of Employees, Disciplinary Records, and Disciplinary Meetings 82

Anti-Discrimination Clauses 84

Class Size, Reduction in Force and Related Subjects 85

Merit Pay and Two Tiered Systems 85

Subcontracting Clauses 87

Grievance and Arbitration Procedures 87

Management Rights Clauses 89

Reopener and Cost of Living Provisions 90

Released Time and Leave for Union Business 91
Leaves of Absence 91
Drug Testing 92
No Strike – No Lockout Clauses 93
Long-Term Substitutes... 94
Automatic Renewal Clauses 95
Union Access to School Facilities and Programs 95

Chapter Five: Strikes **97**
Negotiating in the Context of a Strike 97
Setting the School Calendar 98
Managing a Strike – Operational Concerns 99
Considerations for Board Members 104
Sports and Activities During a Strike.. 105

Chapter Six: Grievances and Arbitration... **107**
The Nature of Grievances and Arbitration 107
Grievance Processing 110
Winning Arbitration Cases 113
Selecting Cases 113
Selecting Your Arbitrator.. 114
Preparation 116
Before the Hearing.. 116
At the Hearing 118
After the Hearing.. 118

A Final Note **121**

Appendices **123**
Glossary of Common School Labor Relations Terms 123
Relevant State Ethics Commission Decisions 129
Superintendent Interview Questions.. 142
BEC 15-1504 (Act 80 Days).. 143
BEC 15-1502 (School Holidays)... 147
Strike Action Checklist... 148
Act 88 150
Public Employee Relations Act... 158

x

INTRODUCTION

This is intended to be a practical book. That's why I prefer to call it a "guide." It is written for school board members, superintendents, administrators, school solicitors, and community members who want to learn something of school labor relations from the practical perspective. It was written by a management advocate, and this bias will be apparent as you read on. Despite this, I have approached this project as I have tried to approach my practice, with an eye toward being realistic and self-critical. My objective was to share my practice experience with those responsible for managing school labor relations in a manner that is both thought provoking and helpful.

I have necessarily drawn on personal experiences, but I fully realize that my way of seeing things and doing things is certainly not the only way, and, in some situations, may not be the right way, or the best way. I'm only sharing with the reader my perceptions, what worked for me, and what I've learned.

I have not written a book specifically for lawyers, and I have attempted to limit, to the extent possible, extended discussion of legal concepts. The practice of labor relations, however, has a heavy legal component, and labor-management relations are heavily regulated activities. Thus, some discussion of the law is unavoidable. I suspect that a general solicitor with no real experience in the labor relations field will find some benefit in what I have done here.

Two caveats regarding the law are necessary. First, the law changes from time to time. To the extent that legal principles are discussed, or are assumed as a basis for the discussion of a particular subject, those principles are subject to change after publication. Second, reliance on this guide is not a substitute for the personal counsel of an attorney experienced in the field of labor relations. Good legal advice is by its nature highly dependent on consideration of the specifics of your situation. Further, it often involves a professional judgment, and not the rendering of a clear answer. In short, I am not advising you professionally through this guide. Rather, I am trying to help you better understand how to deal with the unique challenges that unions can pose for public school systems so that you can work effectively with your professional helpers.

For the same reasons, not all labor relations attorneys necessarily share all the views I express about various matters. That does not mean they are wrong. Rather, there may be more than one way to approach these things, and every lawyer develops preferences based on their experiences and what has worked well for them in the past.

The first chapter sets the labor relations stage by explaining both the context of labor relations and the nature of its participants.

The second chapter outlines the basic provisions of the two statutes – Act 88 and Act 195 – that provide the legal basis for all labor relations activities. It also deals with unfair labor practices and presents a general overview of what they are, how charges are processed, what types of remedies can be imposed upon employers, and how unfair practice charges relate to grievances and contracts.

The negotiation of collective bargaining agreements is really at the heart of labor relations and the third chapter is devoted to a discussion of various aspects of that process. My rough guide for selecting topics has been my experience in explaining to my clients different aspects of the process that they needed to understand to be able to serve in their roles as board members or superintendents. These are the subjects that I most often find myself explaining to the people with whom I work.

The fourth chapter deals with a variety of subjects that are often addressed within the agreements that negotiations produce. The treatment is by no means exhaustive, but, once again, I have selected the topics on the basis of experience. These are the subjects that are either typically addressed in contracts, and/or which I have found frequently to cause problems or misunderstandings.

The fifth chapter of this guide deals with strikes, which, unfortunately, remain with us as a possibility and an occasional reality. Although not as common as they once were, it is important to know how they relate to the negotiation process and what challenges they present from a management and operational perspective when they do occur.

The sixth chapter deals with handling grievances and arbitration proceedings, which are, after all, a direct outgrowth of both the negotiation process and the content of the resulting agreements. In a real sense, arbitration decisions become a part of your agreement with a union, and you will have a strong interest in obtaining appropriate outcomes when arbitration becomes necessary.

Many of the topics in these chapters could have been dealt with far more extensively, but I have tried to keep this work readable and, therefore, useful. I tried to keep in mind that the ultimate objective was to provide useful, practical, "street level" information. Reading this guide, of course, is not a substitute for real world experience, or for having ready access to a competent, experienced advisor.

The final section consists of appendices which I hope you find useful. It includes a glossary of commonly used labor relations terms, several checklists, and full reproductions of some of the important authorities mentioned in the text.

One important aspect of labor relations practice was beyond the scope of this work, but should be mentioned. Over the years, arbitrators have developed a more or less consistent set of informal but generally accepted rules regarding how labor contracts are interpreted. Some of those rules are borrowed from common law legal principles and others are unique to the world of labor contracts. Laymen do not need to have a detailed knowledge of them, but some rudimentary exposure would result in a deeper understanding of some of the issues a district might face, and a better appreciation of why some contract language is written as it is (or ought to be written differently). That is perhaps a topic for a later work.

One note about style is in order. Throughout this work I have used masculine pronouns solely out of convenience and convention. As a matter of style, I've never been a fan of the use of "he/she" and I ask the reader for indulgence on this point. The reader can be assured that no one appreciates the role women play in managing public education more than I do.

Finally, a note to my friends on the other side. I'm sure that more than a few union reps and local teacher union officers will eventually read the pages that follow. Actually, I'll be flattered if they do. I've always believed that anyone who operates in an adversarial environment ought to know as much as possible about the other side. This is particularly true in labor relations, where understanding the other party's needs, wants, priorities, and values is essential to doing a good job. Although I'm sure it often didn't seem so to the union negotiators sitting across the table from me, I've always tried to see things from the other side's point of view. Not because my instincts are any more fair than those of the next person. After all, I've had a job to do. Rather, I engaged in this exercise precisely *because* I wanted to do that job well. To understand what is truly important and what is not, and what is achievable and what is not, it is imperative that you take a look at things from the other side's perspective from time to time. This is hard for ideologues to do, and it is one reason why they often make poor labor negotiators. But being firmly committed to goals, even to the point of allowing serious conflict to develop, is not inconsistent with flexibility and open mindedness. Those qualities will help you to understand what you're really asking others to accept, and will put you in a better position to get the best deal you can. A labor negotiator cannot function effectively without a clear understanding of what his counterpart is trying to accomplish, or to protect against.

There are many good people working on behalf of educational unions, and I respect their role in the process. I've learned a great deal from them over the years. Perhaps they will learn something from me.

The Labor Relations Environment And Its Participants

The Adversarial Nature of the Labor Relations Environment

Labor management relations are inherently adversarial. Even in the best of relationships between employers and unions, this is true. There is sometimes common ground, and there are many situations where the people involved trust and respect one another. There are many relationships where reasonable compromise on issues occurs on a regular basis. Nonetheless, even in these relationships, labor and management have fundamentally different interests, and that hard reality inevitably leads to disagreement and conflict on some level. For a management official to believe otherwise is naive and, potentially, threatening to the interests of the district, its students, and taxpayers.

It can be tempting to oversimplify things by assuming that the job of public school systems and the job of unionized public school employees are really the same, i.e., the education of children. A more accurate and complete description, however, would recognize that the purpose of a school system is to educate a community's children at the least possible expense consistent with whatever standards are adopted for that education. It is not the purpose of the school system to provide jobs, or to provide any particular level of benefits to those it employs. Employment, and the pay and benefits received by those it employs, are only provided as a means to an end. If, magically, an acceptable educational program could be run without employees, it would be. By contrast, while individual educators certainly have as their job the same purpose served by the larger school system they are a part of, when they act *collectively* they act primarily in their own self-interest which will, of course, include maximizing the number of dues payers to support the union's organization, and maximizing the pay and benefits they receive. In these circumstances, tension and some degree of conflict is unavoidable.

While the adversarial nature of labor relations in education is truly unfortunate, it is the inevitable result of the way the legislature structured the law when collective bargaining rights were granted to public employee unions in 1970. The legal framework adopted at that time was largely patterned after the federal National Labor Relations Act which governs such matters in the private sector. The entire philosophical framework is based upon the concept of regulating and managing conflict between contending interests. Such conflict, of course, has long been part of the private sector experience. It's not the system I would have chosen to impose on public schools, and it is not the one adopted in other states, but it's the one that's been given to us.

Given this reality, it is essential to understand the nature of the adversary if you are going to deal effectively with it.

The president of the New York Federation of Teachers was once asked why his organization was taking a certain position which the questioner thought was clearly not in the best interest of students. His response was telling: "When school children start paying union dues, that's when I'll start representing school children."[1] The reality is that whatever the rhetoric the union puts out for public consumption (and for its members' consumption, as well), a union exists for one basic reason and one reason only – to serve the members and to advance their interests as the union perceives those interests. Those interests may, or may not, coincide with what is good for students or other stakeholders in the educational system. In fact, they often don't. But it doesn't matter. Charles Wilson, CEO of General Motors in the 1950's once said, "What's good for GM is good for the country," and this is sometimes the approach taken by education unions. What's good for their members is, in a conveniently self-serving way, always good for education and, therefore, children. A lot of employees really believe this, after having heard it so often, but anyone objective who has worked in unionized education for very long quickly comes to understand that this isn't the reality.

It is not difficult to catalog *how* the union sees its members' interests. What it favors is pretty transparent. First and foremost, it wants to get its members as much in the way of salary and benefits as possible. Period. Since you can't move the district to Mexico to escape labor costs, can't educate your students through contractors, and, for all practical purposes, can't go bankrupt, you're not like a private company, where a union can literally put itself out of business by pricing itself out of the labor market. Indeed, one of the education unions' major reasons for fighting so hard to prevent educational vouchers from becoming a reality is the fear that an alternative to their members' labor would inevitably force them to curb their appetite.

Apart from money in its various forms, unions also are passionately committed to a workplace culture where seniority/length of service is the basis for as many otherwise discretionary decisions as possible. The union is convinced that seniority is a "fair" way to decide things like who works where, who is awarded a vacancy, who is laid off first, and the like. More importantly, whether it is "fair" or not, using seniority to make decisions eliminates management discretion, which is something that unions and their members think lends itself to abuse for any one of a multitude of inappropriate reasons (favoritism, politics, retaliation, or because an administrator just doesn't make good decisions). No doubt allowing employers to promote and furlough whoever they want *would* lead to some bad decisions, but so do systems that require employers to promote or retain the most senior employee, as any employer whose contract requires it can attest.

---

[1] This quote is attributed to Albert Shanker, President of the New York Federation of Teachers and the American Federation of Teachers. Although there is some doubt about whether it is accurate, the quote was attributed to him in a news article in 1985. The Albert Shanker Institute, a pro-union advocacy organization that exists to honor him, believes the quote is fiction. The quote is embarrassingly callous, so it's not difficult to see why an institute named in his honor would be uncomfortable with it.

Unions also believe that it ought to be pretty difficult for a district to discipline or dismiss an employee. They advocate both a difficult standard for dismissal and a plethora of procedural protections. Institutionally, they usually refuse to make any judgment regarding whether a particular employee truly deserves what has been done to him. That is not their job. In their eyes, their job is to make sure you do yours, and that is viewed as in their members' interests. Since unions are run by human beings, there certainly are times when, on a personal level, the union leadership agrees that so-and-so ought to be fired, or has no case. What you can expect to hear, however, is that "we have to represent him" because the union has a legal duty to do so, and, by the way, if we don't, he'll sue us. In reality, the real risk of liability for a union is relatively small. But unions believe the risk exists, and they don't want to deal with even the remote possibility.

When unions make statements like that, they are referring to a legal principle called the "duty of fair representation," sometimes referred to as DFR for short. Somewhat oversimplified, this duty exposes a union to liability if it fails to advocate for a member because of bad faith.[2] The duty is not absolute, nor is liability imposed for mere negligence by the union. There has to be proof of bad faith or arbitrariness by the union in its decision not to press a grievance. This is a very difficult standard to meet. Indeed, unions have been found not to have violated the duty when they failed to press a grievance to arbitration simply because the cost was out of proportion to the amount involved, even when the employee was right. It is rare for a union to be found liable in DFR actions. Still, you hear it all the time as an explanation for otherwise difficult to understand positions. Unions are extremely averse to any risk of liability.

The above are only three examples of the inherent characteristics of your union which make it inevitable that your district's relationship with its union will be adversarial at various times and at various levels. There are many others. By pointing this out, it is not my purpose to incite conflict or belligerency. It is my purpose to keep you from being naive and, therefore, vulnerable.

To deal with unions intelligently, there are several other things about them you must know.

Unions are very conservative institutions. Not in the political sense, but in the cultural sense. They seem to resist workplace change almost reflexively. Innovation and risk-taking are not their cup of tea. Unions prefer things to be run just the way they always have been. It's one of the things about unions that so frustrates dynamic educational leaders. If you took the same approach to running your district, it couldn't function.

Many of them also tend to be top-down, authoritarian institutions. Unions pride themselves on being democratic, and, indeed, they do elect their leaders and vote on contract ratifications. But they fall prey to what the great political philosopher Robert Michels called the "Iron Law of Oligarchy." Michels believed that true democracy was impossible because in any group it is inevitable that a small sub-group will aggregate power and control, either by default or design. "Democracy" only

---

[2] *See Kissell v. Dep't of Corr.,* 1999 Pa. Commw. LEXIS 461, *41 (Pa. Commw. Ct. 1999); *Martino v. Transp. Workers' Union, Local 234,* 480 A.2d 242, 244 (Pa. 1984).

means that the leaders can periodically be replaced with others, who will then behave in the same way. Unions are a classic example of Michels' observation.

Everyone gets to vote on the contract, but what if an employee voted to accept it and was in the minority? How would it go if he decided to cross a picket line and come to work after the union struck over an offer he thought it should have taken? Not very well. Democracy has its limits.

Controlling the flow of information is another way oligarchs run things. In order to keep control of negotiations (a necessary thing, actually), unions often keep their members in the dark about the details of negotiations, including perhaps even what the union itself is asking for. More significantly, the union leadership usually has control over when, or whether, the membership gets to vote on a contract offer. And stories of union leaders manipulating ratification meetings one way or another are legion.

In my college days I was a proud member of a local chapter of the United Steelworkers of America one summer when I worked at U. S. Steel's Homestead Works. The contract was up that summer and I desperately needed to make as much money as I could before I returned to school in the fall. A July steel strike was not a good thing from my point of view. My view that the guys would be nuts to reject the company's offer was pretty well known on the shop floor because we'd all been talking about the possibility of a strike.

I went to the ratification meeting after my shift intending to vote for the contract, and before the meeting my local steward, who was a big burly guy, put his arm around me, squeezed harder than I thought was accidental, and asked whether I was really going to vote for such a bad deal for the guys. The meeting itself was a travesty, with one of the union officials "presenting" the offer in terms that were clearly intended to get it rejected. And it was. Needless to say, I kept my mouth shut, and the news reported that somehow the local had "unanimously" rejected the contract by voice vote. At the time the local had close to 7,000 members, as I recall. Democracy has its limits.

There is yet another perspective on labor-management conflict that I wonder about.

People just don't like change. They resist it. They are creatures of habit, tending to do things in the same way, and to view things the same way, until they see a compelling reason to behave otherwise, or are forced to do so. These human tendencies may have something to do with the behavior of unions and other institutions which, after all, are made up of people. If you take people out of their comfort zone, resistance, and therefore, conflict, often results. Those with the responsibility for educational or fiscal leadership, on the other hand, *have* to be open to change and ready to advocate for it. They are constantly being pressured by a variety of sources to "change" and to "improve" the system, by the state, by parents, by society at large or, by their own sense of purpose. Improvement, or the correction of problems, compels change. The conflict between labor and management is thus inevitable.

Union Representatives

Union representatives come in all shapes and sizes. Some are effective leaders and some are not. Some are honorable, honest people and some not so much. They have a job to do, just as you do, and to the extent that you can maintain mutual respect, yours will probably be easier to do.

Don't lose sight of where the professional union representative came from and how he got his job in the first place. He was a school employee at some point, and almost certainly served as a local union officer as well. He probably sought his current position, at least in part, because of a deep, philosophical commitment to what he sees as the union's positive role in both society generally and education in particular. His values and perceptions are probably different from yours in significant ways.

In what I realize is a gross over-simplification, I offer the following exercise in caricature.

1. The Facilitator

This person wants to get a settlement and will do his best to make a deal, as long as it is not out of balance in favor of the other side and is negotiated with dignity. His operative philosophy is the deal is OK if it is OK with the local. And if the local is being unreasonable in resisting it, he is willing to get in the local leaders' faces up to a point to convince them otherwise. He is not looking for trouble, and will often take an "average" settlement. Don't mistake the absence of belligerence for weakness, though. The facilitator can be very shrewd and very effective, and just because he's not pounding the table doesn't mean he can be pushed around.

2. The Committee Chairman

This person is usually not much help. He exerts little leadership and won't try to talk the local leadership into or out of anything. He views his role as discussion leader, and simply goes with the consensus and tries to keep the union from making mistakes. He often advises extreme caution and thus gets in the way. He abdicates his role as professional leader to the local and may allow things to devolve into "amateur night." Unrealistic union demands are not deterred and reasonable management proposals get no audience. Things tend to take forever to get resolved. He can stumble into a strike that needn't have happened and which he cannot manage.

3. The Antagonist

This person can be a real problem. He has his own agenda, which may be purely personal, or which may take the form of a fight-to-the-death attitude in advocating the parent union's interests and pet issues. If your contract does not provide for agency shop it will be a big deal to him, even though the local has lived without it for decades and only a handful of employees have not joined. He'll fight for the union's right to pick who your vendor is for tax-deferred investments, because he has been told to do so by his superiors because of an arrangement the "preferred vendor" has with the parent union. Never mind that it's not a big issue for the local. He'll try to prevent your local from accepting a settlement that "breaks the pattern" because he's worried about other districts in the region and does not want those employers to press for the same deal when their contracts come up. In his heart, he questions whether management even has a legitimate right to make proposals to change the contract. He's a zealot. You get the picture.

There is a fourth category, but it doesn't really represent a distinct style of leadership. Still, it is worth noting. If you have developed a good personal relationship with a union leader you may find that he is capable of speaking to you candidly about the current issues, without having to always spout the union "party line." Working with such a person can be both pleasant and rewarding. Some reps just can't drop the ideological "union position is always right" rhetoric. Talking to them is like reading a press release. It can be downright tedious. I much prefer, and enjoy, working with people who, while they have an advocate's job to do, can laugh at their own side of the table and its problems, and acknowledge that sometimes *you* have a point, too. Of course, that works both ways.

No one fits neatly into *any* of these profiles, and I have indulged in caricatures in describing them. Often you can see something of each in a given individual at given times, or the person you are dealing with may not resemble any of them. The important thing is to be aware that all union leaders are not the same, and the course of your labor relations, and particularly negotiations, can be heavily influenced by the tendencies of those participating. Apart from tendencies, union leaders are human beings who have their good days and bad days and moods and all of the same things to deal with in their personal lives that you do.

Board Members

Management will have a chief spokesman and leaders in negotiations, too. Some of the same characteristics noted above will inevitably appear on the district side of the table. Often the direction of negotiations is determined not by a single person but by two or more. On the union side, the dynamic is often dictated by the staff rep and the local president or other strong leader among the local union group. On the board side, it may be the professional negotiator and the board president or other prominent board member who has responsibility for negotiations. Together this handful of people often sets the tone, and perhaps the objectives as well.

Most of the board members on negotiating teams take their roles very seriously and serve conscientiously. They try to maintain a balanced, reasonable point of view and do their best to make decisions that will be supported by at least a majority of the full board. If there is one systemic weakness among the board members serving in this role it is probably the lack of experience in negotiations that results from either board turnover or the fact that many board members either cannot devote the time negotiations can take or choose not to.

When board members become problematic members of a negotiating team, I've found they often fall into one of two categories. Once again, I indulge in caricature and over-generalization.

1. The Appeaser

The first is what I call the "appeaser." This person wants peace, and is primarily interested in just getting things over with. Obviously, he will be very flexible and accommodating to the union. If the union side does not have an aggressive disposition, things usually work out fairly easily and "average" contracts result with little conflict. If the union is aggressive, the district loses if this person is influential. This person is well-intentioned and will place a high priority on "cooperating" with the union. He tends to be naïve. He can be dangerous in the long term because of a willingness to compromise on key principles, and he is more likely to act independent of a professional advisor.

2. The Crusader

The second type is the "crusader." This person, often new to the board, or newly in the majority, wants to take a different, stronger approach to dealing with the union than has been taken in the past. Often he reflects a type of "taxpayer revolt" or movement in the community against what is perceived as overly generous spending. The negotiating team will take very strong positions under his leadership and conflict is likely. Unreasonable positions (in terms of what is achievable in a practical sense) may be maintained beyond the point that makes sense. This type of board member can miss opportunities because of a lack of flexibility.

Often the outcome of negotiations from the district's point of view ultimately depends on how much hassle, pain and conflict a board is willing to, or can, endure to achieve its objectives. Stated another way, it depends on the character of board members. Some surprising outcomes are possible, not because of skilled negotiators, but because boards and superintendents had the will to persevere in the face of years of negotiating, strikes, political risk and personal stress and discomfort. The objective was that important to them. For others, it would not have been. Ultimately, negotiating policy is just that...policy. And it's the job of the elected school board to decide what that policy is.

Labor Counsel

At the risk of sounding self-serving, let me emphatically state that managing your district's labor relations well requires that the district establish and maintain an on-going relationship with a competent attorney whose practice is concentrated in the area of labor and employment law. Not all school solicitors are sufficiently equipped to handle this role. Labor law is a highly technical, specialized field, in addition to being one where experience counts for a lot.

Clarification of terminology is in order. There is a difference between labor law and employment law, and in terms of whether your counsel is appropriate, the distinction is significant. Skill and experience in one area is not the same as skill and experience in the other. Fortunately, many practitioners who work in this area deal with both types of issues.

Labor law is the body of law that regulates relationships between unions and employers, and between unions and employees. It includes collective bargaining, arbitration, certification and modification of union bargaining units, and unfair labor practices. Employment law is the body of law that regulates employers whether or not there is a union in the picture. However, whether or not there is a union can affect how some aspects of employment law are handled, especially in procedural ways. Employment law includes many subjects, including, most prominently, employment discrimination claims, Family and Medical Leave Act (FMLA) issues, Americans with Disabilities Act (ADA) issues, wage-hour concerns, unemployment compensation issues, regulation of hiring practices, and compliance with the many employment related provisions of the Public School Code (Code). Ideally your lawyer should be knowledgeable in both fields.

In selecting a labor counsel, great weight should be placed on the candidate's track record. By that I do not mean his "won/lost percentage." I mean whether he successfully already performs the role in a number of other districts. As in most specialized fields of endeavor, experience is important. Has the candidate ever negotiated a labor contract? How many? For whom? Is his labor experience in the *public* sector, particularly, representing school districts? Has he ever handled an arbitration case? How many? What subject matter? You should ask for client references from other districts and talk to them about their experience with the candidate.

Has the candidate handled cases at the Equal Employment Opportunity Commission (EEOC) or the Human Relations Commission? Has he ever litigated an unfair practice case before the Pennsylvania Labor Relations Board? Does he have any experience presenting in-service training to supervisors on personnel-related legal issues, such as professional employee evaluations? Has he handled contested unemployment compensation claims?

You may want to inquire about whether the candidate currently represents any unions, and whether he has represented individual employees in disputes with their employers or former employers. You should not automatically disqualify a candidate because of such experience, but it should prompt you to inquire further. Very few practitioners work "both sides of the street" in the labor field. This is as true of "union" lawyers as it is of "management" lawyers. This phenomena probably reflects the fact that parties to labor issues tend to be invested emotionally in the dispute. Consequently, they don't completely trust a lawyer who does not appear to be philosophically committed to their point of view. I've never represented a union in a labor-management issue and have declined several opportunities to do so. My reasons were entirely personal, as by disposition, I am a management advocate and genuinely admire and respect the people who bear the responsibility for the ultimate success of the organizations they run. The stresses they endure and the obstacles they face are significant, and assisting them is personally rewarding. Conversely, I find some of the behaviors of unions to be distasteful. Such preference for one side or the other is common among both the "management bar" and the "labor bar."

Fees must be considered, although any school board that hires a legal counsel for any complex matter on the basis of hourly rates or cost alone is being foolish. You get what you pay for, usually. Most labor counsel are engaged on an hourly basis, and it is important to remember that the important cost consideration is not how high the hourly rate is, but how much the total bill is. There are two components to the bill – the rate and the number of hours charged. The second component is basically a matter of trust. A school director generally has no way of knowing how long it took to write a brief, or complete a research project. Nor does he know how long it *should* have taken an experienced lawyer to perform these tasks, or whether the research was even necessary. One of the best ways to gauge how much things are likely to cost is to ask the lawyer's client references how much the bills have been over the years, or for particular projects, and whether they are generally satisfied that he was worth what he cost. Ultimately, what matters is not what the work cost, but whether it was *worth* the cost.

Keep in mind that large, time-consuming projects, such as the negotiation of a contract, can be impossible to predict, or to control. The cost of such projects also can vary considerably from district to district, and project to project. Contracts can be negotiated in two meetings in a span of weeks, or in 50 meetings, over three years.

Unions certainly know the value of competent representation. Consider that in a hypothetical school district with 150 unionized teachers and 75 unionized support staff, the union (or unions) representing those workers charge the employees collectively somewhere around $115,000 *each year* for representation. Some of that goes for lobbying, political activity and other support not directly related to dealing directly with the district, but a good deal of it *does* provide direct representation, such as it is. Over the course of a three-year contract, employees in the district will pay around $350,000 in dues and fees to the union. How much did the district spend during that same three years for equivalent service? Unless it is a very unusual district, the fees paid to labor counsel (or the solicitor if he handles labor matters) and to the PSBA (for lobbying and technical support) won't even come close to what the employees pay for similar services.

Finally, there is an intangible quality of your counsel that you should at least be aware of. Many lawyers practice very defensively and place a priority on preventing their clients (and thus themselves) from being exposed to risk. Others, while recognizing the need to alert clients to risk, view themselves more as enablers whose job is to find ways to accomplish objectives at an acceptable level of risk. Lawyers can be very effective at giving clients reasons why they can't, or shouldn't, do things. However, whether to accept risk, and how much to accept, is ultimately your decision, not your lawyer's, and you may not always be well served by a lawyer who effectively makes those decisions for you. Ask your potential counsel what his view is of this subject, and how he views his primary role.

Superintendents

As the CEOs of our school districts, superintendents are central to all important aspects of labor relations and personnel administration, including negotiations. When a district chooses a superintendent, those screening the applicants should address this topic in a very direct manner. In the Appendix, you will find a short outline of questions you would be well advised to address to candidates so that you might gauge the applicant's experience and/or attitude toward this area of district operations.

Superintendents are in a tough spot. They are the educational leaders of the district's professional staff, and, in that role, they must command the respect and, at times, the loyalty of the staff. At the same time, they are responsible for budgets, disciplinary issues, and a host of other matters that can place them at odds with the staff, or significant portions of it. It is a tough job, and superintendents should be protected as much as possible.

One of the hallmarks of a good superintendent is the skillful use of advisors and helpers. One of the key survival skills of superintendents is to know when to pick up the phone, who to call, and about what. Do that well and your odds of success increase exponentially. Try to do it all yourself, and you do it at your peril.

A surprising number of school superintendents do not appreciate the distinction between a general solicitor and a specialized labor counsel. Even in a large firm such as mine, I find myself getting questions about student privacy issues or expulsions. Our general solicitors get questions about employment policies or disciplinary decisions. We can sort these things out internally in cases where we provide both types of service to the client, but I get concerned about labor clients who use a lawyer outside of our firm for general work, as many of my clients do. I wonder what inquiries are misdirected that I don't know about. Someone operating at the executive level as a school superintendent in 21st-century Pennsylvania ought to be pretty savvy about which type of specialized lawyer he needs to talk to about a particular type of problem. Surprisingly, many aren't.

Bargaining Units and Organizational Activity

One of the functions of the Pennsylvania Labor Relations Board is to oversee the process by which local unions are formed. Before an employer is obligated to recognize and bargain with an employee representative, that representative must be "certified" by the PLRB which literally involves the issuance of a certificate bringing the union into legal existence. A union can obtain a certification in two ways. An employer can acquiesce in the creation of the union and participate in a joint request for certification. This represents an agreement by an employer to have a union represent its employees. Almost unheard of in the private sector, it has happened fairly frequently with governmental employers which, for political reasons, may be reluctant to be seen as opposing unionization of their employees. The second method of obtaining certification is to win a secret ballot representation election.

If a union can obtain the written support of 30% of the employees in an "appropriate" bargaining unit, usually evidenced by signatures on cards, it can petition the PLRB to conduct a secret ballot election. If a majority of the employees voting in that election select the union as their representative, a certification will be issued. There is usually a hiatus between the petition and the election of anywhere from four to eight weeks, during which an employer may lawfully campaign against the union and urge employees to vote "no" through letters and presentations. Contrary to what many believe, employer opposition happens all of the time and there are still many school support employees in the state who are not represented by a union. There are fairly rigid rules regarding what an employer may say during such a campaign, but certainly it is not unlawful to point out things like the cost of union dues; the coercive tactics that are sometimes employed to force employees to participate in strike activities; the loss of an employee's ability to speak for himself regarding terms and conditions of employment; the likely loss of the opportunity to have merit recognized as a factor in pay; and many other valid considerations. Generally speaking, an employer may not threaten employees with adverse consequences if the union is successful, or offer to redress complaints or give rewards if employees vote the union down. An employer also is not permitted to interrogate employees about how they feel about the union, or how they intend to vote, or to conduct any type of surveillance of union meetings or other organizational activities. In reality, there have been quite a few opposed union organizational campaigns and many school employers have been successful in resisting the unionization of support staff groups.

Certainly the best way to avoid unionization if your district has unorganized employees is to be careful not to give the employees a good reason to seek representation in the first place. Viewed another way, don't give the union a situation to exploit. School boards who treat their employees unfairly, or who fail to offer their unorganized employees competitive wages and benefits, are simply inviting employees to seek the assistance of a union. Employees who know that they are treated as well as they would be if they had a union simply have no reason to pay hundreds of after-tax dollars per year in dues for assistance they may not feel they need. Good performing, well-behaved employees generally do not come to work fearing that they will be unjustly discharged and feel little need for "protection," which is one of things that unions try to sell to them during organizational campaigns. Competitive wages and benefits without the cost of union dues, fair treatment and good human resource management are the cornerstones of a sound union avoidance policy, just as they are in the private sector. These things take time, energy and resources, but they are well worth the investment they represent.

As noted above, in order to be certified, the union must seek to represent employees in an "appropriate" bargaining unit. Appropriateness depends on whether the employees share a "community of interest" in the terms and conditions of their employment such that it makes sense for them to bargain together as a group. The Board does not mix professionals and non-professionals, but beyond that basic distinction, the clear policy of the PLRB is to favor combining as many types of diverse employees as possible into large units. The Board tends to be very quick to find a community of interest and this creates significant problems with many support groups. It is not at all uncommon to see a "wall to wall" unit of school support staff that includes part-time cafeteria workers, nine-month secretaries and twelve-month, full-time skilled maintenance workers, these groups having very little in common. There can be a lot of politics involved in bargaining, and it is all too common to find one sub group of employees holding an inordinate amount of power at the bargaining table. Since one of the objectives being sought by union organizers is the capture of as much dues money as possible, unions engaged aggressively in organizational activity tend to favor broad, all inclusive types of units without regard to the practical problems that may exist in bargaining for such a group.

Whatever the scope of the unit, it is in the district's interest to insist that the unit description that will go into the certification be drawn with as much precision as possible. During the PLRB certification process, it is usually possible to insure that the description clearly delineates who is in and who is out, and care should be taken to do so for obvious reasons. Certain broad categories of employees will always be excluded, such as confidential employees, guards or security employees, and supervisory employees.

Certifications are not forever. Although complete decertification is quite rare in the public sector, there is a process available to consider or reconsider specific positions and to redefine the unit, either because positions were included but may have evolved into something else, or because they were created after the certification was issued. This process is called "unit clarification" or "UC" for short. A typical example is a secretarial position that was included in the unit but which has evolved into a legitimately confidential position.[3] An employer may seek to have such a person specifically declared out of the bargaining unit. UC petitions, which, like ULPs, involve a hearing before a hearing examiner, involve a claim by either an employer or a union that a position that is in a unit should be taken out, or, that a position that is being treated as outside of a unit should be included. UC petitions, from both sides, are fairly common, and reflect the fact that workforces are dynamic.

---

[3] "Confidentiality" is a much misunderstood term when it is used in connection with union bargaining units. In order to be excluded as "confidential," a support employee must be involved in some meaningful way with those responsible for the employer's labor relations activities. Mere access to information that may be personal, such as payroll on health information, is clearly not sufficient.

The Statutory Framework

Act 88 and Act 195

The Public Employee Relations Act, colloquially known as either the PERA or Act 195, was passed in 1970 and establishes the basic framework for labor relations in Pennsylvania between public employers and unions representing public employees.[4] It was patterned after the National Labor Relations Act, the federal law which has governed labor relations in the private sector since the 1930's. Act 195 contains procedures for the certification or creation of union bargaining units, the placement of employees in, or their exclusion from, those units, and a host of other topics. It defines a type of unlawful behavior called unfair practices (no, an unfair labor practice is not anything that is unfair…it is a specific type of unlawful act, defined in the Act). One of the chief functions of Act 195 was the regulation of the negotiations process, and it set up a specific set of rules and timelines for the process. The Act governed every aspect of school labor relations until 1992.[5]

In 1992, the legislature made a significant change to the rules that apply to negotiations between school districts and their unions. Known popularly as "Act 88," the law did several things of consequence.[6]

Perhaps most significantly, it placed meaningful, or at least predictable, limits on the right to strike. Prior to Act 88, under Act 195 a union could strike at any time, with no notice, and stay out until a judge, after a lawsuit was filed, determined that the strike constituted a threat to the "public health, safety and welfare." These injunctions happened occasionally, and often were accompanied by judicial interference with the bargaining process through orders for "around the clock bargaining" or other such often counterproductive attempts to force the parties to end the process and get the case out of the judge's hair. Some unions also adopted the particularly anti-social tactic of engaging in "hit and run" strikes, con-

---

[4] Act 195 is reproduced in its entirety in the Appendix.

[5] Act 195 still applies to school districts to the extent that it deals with topics not covered by Act 88. Act 88 essentially rewrote the rules for negotiations and related matters only.

[6] Act 88 is reproduced in its entirety in the Appendix. It is a part of the Public School Code and applies only to public school entities.

ducting a series of short, intermittent strikes, with little or no notice, intended to disrupt the lives of the community's children and parents in the hope that these innocent victims of the dispute would in turn put pressure on the board to put an end to it by giving in.

Act 88 changed all that. It required a 48-hour advance notice of a strike, and limited permitted strikes to no more than two per school year. It also established strict limits on exactly how long a strike can last. Generally speaking, a strike must end when it lasts so long that, taking into account all of the available make up days in the school calendar, students will not be able to receive 180 days of instruction by June 15. At that point the employees must return and the parties are required to go through the oddly named process called "non-binding arbitration," which is really a specific type of fact finding (discussed elsewhere in this guide). Act 88 also requires the parties to try to agree on one of several formats for the "non-binding arbitration," although this obligation tends to be overlooked more often than not. Either party is free to reject the result of the "non-binding arbitration," so, in reality, it is just a recommendation.

Following that exercise, the union is free to conduct a second strike, but this one can only last until additional strike days would prevent the students from getting their 180 days by June 30, typically another two weeks. Since support staffs' participation in a strike can rarely be said to prevent students from being educated, it is unlikely that these limitations have much meaning for support groups.

Also of note is a provision that limits a district's right to hire substitutes to replace strikers. In most situations, a district can only employ as substitutes during a strike employees who served at some point during the previous 12 months, thus rendering it very difficult to run limited programs, as had sometimes been done for seniors.

Act 88 also established a firm timetable for some aspects of negotiations, borrowing some aspects that had existed under Act 195 and adding other features. Bargaining must formally begin by January 10 of the year in which a contract expires. The active involvement of a state mediator must occur by February 24. Either party has an absolute right to have the PLRB appoint a fact finder if requested to do so by April 11. After that date, the PLRB may be asked to appoint a fact finder, but is not required to do so.

Finally, Act 88 made clear the right of the Secretary of Education to seek an injunction if necessary to insure the district's students receive the required 180 days of instruction. Districts also may seek such an injunction in such situations.

To my observation, unions have been meticulously following the rules established by Act 88 and court injunctions have been virtually unheard of since its passage. There was an era of occasional lawlessness on the part of some isolated union locals that fortunately appears to have passed into history and Act 88 has now established the basic procedural rules by which the process plays out.

Unfair Practices Defined

One of the most commonly misunderstood features of our labor relations practice is a hybrid type of legal action called an "unfair labor practice." Often referred to as "ULPs," the unfair practices defined by the PERA mirror almost exactly the unfair practices provided for in the National Labor Relations Act, which has been around since the 1930's. ULPs are not simply practices that one may deem "unfair." They are precisely defined offenses against the labor statute which have been further defined through many hundreds of decisions of the PLRB and the courts. Indeed, the PLRB is best understood as a highly specialized "court" that hears ULP cases. That is its principal function.

ULPs can be committed by both employers and unions, although infractions are more commonly committed by employers. Section 1201(a) of the PERA lists the types of employer unfair labor practices:

(a) Public employers, their agents or representatives are prohibited from:
　　(1) Interfering, restraining or coercing employees in the exercise of the rights guaranteed in Article IV of this act.
　　(2) Dominating or interfering with the formation, existence or administration of any employee organization.
　　(3) Discrimination in regard to hire or tenure of employment or any term or condition of employment to encourage or discourage membership in any employee organization.
　　(4) Discharging or otherwise discriminating against an employee because he has signed or filed an affidavit, petition or complaint or given any information or testimony under this act.
　　(5) Refusing to bargain collectively in good faith with an employee representative which is the exclusive representative of the employees in the appropriate unit, including but not limited to the discussing of grievances with the exclusive representative.
　　(6) Refusing to reduce a collective bargaining agreement to writing and sign such agreement.
　　(7) Violating any of the rules and regulations established by the board regulating the conduct of representation elections.
　　(8) Refusing to comply with the provisions of an arbitration award deemed binding under Section 903 of Article IX.
　　(9) Refusing to comply with the requirements of "meet and discuss."

While it is beyond the scope of this work to provide a detailed discussion of what types of employer behaviors constitute unfair practices, certain types of ULP claims are so common that any school official with a working knowledge of the legal framework of school labor relations ought to recognize them and understand what their consequences are.

By far the two most common types of ULP claims are claims of discrimination and claims that an employer has not satisfied its obligation to bargain in good faith. With respect to discrimination, alleged violations can take a myriad of forms, from the discharge of an employee which is claimed to be in retaliation for legitimate union activity, to the favoring of employees who are ill disposed toward the union. Remember that a single act of an employer can constitute both a violation of a contract (for example, the "just cause" clause which regulates disciplinary action) and the PERA, giving rise to claims under both the contract and the law. Essentially, any adverse employment action can be viewed as unlawful discrimination if it can be shown that the employer was influenced in any way by the employee's union activity.

Refusal to bargain claims can arise in several different situations. Generically, if an employer conducts itself during contract negotiations in a manner which establishes that it lacks a sincere desire to reach an agreement, it can be guilty of bargaining in bad faith. Evidence of such behavior can consist of shifting positions without a sound reason, withdrawal of agreement from items previously deemed acceptable, adding new proposals after negotiations have progressed, simply refusing to meet at reasonable times and places, or placing unreasonable pre-conditions on negotiating sessions.

Employer decisions to subcontract often give rise to bargaining claims, with the union alleging that prior to implementing a contracting proposal the employer did not bargain sufficiently over the subject. If an employer changes a pre-existing "working condition" without bargaining, even if it relates to something not addressed in the contract, it also violates the provision in section 1201(a)(5) which requires bargaining in good faith. It also is an unlawful refusal to bargain to refuse to process a grievance, no matter how meritless it is, or to refuse to provide the union with information reasonably necessary for the union to either assess or prosecute a grievance, or to prepare for or conduct contract negotiations.

Finally, it is an unfair practice to fail to comply with an arbitration award. Awards can be enforced through a court petition, but the PLRB also has jurisdiction over such claims.

On the union side, ULP claims are fairly unusual, but not unheard of. A union which ratifies a contract and then refuses to sign it, claiming the agreement is other than what was actually agreed upon, commits a ULP. And the duty to bargain in good faith works both ways, requiring that a union behave with respect to bargaining in the same way that management is required to behave. There have even been cases where unions have been required to provide information to an employer that was necessary for an employer to assess the merit of a grievance or to prepare for negotiations. Finally, it is a ULP for a union to try to control who the employer sends to the bargaining table as its representatives.

Procedure

A charge of unfair practices must be filed within four months of the event giving rise to the charge. Any later than that and it is too late.

When a charge is received in Harrisburg it receives a generalized review by the office of the Secretary of the Board to determine if, on the face of it, it states a claim that, if true, really is an unfair practice prohibited by the PERA. Once in a while the Secretary will determine that the claim set forth in the charge, even assuming all of the alleged facts are true, simply relates to something that the Board cannot, as a matter of law, say is a ULP. Or it may be apparent that the charge is being filed too late. In these situations, the Secretary will issue a notice saying she is refusing to issue a "complaint."

Typically, the filing is in order and timely, and the Secretary issues a complaint and notice of hearing. The complaint is really nothing more than a copy of the original charge, and the notice tells you when and where the Board will conduct a hearing to receive evidence on the charge. These hearings are usually months away from the date of the notice, and are held at the Board's offices in Harrisburg, Pittsburgh or Philadelphia, depending on where the parties are located. No formal answer to the complaint is required to be filed, and there is really no such thing as a default judgment on an unfair practice. A failure to formally answer the complaint only constitutes an admission of the identities of the parties and their status as a public employer and or an employee representative within the meaning of the law.

Sometimes, but not always, a representative of the Board will conduct a pre-hearing conference with the parties by telephone to try to settle the case or narrow down the issues. As is the case with arbitration hearings, there is no formal discovery available to the parties, and preparing for the hearing can be challenging. A pre-hearing conference can be a good way to learn what the evidence will look like.

Eventually you will have a formal hearing before an official called a hearing examiner. This is your trial on the facts. You probably won't get a second chance to prove anything, so the hearing must be approached seriously, like any piece of litigation. The technical rules of evidence used in a courtroom do not apply, but the hearing examiner will apply a general rule of relevance, will require that documents be properly authenticated, and will sustain hearsay objections. He will accept post-hearing briefs and they are usually a good idea. In the brief you can argue your position on what the facts were, if they were in dispute, and what the law says about the particular circumstances. A transcript is essential in order to prepare an effective brief.

Within a few months of the hearing, the hearing examiner will issue what is called a "proposed decision and order." This is the outcome of the case unless one of the parties files what are called "exceptions" to the proposed decision. The exceptions must be filed within 20 days, and must be accompanied by a brief explaining why the hearing examiner was wrong. The exceptions go to the

PLRB itself, a three-member board appointed by the Governor and confirmed by the state senate. The PLRB never conducts any type of hearings or oral argument, and makes its decisions by reviewing the record and the briefs of the parties. It can make one of a number of decisions. It can simply affirm the hearing examiner's decision and reasoning; it can affirm his decision but use different reasoning; it can remand it to the hearing examiner for an additional hearing on some point it feels was not covered adequately in the record; or it can reverse the hearing examiner and go off in a totally different direction with a different result. In the vast majority of cases the PLRB simply affirms the decision of the hearing examiner.

Once the PLRB has ruled on any exceptions, its decision becomes final unless one of the parties appeals the decision to the Commonwealth Court. Ultimately, the Commonwealth Court's disposition is subject to review by the Supreme Court of Pennsylvania.

Remedies

The PLRB has no authority to impose any type of punitive damages on an employer, nor can it award counsel fees to the party filing a charge. It can issue "make whole" remedies. Such remedies may, for example, require that an employee who has been the object of a ULP be made whole economically for any loses suffered as a result of the infraction. The classic example is the case of an unlawfully discharged employee, who may receive back pay and reimbursement for medical expenses that would have been covered by employer-provided health insurance had he not been discharged. If the nature of the case is such that no monetary claim is involved, then the offending employer simply has no financial exposure from the process.

Occasionally, a ULP can present very significant financial exposure for a district. A good example of a very risky ULP is a charge alleging that a district improperly subcontracted bargaining unit work without first fully discharging its duty to bargain in good faith. An adverse result in a case of that nature can be very bad news indeed, as it may carry with it a bill for back pay liability for an entire bargaining unit of discharged employees.

An employer also can be subjected to what is called affirmative relief, in the nature of an order to take certain action, or to refrain from doing certain things. Again, the classic example is an order to reinstate an employee who has been unlawfully discharged. Similarly, an employer can be ordered to restore conditions of employment that may have been unlawfully modified without bargaining, and the like.

Finally, the Board will always require that the employer post a notice on employee bulletin boards if it has found that an unfair practice has been committed. The notice is usually simply a copy of the decision in the case, which will include in its "order" section whatever relief the PLRB has determined is appropriate. Such notices are, if nothing else, a bit embarrassing. They make the district look bad, and the union look like a winner.

Deferral

Occasionally a union will file both an unfair labor practice charge and a grievance over the same employer action, and, indeed, it is possible that a single act of an employer can constitute both a ULP and a violation of a contract. The PSEA is particularly fond of arguing that virtually anything a school district does that is negatively perceived by an employee or group of employees violates the typical "just cause" clause, even if the action in question had no disciplinary purpose. The PLRB has adopted, in part, a doctrine of deferral long used by the NLRB in such situations.[7] Under the Board's deferral policy, if a grievance relating to the same subject is, in fact, filed, the unfair practice charge will be held in abeyance if the Board determines that the charge is "rooted in the parties' contract" and does not allege unlawful discrimination or "enmity toward the exercise of employee rights."[8] Upon disposition of the grievance, the Board will examine whether the grievance was amicably resolved and, if not, whether it proceeded to arbitration where the proceedings were "fair and regular." Finally, the Board will review the result (either settlement or arbitration award) to determine whether the result was "repugnant to the (Public Employee Relations) Act." If none of these issues are present, the charge will be dismissed.

The theory behind the deferral policy makes sense. If the union prevails in the arbitration process the charge is likely moot, since the union can't receive a double recovery or redundant remedies. If, on the other hand, the employer prevails on the contract-based claim, it is very likely that the charge would be found to lack merit as well. Thus, the Board lets another decision maker shoulder the burden of resolving the dispute. Viewed another way, the policy often prevents a union from having two bites at the apple. As a practical matter, where the deferral doctrine applies, a union can elect to process a grievance, or it can abandon the idea of pursuing arbitration and place its faith in the Board's processes. It can't have both.

---

[7] *See Pine Grove Area School District,* 10 PPER 10167 (BD., 1979).

[8] The principal difference between the PLRB's policy and the federal version adopted by the NLRB relates to the deferral of charges of discrimination. In many situations, the NLRB will defer where discrimination is alleged. The PLRB will not.

The Negotiations Process

Preparing for Negotiations

1. Selecting the Committee

Although it is not legally required that board members be in attendance at negotiations as part of the employer's bargaining team, it is almost universally the case that at least some board members are directly involved in the negotiations. Certainly such participation is recommended. Board representation can be effectively accomplished through a single member, or through a larger contingent. My preference typically is to have the board appoint a negotiating committee of three members to attend negotiations, the thought being that we need enough of a cross section of the full board to be confident that if the three of them concur on a proposal, or course of action, a majority of the board would likely agree if the full board were present. In other words, you need three people who can effectively speak for five. We are speaking here of tactical decisions, not strategic ones. The negotiating committee (and its labor attorney) should consult with the full board at appropriate times, and certainly on major parameters for negotiations since, ultimately, a majority of the full board will have to ratify the agreement, and live with it.[9]

The superintendent should be discouraged from being a member of the committee that attends bargaining sessions. Certainly, the superintendent needs to be seriously involved in the process, and should be physically available to consult with the committee during breaks in the negotiations. However, if things get very contentious, and certainly if there is a strike, sometimes the superintendent can become a target. Unions know that in order to be an effective leader of staff on a day-to-day basis, the superintendent needs to avoid being made into a "bad guy," and, consequently, unions sometimes assume that superintendents will tend to encourage the district to do whatever is necessary (whether prudent or not) in order to avoid (or end) conflict. The superintendent thus becomes an unwitting ally of the union by being made to feel uncomfortable. In some districts (particularly smaller ones with few central office

---

[9] Regrettably, there are occasions where board members inappropriately share confidential information regarding negotiations with outside parties. The extent and frequency with which the negotiating committee involves the full board in reviewing negotiations may be influenced if this is a concern.

staff), it simply does not make any sense for the superintendent to be physically absent from the meetings. Still, *if* it can be avoided, it is preferable that other central office administrators serve in that capacity.

Sometimes things become dysfunctional at the bargaining table, and the parties simply aren't communicating on a useful level, or perhaps they are not meeting at all. When this happens, but one of the parties has something constructive to say, it may be necessary for the parties – district and union – to find a different away to communicate. The superintendent (particularly one who has not been at the table) is a logical point of contact for the union to reach out to in such circumstances, and it is not unusual for the union president and the superintendent to privately address negotiations. The superintendent should be prepared to assume this quiet but important role, if necessary.

An assistant superintendent, personnel director, or business administrator can all be useful members of the bargaining committee, as can anyone who just knows district operations well and has a good head on his shoulders. Sometimes a special education director, or a curriculum director can be a useful participant. Senior building administrators who are viewed as respected leaders also can be helpful. Exactly who it makes sense to place on the committee varies from district to district, but some significant administrative presence is essential, for obvious reasons.

2. Assembling Information

Obviously, you will need to know what you are talking about during negotiations, including where you stand on salaries and benefits vis-à-vis neighboring and area districts. Even though financial circumstances do vary from district to district, it is in the nature of negotiations that comparisons to other employers are inevitably made, by both or either side, as they advocate demands or justify offers. The necessary information typically can be obtained from two sources. Most intermediate units compile and share such data from constituent districts. Also, your professional advisor/negotiator should have useful information on your area. Our firm, for example, keeps detailed information on salaries, salary increases, and other major features of contracts in northwestern Pennsylvania and some adjacent areas. Anyone who is seriously engaged in the business of negotiating school labor contracts will have his fingers on the pulse of the area. I actually freely share some of my information with my counterparts in the local regional office of the PSEA, and they do the same with me. None of it is confidential, and our data is usually fairly consistent.

3. Preparing Proposals

How extensive the district's proposed changes to the contract will be, and exactly what those proposals will consist of, are major decisions in bargaining. Factors influencing these decisions are discussed elsewhere in this guide, but, for purposes of preparation, certain things should be done even if the district's agenda is not going to be aggressive.

The administration should consider whether, based upon operational experience, any particular portions of the contract have created issues or problems. If any are identified, they should be reviewed in detail as potential subject matter for contract proposals. Building administrators can be asked to participate in such a review as well, although they tend to suggest that the district rewrite the contract on a wholesale basis. At least their hearts are in the right place.

Ground Rules for Negotiations

Negotiating parties sometimes agree on a set of "ground rules" for negotiations at the outset of the process. It seems as though unions are more interested in this device than are employers, although some districts have embraced the concept. Often some type of formal looking written agreement is offered memorializing these procedural understandings. The following items are sometimes included in such "rules."

- Limits on the maximum amount of time for a session
- Restrictions on public comment or disclosure of proposals being made
- Limits on the number of people who attend sessions
- Designation of who is permitted to attend
- Acknowledgement that parties can add new proposals at any time
- Agreement that the fact that a proposal was made and withdrawn cannot be used as evidence in an arbitration
- A time limit on caucuses

There is little reason for a board to agree to such restrictions. Of all of the things on this list, the one the union is likely most interested in is preventing public disclosure of what they are asking for, or what they already have, for that matter.

The other items are either just bad ideas (such as sanctioning the addition of new proposals) or create artificial regulations that may not make sense when they have to be applied. You can politely decline to agree to anything formal that restricts how negotiations will proceed, along with a comment to the effect that although "negotiating in the newspaper" is not a procedure that you typically endorse, the district reserves the right to inform the public if it becomes necessary. And it may become necessary for several reasons. You might have to correct misinformation, or to prepare the public for a potential strike, so that it understands and, therefore, supports the positions the board is taking in its name. These considerations are discussed in detail elsewhere in this guide.

Sometimes a question arises concerning when each party should present its initial set of proposals to the other party. Unions usually prefer, and sometimes insist, on exchanging them simultaneously. Other than perhaps a sense of fair play, the reason for this preference is not clear. A union is far more likely to get an aggressive proposal from management if management has to guess about how aggressive the union's proposal will be. If, on the other hand, management receives the union's proposal first, and it is fairly modest in scope or content, management has to at least consider taking the same approach. If the district wishes to insist that it receive the union's proposals first, after a period of grumbling from the union, it can usually have its way, because ultimately the union has a much more immediate interest in negotiating changes in the contract than does the district. After all, if no new agreement was ever reached and things just remained unchanged, the district never has to provide any improvements. Nonetheless, a district that seeks to make significant changes in its contract can make a strong case for bringing its proposals to the table at the first meeting, without regard to anything the union might propose, as a means of demonstrating that the district is really serious about the proposal no matter what the union's approach to negotiations is.

Some negotiations advocate separating issues into two categories – economic issues (things that have a direct cost) and language issues. This is commonly done in private industry. When this is done, typically the party inclined to separate them (usually the district) will want to address the language issues first. The thought here is that language issues will be easier to dispose of if one has to resolve them before getting to the truly important things. The extent to which this is true depends largely on the circumstances, but the approach does not make sense if management is proposing concessions and it is the *district* which wants to get to the economic issues quickly.

Common Errors of District Negotiators

Some mistakes tend to show up over and over again. To be sure, not all districts have committed these errors, and many who have also learned from them. Still, the list is worth reciting, if for no other reason than the fact that school leadership experiences frequent turnover.

1. Misjudging the Loyalty of Employees

For practical purposes, you should always assume that employee loyalty is to the union, *not* to the district, its students, or even the cause of education. Many individual employees may have misgivings about the union's positions or leadership, or just dislike the idea of confrontation and conflict. But in the end, they will do as they are told to do, and, if necessary, walk the picket line like good soldiers. Count on it.

From the employee's point of view, this is a reasonable approach. After all, the union is the employee's representative and is paid to look out for the employee's interests. And, of course, all that employees are told by the union about the employer's positions, tactics, and motives is designed to disaffect the employee from the district's point of view and cement his loyalty to the group. The employee is conditioned to be suspicious and cynical about his employer's actions. Who is he going to trust, after all?

It is important as a district leader that you understand this perspective and not naively hope that, in the end, "cooler heads" will prevail and things will work out because the staff is really "good

people" and will accept reasonable terms, as *you* see them. Remember, you are dealing with two groups in trying to reach a settlement, and you must satisfy both groups, *in the following order*:
- Union leadership/bargaining committee
- Union membership

The union leadership can almost always get a union membership vote to produce the outcome it wants.

2. Meeting Too Often and/or For Too Long

Progress in negotiations is not a function of the amount of time spent in negotiating sessions, or how frequently they are held. This is a reality that is lost on John Q. Public and, unfortunately, the news media, who often think that the district isn't trying hard enough if it isn't negotiating on a daily basis or, God forbid, "around the clock." Newspaper editorial writers, in particular, seem to think that when there is serious labor trouble it will help if those involved simply try harder and meet more often. It makes for good, high sounding editorials. This view reflects a serious naiveté, because, in fact, spending too much time at the table, particularly at the wrong time, can actually impede a settlement. Contract settlements are heavily influenced by the timing of actions and decisions, and by the relative bargaining power of the parties at a given time. Actually, a meeting of the negotiating teams often isn't even necessary to reach a settlement. Contracts can be settled over the telephone, or, more commonly, at a very small private, off-the-record meeting between a few key players on each side, sometimes called on a very impromptu basis. Sometimes they are settled by nothing more than a private visit by the union president to the superintendent's office. The point is, parties settle contracts when the conditions are right for *both* of them to do so, and not before, no matter how often they meet for appearances sake.

Indeed, a desire to meet too often is sometimes interpreted as over anxiousness and weakness. So perceived, it may actually *lessen* the chances for a settlement as the other side senses that it can press an advantage. It's usually when *both sides* feel that nothing further can be gained that negotiations are concluded. You should avoid the feeling that you have to be "doing something" all of the time. Standing pat and conveying that you are resolute can be a good strategy at times, and can actually facilitate settlement. It is no accident that *the union* is usually in favor of "round the clock" bargaining when things get dicey. It makes good press and puts pressure on well-intentioned people in the district to "do something." Don't fall into that trap. If you can stand a little public criticism from those who don't understand negotiations, you can help yourself by conveying to the union that you'll meet when someone has something new and productive to say, and not before.

3. Sending Inconsistent Messages

Signals and subtle forms of communication often are more important than pretty speeches or fiery rhetoric. And nothing will complicate or confuse negotiations more than inconsistent or changing signals.

One way to give a negative signal is to change the personnel in mid-stream. Any change in the composition of the negotiating team, or the identity of the district's public spokesman may be viewed as very significant. Certainly anything that suggests that the full board lacks confidence in those it has been sending to negotiate on its behalf will cause an aggressive response from the union, as it senses weakness and, therefore, an opportunity. Personnel changes will be viewed as signaling a change in policy, often in favor of conciliation or concession.

4. By-Passing the Designated Negotiators

Unions naturally prefer to deal with a district that does not have access to competent, experienced advisors. They prefer to deal with well-intentioned, but unsophisticated amateurs and board members whom they can take advantage of. The unions, of course, *rarely* make any significant moves in negotiations without the close involvement and/or participation of their professional advisors, who are well-paid and experienced. In short, they want an advantage. Consequently, if you let them, they will often try to separate a district from its counsel or professional advisor. A variety of means are used to accomplish this.

The most common, and least sophisticated method is simply to try to negotiate privately, by-passing the professional. This can take the form of a direct approach to an individual board member or the superintendent by a union leader, a respected rank and file teacher, or even a recruited public spirited citizen or union sympathizer. An unspoken appeal is thus made to the target's natural desire to be a hero and to solve the problem for the district.

Another common union approach is to suggest that both sides negotiate without either one having professionals involved. As friendly and cost-saving as this proposition may seem, it is critical to understand that the people you would be facing on the other side of the table are not simply some teachers who raised their hands last month to volunteer for this, but more likely are people hand picked long ago for the negotiation role and given years of intensive training for it. On top of that training, they will have behind-the-scenes guidance from their professional advisors at every step of the process. Thinking you can survive on your own in this scenario may be like thinking you can take on a black belt in karate just because you have watched a few martial arts movies.

A related, alternative method is simply to attack the negotiator, usually publicly, but also, privately with board members, to undermine confidence in him and to convince the board that he is the problem and, if he's removed, everything will work itself out. When these attacks occur at the table, in front of the management committee, sometimes they can be particularly effective, because they create the appearance that the union is just refusing to move the negotiations forward as long as "that man" who is costing the taxpayers so much money is in the room.

5. Mishandling of the Management Proposal

Management, of course, has just as much right to propose changes to the contract as the union does, although unions hate acknowledging that. Some particularly aggressive union negotiators actually dispute that right and say point blank that management has *no* legitimate right to propose *anything*. It sometimes takes a while to convince them that the natural order of the universe isn't that negotiations exist for the purpose of seeing how much the union can get. Eventually, they come around.

When management proposals tend to the extreme, they seem to fall into one of two categories: districts that typically have *no* proposal, and districts that submit a lengthy "wish list" of pie-in-the-sky ideas. Neither approach is recommended.

Having no proposal, or very few items, is not necessarily bad, if the union is taking the same approach. This is often the approach necessary for an "early bird" type of quick settlement. It is inherent in such a process that you don't complicate things, since the objective is to get it done relatively quickly. However, in "normal" negotiations it would be most unusual for a district to have no significant issues worthy of discussion.

The "wish list" approach usually doesn't work, simply because a proposal like that often isn't taken seriously. Credibility is everything in negotiations. Before you can ever expect to obtain a significant concession at the bargaining table you have first to convince the union it is going to have to give it to you if it ever wants a contract, and that you are prepared to do whatever it takes, wait as long as you have to, and endure any unpleasantness it can inflict, in order to get it. When you've accomplished *that*, success is assured. Such an approach is much, much easier if you concentrate on a very few priority items and invest all of your time convincing the union that you are really serious about *them*. It is exceedingly tough to do that with a long list. Districts may be well advised to isolate on at the most two or three items of significance, carefully chosen because (1) they really do matter, and they will help the district in some real way and, therefore, are ultimately worth fighting for; and, (2) there is a great case to be made for *why* we need them, i.e., we don't want them just because we want them, and there is a moral case of sorts, or at least a very good reason for them. The union doesn't have to like your proposal. It just has to believe you are serious about it, and that there is a good reason for it that they can understand.

There is, of course, often a bit of "horse trading" that goes on, and the strategic withdrawal of a proposal can be a significant event in negotiations. Consequently, there is often nothing wrong with advancing items knowing they will likely have to be abandoned at some point. Just be reasonable about them. Indeed, proposals can be advanced and pushed pretty far before being dropped just to make a point the district wants to make about something or other. Sometimes that approach has a beneficial effect. Unions employ the same tactic, making proposals they know full well they won't hold up a settlement over, just to let the district know something has really bothered them, or is worrying them. It's another of those "signals" you should pay attention to.

6. Trying to Do Too Much

Labor contracts are a continuum, literally stretching over decades.

Change, if that is your objective, is usually achieved incrementally, over time. That's why good negotiators take a long-range view and often define success as getting a "foot in the door" where previously the door was shut tight. Failing to see the virtue of this approach can be counter-productive. Insisting on a sea change and showing little willingness to compromise toward your ultimate goal can actually result in more resistance than you might otherwise encounter. Show the other side a way out that still helps you, and you might get a more positive response.

A good example of this is provided by the oft visited issue of health insurance deductibles. If your district has a very low, or even zero, deductible, obviously something has to be done going forward. But if you try to go from zero to thousands of dollars a year in one contract to mirror what may be common with private sector employer plans in your area, you're likely to encounter vehement resistance. Five hundred dollars a year might get their attention, and if you can achieve it, even if you stage it incrementally in a few hundred dollars each year, you are headed in the right direction. Negotiating postures aside, when it comes time to show the other side what it will really take to get you to settle the contract, an overly aggressive position on the types of things (like deductibles, and premium contributions, for example) that are susceptible to incremental change can actually hurt your chances of making meaningful changes to your contract.

Going Public

An issue that often arises during negotiations is whether, and when, to make the negotiation process publicly visible. Interfacing with the public can take many forms, from carefully controlled briefings and press releases focusing on the issues and developments, to proposing the actual negotiating sessions be open to the public or the press.

On a philosophical level, it is hard to argue with the notion that negotiations are the public's business, since it is the public's money that is being spent, and the welfare of the community's children is directly affected by the outcome, and, at times, by the process itself. Nonetheless, there are times and places where the public interest is *not* well served by "negotiating in the newspaper," as the union will refer to it when it suits the union's purpose to denigrate public attention to bargaining. Negotiations are a complex process, not easily understood by the average journalist, let alone the average citizen. Much of what is said or done in the process is not to be taken at face value, and getting to an agreement is often difficult enough without adding the need to posture for the media and its larger audience. Whether and when to inform the public about any aspect of bargaining is a judgment that has to be made as the situation warrants. There are times when a great deal of visibility is a good idea and others when the process is best served by proceeding quietly. That is essentially the view taken by the unions, as well. The PSEA will often take great exception to a district aggressively sharing information about bargaining with the press, all the while maintaining a highly paid public relations flack in its regional office whose main function during bargaining is to do whatever he can to make sure the public is selectively informed and fed the appropriate rhetoric and half truths. In public relations wars, sometimes the union tosses the first grenade, sometimes the district does.

Despite the virtue of taking a case-by-case approach to releasing information, there are a few unalterable truths when it comes to public relations. First, and foremost, is the public's undeniable right to know what has been *done* in its name, and with its money. Do not confuse conducting negotiations in private with keeping the *results* private. The latter is not only indefensible on a philosophical level, it is essentially illegal. When it comes time to ratify the contract and to disclose its contents, the public must be informed fully and honestly. To their credit, there are very few school board members who feel otherwise.

Second, do not allow concern over derailing the negotiations process to cause you to fail to defend yourself. Near the beginning of bargaining, you may be asked by the union to agree not to release proposals to the media, or to make some similar commitment. Your response to a request that you agree to limit media comment ought to be "no," and the explanation is simple. There may be a time when it is necessary for the public to know what is going on and why an agreement has not been reached. When asked to explain, you should point out that the instant the union threatens to strike and to interrupt the education of the community's children, the public has a right to know why things have gotten to that point, i.e., what the parties are disagreeing about, and why. Further, the district has no intention of letting the public misunderstand what is happening, or why, and when a sense develops that misinformation is being circulated, either officially or unofficially, either to the public generally, or to the rank and file of the bargaining unit, the union should expect the district to correct it. In other words, concern about the confidentiality of the process has reasonable limits.

Unions are often very vulnerable when details of negotiations are visible to the public, particularly in the early stages when pie-in-the-sky proposals and unrealistic salary and benefit demands may be on the table. Releasing such material to the media can make the union look unreasonable and place it on the defensive.

So why not just do it right out of the gate? Well, consider that after all of the fun of reading the anti-union letters to the editor in the newspaper has died down, you'll have to sit down with these people and actually try to get them to agree on a contract. It's a tough job as it is. It can get a lot tougher when everyone is angry. And remember one of the other fundamental truths about public relations: At the end of the day, the union doesn't *need* to have the public on its side. In fact, the union can be wildly successful in the face of public hostility. The union *likes* to have the sympathy of the public, and will do what it can to secure it, but that sympathy is not essential for union success.

The union only seeks public support because it knows that to the extent it can gain public sympathy, the board loses that sympathy in nearly direct proportion. But the union doesn't have to get re-elected, and is not accountable to the public. Its members are public employees, not public servants. For school boards, however, public relations is a critical matter of defense. To make it through a protracted period of labor dispute, a school board needs to maintain a certain level of public support for its objectives. The union does not.

Keep in mind that different news media operate differently. Television reporters tend to be looking for brief sound bites of a few seconds duration which do relatively little to inform the public. Print media folks tend to be more engaged in the event they are covering and need to be educated to a greater extent about what the issues are and what positions are being taken. Address each according to their role and how they function. With print media, be prepared to sit down and go over information in detail. Most print reporters will appreciate it and will treat you fairly once they understand the district's point of view. When dealing with broadcast media, be sure your spokesman understands that all that may run on the news is 10 or 15 seconds of an interview. Keep it simple and to the point.

Increments, Jumps and Bumps

The salary schedules we see in teachers' contracts are the result of both history and the now obsolete statutory pay scheme placed into the Code back in 1949. In the days before collective bargaining, the legislature deemed it appropriate to provide for some type of minimum salaries and minimum annual raises for teachers and other professional employees. These provisions, long outstripped of real meaning by the results of collective bargaining and inflation, can still be found in the Code. One of their prominent features was a mandate for annual increments as staff accrue service.

As collective bargaining resulted in significant annual increases, most districts applied the increases more or less uniformly, including to those already at the top of the scale. This practice necessitated adding another step each year in order to give the person at the top the same, or nearly the same, raise as the person at the step next to the top. Some salary schedules grew to in excess of 30 steps, a fundamentally irrational system bearing no relationship to an actual learning curve for the job. Something had to give. Enter salary schedule "compaction" proposals from the union and the accompanying rhetoric about the importance of the "career salary."

Compaction proposals were simply requests to reduce the number of steps to anywhere between a dozen to about 18, where the numbers appear to have now stabilized. Sometimes when districts resisted these proposals, the unions settled for simply not adding any new steps. In either event, with a constant or reduced number of steps, it is obviously mathematically impossible to give each employee an identical raise, or even a nearly identical raise. Another way of looking at the effects of compaction is an analogy to a tube of toothpaste. If you shorten a full tube of toothpaste and added more toothpaste to it at the same time, you're going to have a bulge or two somewhere, and it may well burst. In a sense, that's what you do to a salary schedule when you stuff it full of money and then make it shorter. You get what are sometimes referred to as "jump" or "bump" steps. These steps are nothing more than unusually large increments, or, distances between steps. Employees fortunate enough to be moving through such a step in a given year will receive a very large increase. I've seen them reach amounts in excess of $10,000 in my area, and some schedules have several of them. Some school directors have become very upset about these very large increments because of the obvious difficulty in explaining to the public why any employee got a $10,000 raise in one year.

Another problem created by jump steps is really an issue for both sides as they struggle to distribute limited dollars across a salary schedule. Depending on demographics, jump steps can soak up a lot of the money available to fund a settlement. If no one, or only one or two, staff members are going through a jump step in a given year, the amount can be manageable. Put five or six of them there in a single year in a district with only one hundred or so teachers, and a $7,000 jump step, and the amount of money left for everyone else can get very tight. Remember, the union ultimately has to get a majority of its members to approve whatever schedule you come up with. Telling the folks to accept small increases because their day at the jump step will come later sometimes is a tough sell. Telling it to those who have *already* received the benefit of the big raise and who are looking ahead to retirement based on their highest years of salary can be an even harder sell. Such is human nature.

There is no really good "fix" for jump steps from a district's perspective. Reducing the size of the jump step, or generally evening out the distances between steps costs money and is often impractical to do in a usefully short timeframe. Correcting a jump step can take a very long time.

In addition to creating jump steps, compaction also had the inevitable effect of vaulting a teacher to the top salary paid in his district considerably faster than would occur with a longer schedule, thus increasing his "career total earnings" by quite a bit over what they would have been if it had taken decades to work up to the top, whatever the top happens to be.

In response to the pressure to produce an agreement in a given round of bargaining, most districts focus on the total cost of a potential settlement. Proposals are typically made in terms of an average dollar increase per teacher over the previous year's average salary. Averages, averages. The average per head increase can just as well be expressed as a percentage increase over last year's average salary if the parties prefer, but it's the same thing. By dealing with averages, the district can keep control of the predicted total cost of the settlement (assuming a given number of anticipated staff), a critical matter for the district. Salary agreements almost always begin with an agreement in principle on an average dollar (or percentage) per head increase over the prior year's salary. Often proposals take something like the following form:

An average increase of $_____$ per year in each year of a three-year contract, inclusive of the amount of any incremental increase resulting from advancement on the salary schedule. Specific salary schedules resulting in such average increases shall be subject to agreement of the parties. In developing the schedules, the parties shall assume a constant population of staff, with the population as set forth in a staff matrix already exchanged between them, and schedules consisting of 18 steps.

Take a careful look at the sample wording above. It takes into account several important things about a salary offer and the ultimate agreement it may produce.

First, it honestly depicts some measure of the real cost of the proposal, because it expressly includes within the scope of the dollar commitment the very real cost of the incremental movement that will be experienced by everyone except teachers already at the top step. Whatever increase in salary "built in" to your schedule certainly represents real dollars to you. In many districts – particularly those with fairly short schedules with larger distances between steps – this amount can easily represent 2% or more of the average teacher salary before an additional dollar is put on the table.

Union compensation experts will argue that by counting the cost of step movement "against" the raise being offered, you are asking employees to "pay for their own increases." They also may point out, correctly, that in industrial negotiations such a costing device is almost never used, and the negotiating parties simply agree on a percentage or flat cents per hour increase and add it to the top, or "journeyman" type rate for each classification. Learners simply start lower, and the periodic increases they may receive every six months or year are not "counted." There is some philosophical merit to the first point, and the second point (really only an observation), is certainly true. Indeed, in school support negotiations, the cost of learner's rates *is* typically ignored, in contrast to teachers' settlements. What these arguments fail to take into account is that *so much* of your professional compensation system is driven by seniority (i.e., the number of years a person has in) that it is impossible to ignore the cost of the system itself, which, by the way, the union is as responsible for creating as is the district. Buying their philosophy will turn your 3.5% raise into a 5.5 or 6% raise each year. If, in private industry, the wage progression for a machinist was 18 years long, and a majority of the company's workforce was working its way through the progression at a given time, private industry negotiators would take the same approach school districts usually take in bargaining. In private sector employment, a typical wage progression is a few years long at most, and the top rate rarely reaches two times or more of the entry rate. In education, the "progression," with its associated costs, is closer to two decades and the spread between top and bottom is often 2.5 times.

You can determine the incremental cost built into your existing schedule very easily. Simply place every staff member on your schedule and then age them a year each. Everyone moves up one step except those at the top, who have nowhere to go. Compare the total existing payroll to the new payroll generated after the exercise, and the difference is what simply re-signing the old agreement for a year with no change will cost you, assuming no retirements or new hires. If you think you know how many retirements and new hires you will likely have, you can refine the calculation, but that's guess work.

The second thing to notice about the offer format is that it does not propose a specific salary schedule. The schedules will come later, after an agreement in principle on the average increases (their point of view) and the average cost (your point of view) is reached. You should be careful, though, to say that each side must agree on whatever schedule is settled upon. Some districts have foolishly agreed to accept *any* schedule the union developed, as long as the cost ended up at the amount agreed upon. This is sometimes referred to as the "pot of money" approach. This is a huge mistake. There have been some very strange and some thoroughly unfair salary schedules proposed that nonetheless produced agreed-upon average increases. Ultimately, you will be asked down the road to fix the resulting inequities and problems, probably at significant cost. The district has a clear interest in *how* the money is distributed, in addition to *how much* is distributed. If nothing else, you need to pay attention to your starting salaries for recruitment purposes, as senior union leaders often do not seem to care greatly about those at the bottom of the food chain. Notice also that the district's position on the number of steps is clear. You want no confusion there.

Finally, the offer format specifies the staffing assumption that must be used in constructing the schedule, and referred to an earlier agreement (which I recommend obtaining) on the current staff distribution, often referred to as the "matrix." The "matrix" is nothing more than a chart which shows where every staff member is on the salary schedule as of a given time. It is impossible to say whether a particular salary schedule will cost a certain amount without knowing who is on it, and where, in each year. Notice I also have specified we assume a constant population, meaning we are assuming (somewhat unrealistically) no one retires, quits, gets fired, or is hired. In this regard, there is a choice between speculation and being unrealistic. Generally, it is in your financial interest to make the constant population assumption, because, in terms of gross payroll (the budget number) as soon as the first retiree is either replaced with a first-year teacher or not replaced at all, your total compensation number goes down. This is sometimes referred to as "attritional savings" and it is real. From the average teacher's point of view, though, there isn't much effect because they're all still getting the advertised raise, on average, more or less. In fact, those retiring from the top of the salary schedule typically get *less* than the average increase, with more of the money being distributed to those working their way up.

Binding Arbitration of Contract Terms

When a district and its union cannot reach agreement on a new contract, you sometimes hear the suggestion that the parties ought to agree to allow an outside arbitrator to decide what the contract should say. This process is sometimes referred to as "interest arbitration" and is the process routinely used to create labor agreements for public safety employees in Pennsylvania. It is fundamentally different from "grievance arbitration," discussed later in this book, which relates to claims that an existing contract has been violated. "Interest arbitration" sounds like it might be a sensible idea, particularly if a strike has occurred or has been threatened, or if a very long and protracted period of negotiations has failed to produce an agreement. After all, the arbitrator is presumably neutral, and, also presumably, is knowledgeable about what is "fair" in such matters. Taking your chances with the arbitrator is considered preferable to a continuation of labor unrest with all of its attendant negative consequences. It is no coincidence that such calls for settlement through binding arbitration almost always come from the union and its allies, or from well-intentioned, but uninformed community members who have taken a sudden interest in negotiations for one reason or another. The reality of binding arbitration is sometimes quite a bit different from the sales pitch described above, and, there are some situations where it is virtually guaranteed that the result will not be in the district's interests.

Arbitrators tend to compromise between positions. They also tend to award what they perceive as "typical" or "average" contract terms. They tend not to award things that are novel, or that change the status quo in a significant way, particularly with regard to contract language. Thus, if what is causing your impasse is the union's refusal to agree to one or more aggressive management proposals for significant changes to contract language, or significant changes to overly generous traditional benefit programs, odds are an arbitrator will not give you what you want. The union might, eventually and reluctantly, agree to such changes after a long battle, but an arbitrator probably will not place them in an award. Similarly, if you are resisting a union salary demand by offering a much lower than "average" pay increase because your particular district is in financial difficulty, an arbitrator is not likely to give you what you want, simply because it departs so much from the norm. Indeed, the only time binding arbitration might appear to be a viable option, given these tendencies of arbitrators, is if your particular impasse is being caused by the district's resistance to excessive and/or peculiar *union* demands. You should be skeptical, even in those circumstances.

On a philosophical level, an agreement for binding interest arbitration (and it has to be agreed to – the law *never* compels a school district to participate in it) represents the surrender of control over what goes into your contract, and, in a larger sense, an abdication of the responsibility of the elected school board to make fundamental policy decisions for the district.

Police and fire contracts, transit contracts, and contracts for some court-related employees have been dictated by the binding arbitration process for many years, because the legislature felt these employees provide such vital public services that strikes are intolerable. Unlike school districts, cities and municipalities have no choice but to submit to binding arbitration for public safety workers. Education has not been considered to be as essential a public service as police and fire protection, or the operation of the court system, so *binding* interest arbitration is never mandatory. I have been involved in a number of negotiations involving municipal public safety employees and, almost uniformly, the mayors, township supervisors, and public administrators I worked with found the arbitration process to be unsatisfactory, in part for the reasons discussed above.

Can We Learn Anything from the Private Sector?

The private sector has been dealing with labor issues and labor unions for a long time, much longer than school districts. Can we learn anything from the private sector experience?

To appreciate what we can (and can't) take away from the experience of the business community, we must first understand the fundamental differences that exist between private and public enterprises. It is a matter of context.

The first and most fundamental difference is that private business has been doing it a lot longer. Experience is the best teacher in this field, and business has a lot of it. Closely related to this observation is the fact that those who are responsible for labor relations in the private sector not only are more experienced on a personal level, but the cast of players is far more stable. One of the problems we face on a regular basis is the high turnover rate of both school board members and, unfortunately, superintendents. It seems that school labor policy makers are constantly being re-educated and broken in. Business also recognizes the importance of having a professional human resource/personnel office, even if the business is fairly small. Although schools are doing a better job of recognizing this, it is still quite common for no one other than the CEO (i.e., the superintendent) to have responsibility in this area. So, the nature of the enterprise is very different in the private sector with regard to who is in charge of labor issues.

The second key difference relates to decision making. It is much easier for business. Typically only one person – the CEO or president – calls the major shots. Decisions can be made quickly, and the information necessary to make them can be quickly and efficiently transmitted and assessed. There is typically no "board" involved, and certainly no public input. Lines of authority and responsibility are clear, sometimes brutally so.

Third, negotiations in business are private matters. The public has no right to know anything, decisions do not have to be made publicly, and, typically, the news media pays no attention to the process. And, if it did, it really doesn't matter what anyone outside of the business thinks. How much simpler life would be if there were no public meetings, no public documents, and no sunshine law.

Fourth, private business can go *out* of business – or move to Mexico – or contract out many of its functions – things that realistically cannot happen to a public school system. Those possibilities make a huge difference in how unions conduct themselves.

Finally, the law is fundamentally different in the private sector. Although the Public Employee Relations Act (PERA) is patterned after the National Labor Relations Act with respect to what constitutes an unfair labor practice, the similarity ends there. Fact finding, mediation timetables, mandatory starting dates for negotiations, restrictions on hiring strike replacements…all of these things are unique to government negotiations.

Still, there are some things schools can learn, even from this very different world.

The first thing you'd notice if you observed business go about negotiating is how well it prepares. Little is left to chance. Industry patterns are studied, as are competitors' labor agreements. Every proposal with economic consequences for both sides is carefully costed out and evaluated.

The next thing you'd be impressed with is how vehemently management will resist any attempt to encroach on its ability to manage the business in the most effective way. Most companies will fight to the death to defend management flexibility and, in particular, the ability to innovate and change how things are done. They are aware that the loss of managerial freedom is often incremental, and subtle, and they take a long-range view of things. They know if they lose the ability to manage, they lose the ability to control the quality of the work, and, eventually, the bottom line is impacted. I see provisions in school contracts all of the time that most of my private sector clients would have taken a strike over, if necessary. Many of those provisions were surrendered without a fight, and perhaps without even a very good idea of what they really meant.

What types of things? A private firm is not likely to have something in its contract that says an employee cannot be evaluated on certain days, or unless he's told in advance he's being watched. Or that he won't lose any "advantage" without "just cause." Or that he will never be criticized within hearing distance of someone else. Or that any of his employer's policies can be grieved if they are applied "unfairly" or "inconsistently." You can find all of those things in school labor agreements.

Studying the private sector also teaches the virtue of stability. Neither employer philosophy nor personnel is likely to change much and what the union sees one time is very likely to be what it sees the next. There are no "liberal" or "conservative" cycles in leadership groups, and managers and policy makers tend to be around for a while.

Business also is acutely aware that an employee's time equals money. It is much less likely to agree to generous paid leaves or vacations or personal time. It recognizes that paying an employee when he is not producing has a cost. How well the enterprise accomplishes its purpose is affected by such things. Thus, companies typically see no real difference between paying someone a higher wage and giving them more paid time off. In fact, when companies do their internal costing analysis of various contract proposals, time off issues are *always* converted into a cash equivalent for purposes of analysis. Time off in the public sector also means quality is affected, i.e., the quality of education is impacted by the absence of a child's regular teacher, just as, in business, the profitability of the company is affected.

"We Just Want What All the Other Teachers Have"

One of the most difficult challenges facing district bargainers is getting the union to accept an "outside the box" settlement on issues of consequence – outside the box meaning something that departs from the "teacher contract" pattern. Thus, districts struggle to gain contracts that contain health benefit terms that even remotely resemble what is commonly seen in the private sector, or to achieve wage settlements that reflect what local taxpayers experience, if they see increases at all. The union response to such proposals is to make sure the debate is framed in terms of what is typical *in other teacher contracts*, not what is typical in the general economy. They thus define their own market, narrowly, and to their advantage. They prefer to live in a world populated only by unionized teachers.

There is a certain logic to the union's position. After all, why isn't it sensible to compare your teachers to other teachers similarly situated, and to give them what other teachers typically have, as opposed to some other occupation? Isn't the "market" for teachers defined by what other teachers get? It's a sweet deal, of course, because it guarantees the union remains immune from the influence of the larger society within which it exists and upon which it depends. If your teachers have to be treated like all the other teachers, how does anything ever change for the worse? Quite simply, it can't. No one ever has to go first, when it comes to negative changes. This is an over simplification, but it captures the essence of the situation.

There are, of course, compelling arguments against this point of view. Why isn't it just as sensible for teachers' terms of employment to reflect the circumstances of the community whose resources are coercively taken, through taxation, to support those terms? Indeed, why *should* teachers be a privileged group, with benefits so far out of step with what prevails in their communities? Why shouldn't the economic fortunes of other groups of degreed professionals in the community at least be considered? One of my client school directors likes to put it this way: Why should the district agree to give teachers Cadillac health insurance when it has to be paid for by the taxes of people who can't afford to have any at all?

I have no easy solution to resolve this philosophical confrontation. I merely identify it and comment upon it because it seems a permanent part of the bargaining dialog, and you will need to deal with it. Ultimately, the school board will have to decide, on behalf of the community, how to resolve this fundamental difference of opinion and translate that decision into bargaining policy.

Changing Arbitration Outcomes Through Negotiations

When you've received a grievance arbitration award that applies or interprets your contract in a troublesome way, the only realistic way to reverse the outcome is to alter the contract language on which it was based, or add something new to the contract that has the same effect. This is often easier said than done, since the union has invested time, money, and emotional capital in doing battle in arbitration. You will be asking them to give up something they have fought for and won, and it is human nature to resist doing that. Given this reality, one should not assume that "if we lose, we can always fix it in negotiations." It may be more difficult to get a misinterpreted contract provision clarified to your liking than it would have been to get the provision in question re-worded absent any arbitration over the meaning. This observation cuts both ways, of course. When the union has put management to the test over a disputed provision, you should be most reluctant to surrender your victory to help get an agreement on unrelated matters.

The Consequences of Unsuccessful Proposals

Be careful what you ask for, because if you don't get, it the fact that you asked can hurt you later. One of the risks inherent in an overly aggressive contract proposal is that much of it will inevitably be withdrawn as the negotiations take their course. One of the most compelling pieces of evidence that can be used in arbitration is proof that a party tried to get agreement on a contract proposal that would clearly give it what the same party now claims the contract gives it anyhow. Arbitrators seem impressed with the argument that a party should not be (in effect) awarded in arbitration what it unsuccessfully tried to get in negotiations. This is more often a problem with union proposals, as they typically ask for all kinds of things they can't realistically expect to get.

Ethics Issues and the Negotiating Team

There are two sources of possible concern when it comes to ethics issues. The PERA prohibits any school board member who is a member of the same union that the district is negotiating with, or who has an economic interest in the outcome of bargaining that is in conflict with the district's interests, from actively participating in negotiations, although such a person is permitted to vote on the question of contract ratification.[10] The Ethics Act also generally prohibits any public official from engaging in conduct which constitutes a "conflict of interest" under the Act.[11]

For a number of years the Ethics Commission held the opinion that a school board member who had an immediate family member in a union bargaining unit was barred by the Ethics Act from actively participating in negotiations with that unit. Because it is not at all uncommon for board members to have spouses or children employed by the district they serve, this often created issues related to participating in executive sessions, conferences with labor counsel, or even serving on the district's negotiating committee. The Ethics Commission has in recent years reversed its position and now allows a board member with an employed family member to participate fully as long as the family member can only benefit from the terms of the settlement as a member of a larger group and not in some identifiable *individual* way.[12] The Ethics Commission, as of this writing, has not ruled on a situation where the family member is in a leadership position with the union, and the Commission might still have problems in certain specific situations like that. But, generally, board members are free to serve.

---

[10] 43 Pa. Stat. Ann. § 1101.1801 (2012).

[11] 65 Pa. Cons. Stat. §§ 1102-03 (2012).

[12] *See* State Ethics Commission Advice of Counsel 09-549 and Opinion 08-006, reproduced in the Appendix.

It is sound practice for a board member who has an immediate family member in the bargaining unit to abstain *voluntarily* from active participation in the negotiations process. This includes participation as a member of the district's bargaining team, as well as participation in sensitive discussions of strategy or planning. The basis for this advice is simply the protection of the reputation of the individual board member and a concern about public confidence in the process. There are sometimes situations where the leadership position, skills or services of a particular board member are deemed critical to the successful conduct of negotiations and such considerations may override the need to avoid even the appearance of impropriety. This is typically not the case, however, as most school boards have sufficient personnel capable of serving in these roles that do not have personal circumstances that raise the conflict of interest issue. Ultimately, it is up to the school board to determine who will participate in negotiations and related decision-making, after considering not only the law but who the board is comfortable with in the various roles.

Negotiation and Past Practice

It is certainly possible to deal specifically with the subject of past practices in your contract language. Indeed, unions covet language in contracts that obligates employers to follow past practices. But there is a little appreciated aspect of past practice relating to negotiations that can be used to the advantage of an employer which yearns to be free of the bonds of history.

There is an extremely well-established line of reported arbitration authority which holds that an employer can jettison past practice if, during negotiations, it identifies the particular practices it wishes to disown and so informs the union in time for the union to propose, during negotiations, that the practices be enshrined into the contract. If, after being so notified, the union does not manage to get the practice converted into contract language, the practice need not be followed when the new agreement takes effect.[13]

To understand why this makes logical sense, you have to understand how arbitrators use the concept of past practice. Past practice can, of course, be used to help interpret ambiguous contract terms. Has your labor counsel ever asked how you have handled a certain type of situation in the past when you ask for advice about a grievance? I'm not only talking about those types of situations necessarily. Arbitrators also refer to past practice to create *independently enforceable* contract terms that you never actually agreed to.[14] It doesn't seem to make much sense to require you to pretend you agreed to something that you never agreed to, or that maybe the union never even asked for, but that is, in fact, what happens. But if you place the union on notice during negotiations that with the start of the new agreement things are going to change, you impose on the union the burden of getting you to agree not to make the changes.

---

[13] For an excellent discussion of this subject and citations to the many reported arbitration decisions in this area, *see Elkouri and Elkouri, How Arbitration Works, Sixth Ed.*, at p. 619. *Elkouri* describes the weight of this authority as "impressive."

[14] This notion is further discussed in the section titled "Maintenance of Standards" in the context of contract clauses dealing with past practices.

A blanket statement during negotiations that all past practices will be abrogated going forward simply will not work. But, if you can identify *specific* habits of management behavior you'd really like to discontinue, placing those practices on the table can be an effective way to deal with them prospectively. And, it places the burden on the union to get YOU to agree to reinstate the practice.

The Union's Back Room Committee

It has become fashionable for educational unions to construct an elaborate decision-making process affecting negotiations, involving two or more "tiers" of committees or reviewing bodies who have a direct role in approving positions taken at the table. It is not uncommon for district negotiators to meet with one group at the bargaining table face to face, and for another, different group of employees to be closeted away with the function of reviewing and perhaps approving/disapproving/authorizing decisions made at the table. You never see this second group, which may very well be on site during negotiations. The obstacle this may create to achieving a settlement is obvious, although it apparently isn't so obvious to the union. I have no idea why a union would think this is a good way to conduct negotiations, unless the thought is that if everyone who has a meaningful point of view is actually personally involved in the process, it makes ratification painless. Perhaps they think it is more "democratic" and serves some such lofty goal. Still, it can be very, very frustrating to have to obtain approval from a small group of perhaps agenda-driven individuals who you never get to see or talk to. Everything they know and think has to be filtered and translated through others.

If you find yourself confronted with this structure, there is not much you can do about it. An employer has little ability to influence how a union goes about handling its internal decision-making process.

Fact Finding and Non-Binding Arbitration

Under the current state of the law, either party to school negotiations has the absolute right to insist the parties go through fact finding by making a request for it by April 11 of any year in which bargaining is occurring. Additionally, the PLRB can order parties to participate in fact finding at any time if it chooses to do so, usually at the request of one of the negotiating parties.

Fact finding is a procedure somewhat similar to the "interest arbitration" process under which municipalities in Pennsylvania settle their police and fire contracts. The only difference is that the result of fact finding is a "report" of the fact finder that is non-binding, i.e., either side is free to reject it. It is merely a recommendation for what the fact finder thinks would be a fair compromise of the outstanding issues.

Fact finders are appointed by the PLRB with no input from the parties from a fairly small panel of people whom the PLRB thinks are qualified to handle the job. They always conduct a "hearing" of a sort in which each side gets to explain what it is asking for in the new contract and why, and why it hasn't agreed to what the other side is asking for. The hearing is usually heavily laden with economic data and you'll need an expert to help you make the presentation. It's rather different than a grievance arbitration hearing in the sense that each side is often left essentially unimpeded to present its "case." The PSBA can provide helpful support in making hearing presentations. Most fact finders try to function as mediators, working to try to forge a compromise settlement that the parties can just accept. They often will make one or more visits after the hearing to try to work out an agreement and avoid issuing a formal report.

The PLRB has fact finders on a very short leash time-wise. They are required to issue their reports within 45 days of appointment, no exceptions. The process moves along quite rapidly.

As you might suspect, fact finders tend to "split the difference" in their recommendations and tend to be loath to recommend major changes to your contract. They like to recommend "average" settlements.

Fact finding is requested much more often by unions than by management, often as a way of "doing something" when they don't know what else to do with a difficult board.

Although neither party is required to accept a fact finder's recommendations, a party which has requested fact finding is in an awkward position if it chooses to reject the report, since, after all, it requested the process in the first place. A party which was not in favor of fact finding suffers from no such pressure to accept the result. Keep in mind that a party which accepts a report's recommendations has effectively modified its contract proposal to whatever is in the report since, by accepting it, it is manifesting a willingness to live with the recommendation as its contract, regardless of what its position was going into the fact-finding process.

There are very specific requirements that must be followed to "reject" a report you don't like, so you need to be careful to handle the rejection properly if that is your disposition. If the report is accepted by both sides, of course it becomes the new contract. That's actually the idea behind the law. The PLRB will release the rejected report to local media if it is rejected by either side, so the fact-finding process can result in the larger community being informed of the details of what is being offered and demanded in negotiations, which may be helpful if the fact finder's particular style involves providing a lot of detail in the report on the parties' respective positions. After the report is released by the PLRB, the parties are required to "reconsider" their rejections and have a second opportunity to accept or reject. Typically the result does not change.

Act 88, enacted in 1992, added the interestingly named process of "non binding arbitration" to our negotiation vocabulary. In reality, "non-binding arbitration" is just fact finding under another name, since the process is identical to what you experience in fact finding and is non-binding. This ersatz "arbitration" procedure is mandated by law in several situations, most notably when a teachers' union has struck for so long that students cannot be assured 180 days of instruction by June 15 if the strike continues any longer. Under such circumstances, the union is required by law to return for a period of time and to submit to "non-binding arbitration," after which it can strike again during the same school year for a fairly brief period of time. This and other aspects of Act 88 are discussed elsewhere in this guide.

As if fact finding and "non-binding arbitration" weren't enough, in July 2012 the legislature created a third procedure under which the Secretary of Education "may" conduct a "public hearing" in cases where a "contract impasse" has lasted for a full year.[15] The rules for these hearings are not spelled out, other than a requirement that "testimony" is to be taken from the interested parties, and a "report on recommendations" is to be issued within 90 days of the hearing. The new provision does not define when the one-year measuring period begins, and a number of interpretations of the timetable are possible. It remains to be seen how often the secretary will choose to invoke this procedure.

"Early Bird" Negotiations

Sometimes it is possible to achieve a settlement fairly quickly, well before the January to September time frame that describes the "normal" negotiations calendar. Sometimes parties can quietly reach agreement on a contract "extension" well before their current agreement even expires. Such exercises are usually referred to by the somewhat quaint term "early bird" negotiations.

There are several reasons one party or the other might suggest early bird negotiations. Often it simply reflects a desire to avoid the long, potentially contentious and stressful process of "normal" negotiations. Sometimes it is suggested as a means of avoiding media attention to what is being given, or to generally place a settlement under the community's radar and thereby avoid criticism of either the union or district management.

There is nothing magical about early or streamlined negotiations. They are neither good nor bad, and they have been suggested by both unions and management, although it seems more often proposed by the union side. The key to conducting successful early talks is to keep control of the scope of the agenda. The exercise will have little chance of succeeding if either side has an aggressive list of proposals, or ambitious objectives. Early settlements tend to be very "average" and to have very few items in them. They tend to be conducted without professional helpers at the table on either side (although they should be assumed to be in the background) and, for that reason, school districts need to tread carefully. There is nothing wrong with having your labor counsel deeply involved with the talks behind the scenes. You can be sure the union is doing the same thing with its professional staff resources. There also is no reason professional negotiators can't participate directly in the "early bird" format.

If you engage in early negotiations, do not be naive about being able to "start from scratch" in January if things don't work out. No matter what sort of understandings you have with the union about how informal or off the record the early discussions are, once the genie's out of the bottle,

---

[15] *See* 24 Pa. Stat. Ann. §11-1131-A.

he's out of the bottle. If you offer "X" as a salary increase in October, don't think you can credibly tell the union in January that you're only willing to pay "Y." Unless the district's circumstances have changed drastically in a few months, the union knows better. As a rule of thumb, don't offer anything early that you won't be willing to offer later.

A cautious approach to early bird negotiations acknowledges that it is possible that a union's interest in them may be a ploy to try to draw out the district's position on salary prior to the normal start of negotiations in January. The best way to guard against this possibility is to say nothing specific about what the district might be willing to do until after the union makes a specific early bird proposal. If it's reasonable, the district can safely respond. If the union's proposal seems unrealistically high, and too high to work with, end the process at that point.

Final Offers and Union Committee Recommendations

There was once a well-known, elected municipal official in my town who was famous for negotiating with his employees' unions by opening negotiations with his "final offer." He would tell them he had carefully considered his finances and thought he knew what he could, and could not, afford to give. He would announce that he saw no purpose in beating around the bush and playing games with ever-increasing offers until the process arrived at a conclusion. Of course, no one believed him when he said his first offer was "final" and he always revised the "final" offer several times before he ever finished a set of negotiations. You don't want to negotiate like he did.

There is a time and a place for a "final" or "last best" offer. However, it is a step that should be taken reluctantly and only after careful consideration of the circumstances. It is much better to leave the table with a handshake instead of an ultimatum which may, or may not, work. Making a final offer places the employer's credibility at risk unless you are very, very sure that the offer is, in fact, final, at least in the sense that you are willing to let the employees strike before you'd change it. It should never be used as a bluff, lest, going forward, the employer's "line in the sand" will never be taken seriously. Credibility is perhaps the most important commodity you can have in negotiations and once it's lost it is extremely difficult to re-establish. Making final offers lightly is guaranteed to compromise it.

You can almost certainly expect the union to test you to see if your "final offer" is really final. This test may occur at the meeting where you make the proposal, or it may extend over a long period during which the union repeatedly tempts you with this or that change in its positions, perhaps even coming tantalizingly close to your "final offer." If you don't have the stomach to resist such temptation, you may want to rethink whether a final offer is really a good idea.

You can agree to modify final offers, but should only do so with respect to minor terms that do not materially affect the overall settlement. You also can "rearrange" settlements by expanding or contracting the terms as long as the changes have an equivalency to them, i.e., you are giving more than your final offer provided for but you are getting something more in return as well. The essential calculus of the deal, however, remains.

The best "final offer" is one you think has a reasonable chance of being deemed acceptable by the other side, the thought being that your counterpart's approach to negotiation is just to drag things out until he is as sure as he can be that he has not left any money or anything of value on the table. The final offer is a way of saying the party's over and it's time to go home. If you have credibility, it may work. Indeed, there are some union representatives who simply will not settle until they have your "final offer," as though it were some type of code for saying "that's all there is."

One of the things you should consider before making a final offer is just how far apart the two sides are. If, in your best judgment, the distance between the parties' two positions is not enough to be worth fighting over *from the union's point of view,* then, indeed, the party *is* over, there won't be a strike if you just hold your ground, and that is exactly what you should do. A final offer may well be appropriate in such circumstances. Just remember that to make this assessment you have to see things from the other guy's point of view, and not just yours. You can relax a bit once you are convinced that what's left is not worth striking over, with all of the negativity that goes along with that. Whether the union fully realizes it at that time or not, the game is finished and no further concession should be made.

Just as consideration of making a 'final offer" to bring closure to negotiations is sometimes a part of the end game of bargaining, so too is the concept of buying the union negotiating committee's "recommendation" that the membership of the union vote to ratify the proposed agreement when it's taken back. Often, when a union knows the end of the process is at hand, it will try to squeeze just a bit more out of management by announcing that its negotiating committee will be willing to "recommend" the offer to the membership, or "sell" it, if only the district will add a little more to one item or another. The suggestion is that without that recommendation there is a greater risk the membership will vote to reject the agreement than is the case if the offer has the committee's recommendation. Often this is used as one of the ways to test whether a final offer is really final.

How much weight a committee recommendation actually has in these situations is hard to determine. Although there are occasionally situations where a ratification vote is actually very close, you should be skeptical that buying a union committee recommendation materially improves the odds of a successful ratification vote. If a package is good enough, and it makes sense to approve it, it probably will be approved, with or without an endorsement, unless the union leadership sabotages it. This is not to discount the very real threat of a rejection if, in fact, the union negotiating committee decides for whatever reason that it *wants* the contract to be voted down. You should respect the reality that even with a good offer on the table, if the union leadership wants the membership to vote it down because it thinks it can do even better, it can usually accomplish that result.

Retroactivity, Contract Extensions and the Status Quo

When the parties fail to reach an agreement by the time a contract expires, as is often the case in school negotiations, a question sometimes arises about the retroactivity of the eventual settlement. If settlement occurs fairly quickly after the expiration date, retroactivity is usually not much of an issue. If things drag out for a significant period, though, it can become a major concern to both sides. The union, of course, will want some assurance the eventual settlement will, in fact, be retroactive if it provides for any meaningful economic improvements. Management, on the other hand, may feel it is entitled to retain for itself the delay cost associated with a union it views as being recalcitrant in settling on reasonable terms. In addition, the threat of withholding retroactivity is often the only real means available to an employer to pressure a slow-moving union into bringing closure to the process on acceptable terms.

The important thing to remember about retroactivity is that it is negotiable and your settlement needs to specify whether it is, or is not, retroactive, in whole or in part. If you don't say anything, the union will assume your offer is retroactive. Despite what some union folks would have you, or their members, believe, retroactivity is neither universal nor inevitable. I've settled a number of agreements without it, or without all of it. Taking the position in bargaining that an offer is not retroactive, however, may be viewed as a provocative move, particularly if, despite the long, drawn out negotiations process, the union has not interrupted service by striking. Keep in mind that taking the position that an offer is not retroactive can create a serious obstacle to settlement.

When negotiations fail to produce a settlement by the date a contract expires, the union will often send the district a letter declaring the employees will continue to work under the terms of the old contract until or unless the district is notified otherwise. In order to help avoid a later accusation that it engaged in a "lockout," most districts respond by saying they intend to let work continue. These communications, in effect, create a sort of open-ended contract extension, subject to cancellation if things go badly. There is usually no need for a more formal type of contract extension, although occasionally formal extension agreements are used, either for a fixed length of time or incorporating some provision for cancellation after a defined period of advance notice.

Regardless of the device employed by the parties, the district should act as though the contract remains in effect as it was on the last day of the original term. This means that in most cases, employee salaries should also remain unchanged from the last day of the old agreement, with no step increases or increased pay for earning graduate credits taking effect until a settlement is reached. Believe it or not, even such *increases* in compensation can be viewed as an unlawful unilateral change in working conditions, an unfair practice, or a constructive "lockout" for unemployment compensation eligibility purposes.[16] Absent a specific agreement with the union regarding such matters, all changes in compensation, except those dictated by transfers, reassignment, the

---

[16] See *New Castle Area School District v. Unemployment Compensation Board of Review,* 633 A.2d 1339 (Pa. Commw. Ct., 1993).

acquisition of new duties, or promotion, should be deferred. You need to pay attention, however, to exactly when your old contract expired and when the first work day of the following school year fell. In most cases, the first teacher work day will fall *after* what is technically the final day of the old contract (often June 30 or August 31). In such cases, compensation should not change. If, however, in cases where the old contract was technically in effect on the first work day of the new school year, even though a scale for that year was still under negotiation, at least one arbitrator has sustained a grievance claiming that all teachers not at top step, and those who earned credits entitling them to column movement, were entitled to move, albeit based on the old salary schedule (and temporarily). The Commonwealth Court refused to vacate this award.[17] This is a significant issue since the effect of moving everyone up one step on a salary schedule can be a 1.5 to 2% salary increase, even without a change in the schedule itself.

Apart from compensation issues, a district is obligated to maintain *all* terms and conditions of employment as they existed when the agreement expired, until *either* a new agreement is reached or the parties have bargained to impasse over a proposed change the district wishes to make. To fail to do so is an unfair practice. This burden, imposed by the PERA, is often referred to as maintaining the "status quo." It is somewhat easier to articulate than it is to apply, since sometimes the "status quo" cannot be defined with precision. Although not relevant until the employees strike, if an employer alters the "status quo" and employees subsequently walk out, the employer also runs the risk that, for unemployment compensation purposes, the employees will be considered "locked out," and not simply on strike, and, therefore, eligible for benefits.

Tentative Agreements and Documentation

"Tentative agreements" are really just agreements. What makes them "tentative" is the fact that they have been reached along the way toward an overall settlement that has not yet been achieved. Because negotiations often involve discussion of a multitude of different issues, it is common to resolve some along the way, either as standalone agreements or as a part of a package of understandings concerning related (or even unrelated) subjects. Once agreed upon, they are usually put aside until the overall settlement is achieved and they then become part of the new contract. They are "tentative" in the sense that they *can* be revisited later in the negotiations process without committing an unfair labor practice, although they rarely are.

It is important to carefully document any such agreements to avoid later misunderstanding about what, exactly, was agreed upon. Some parties follow the practice of actually initialing or signing off on precise drafts of such items, and you should not be offended if you are asked to do so. Even absent signed agreements, you should be careful to reduce to writing every proposal and every agreement made as negotiations progress. Carefully document the precise changes that are being proposed or which will be made to the contract and make sure your counterparts have that

---

[17] *Northwest Area School District v. Northwest Area Education Association*, 954 A.2d 111 (Pa. Commw. Ct., 2007).

document and have been asked to tell you whether it accurately reflects what has been proposed or agreed upon. Nothing is ever left to be "written up" later.

When a final, overall settlement is achieved you should construct a comprehensive summary of exactly what has been agreed upon throughout the process *prior* to any ratification meetings and to share that with the other side so that there is absolutely no possibility of any disagreement over what the respective groups are voting on. There is simply no excuse for professional negotiators to leave the table with any ambiguity whatever about what the settlement is, down to the last comma and period. That's a mistake amateurs make, and they sometimes end up paying for it.

Tentative agreements should be viewed as serious commitments. Although they often can be lawfully withdrawn or reconsidered, they ought not to be without a good reason. Treating them as whimsical or halfhearted commitments can be viewed, with justification, as indicia of bad faith and, potentially, an unfair practice. Even absent legal consequences, backing out of agreements is sure to interfere with achieving a settlement.

Ratification Votes

The very last stage of labor negotiations involves the formal votes of approval of the two groups represented by the respective negotiating teams – the school board and the union membership. In strictly legal terms, the district cannot be bound to a contract that has not been approved formally by the school board. Internal union governance is really the union's business, but every union requires some kind of ratification vote of its membership to conclude a contract.

If a school district's negotiators are competent, there should be almost no possibility that the full board, when it votes, will not approve the tentative contract settlement. That is because good negotiators are very sure of their authority and their client's wishes before any significant moves are made, and they've taken the time to consult along the way when it was appropriate to do so. Experienced, competent negotiators know what they can safely commit to, and when. The vote should be truly only a formality. In my entire experience as a negotiator on behalf of school districts, I have never had a board reject a tentative settlement I reached at the table, not because the settlements were so great, but because my committee did its homework.

Not quite so on the union side. Although most of the time – indeed almost all of the time – you can expect the union's rank and file membership to vote to approve a tentative settlement (particularly if the union leadership is sincerely recommending it), there is always at least a chance something will go wrong at the ratification meeting and the deal will be voted down. Certainly, the risk of the union's vote going bad is materially greater than the risk a school board will turn on *its* negotiating committee. For this reason, you should always ask that the union conduct its vote first, to get any uncertainty out of the way before the board makes a commitment to the deal. If, for some reason, the union's membership rejects the contract, the board should not vote, since its action serves no useful purpose and unnecessarily commits the board publicly to whatever was in the offer. In a situation that fluid, you want to keep your options open.

Union ratification votes can go bad for one of two reasons. The union leadership may have simply misread its membership and is as surprised by the rejection as you are. Something untoward may have happened at the meeting and the leadership just lost control of the group. Group dynamics sometimes work that way. It also is possible that you've been "had," and are the victim of bad faith on the part of a union negotiating committee that sabotaged the vote in order to get you to sweeten the deal *after* the rejection. Fortunately, this is not very common, but it has happened. If the union leadership is recommending against accepting an offer, and makes it perfectly obvious that it is doing so, there is absolutely no reason for the board to schedule a vote, because if the union conducts a vote under these circumstances, it is almost certainly for the sole purpose of showing you how solidly the membership is behind the negotiating committee in its feeling that your latest offer is unacceptable.

Once an agreement has been rejected by the union, there will inevitably be at least one more bargaining session, since you have to go back the table to try to pick up the pieces. Whether or not the failed agreement involved a management "final offer," the district should be most reluctant to make any improvements in order to change the outcome of the vote. Quickly sweetening the deal rewards, and therefore encourages, that sort of behavior, and may actually make the union leadership look bad to its membership. After all, they may have just recommended acceptance of a contract that was quickly proven not to be the best available deal after all.

When faced with this situation, you should try to get the union folks to explain exactly why the vote went bad in order to see what changes might be necessary and/or possible. The preferred approach to repairing the deal is to see if it can be rearranged, as opposed to improved. Perhaps you can move money around from one area to another, or replace a concession with something different, but of equivalent value or importance. Maybe you can add something new of value to the union side of the deal, but also secure some new concession in your favor as well. Balance is the key. If the settlement involves a number of items, as they often do, there is usually some way to rework it so the union leadership can justify resubmitting it to the rank and file, hopefully with a better outcome. Working through situations like this really puts the quality of your relationship with your union counterparts to the test.

Mediators

Mediators are employees of the Commonwealth who work for the Bureau of Mediation, a part of the Department of Labor and Industry. Every public sector negotiation is assigned a state mediator whose job is to do whatever he can to facilitate an agreement. The mediator has absolutely no interest in whether the settlement is a good one or a bad one for either side, and he has no authority to make either side agree to anything. His only concern is that there *be* a settlement and that no interruption of public service occurs. He won't help you get a favorable settlement, and likely won't offer an opinion one way or the other on whether you are about to do something ill advised, unless he thinks the greater good of achieving a settlement may be harmed by your actions. Mediators are facilitators.

Because of their neutral role, it is essential that mediators maintain the respect and trust of both sides. It is important to understand that the mediator cannot be effective if he simply berates the other side into seeing the wisdom of your proposals. He also loses his effectiveness if either side concludes that it can't trust him to keep a confidence. Don't ask him to do your job for you, or to let you in on the other side's secrets, and don't expect him to do those things.

That is not to say that mediators won't, at appropriate times, tell a negotiating party its proposals are unrealistic, or unachievable. They do that all the time, and it is an essential part of the assistance they provide to try to get the contending sides to view things realistically. Don't resent it if the mediator does that to your side as well. Their reward is surely in heaven.

Mediators employ a variety of techniques. Often, they shuttle back and forth between the two sides who are holed up in separate rooms, sending out feelers or acting as messengers, communicating proposals that are "unofficial" but very real. Sometimes they invent proposals of their own, based on what they think might be acceptable, in the hope they can construct a settlement both sides can live with. And don't be surprised if an idea that the mediator presents as his own really had its origins in the other side's caucus room, but for some reason, your opposite number was reluctant to stick his neck out. Often mediators are made privy to information about what one side is willing to agree to that they are not at liberty to divulge. With very rare exceptions, they are trustworthy and able to keep a secret. They are generally helpful sorts. And, incidentally, mediators are immune from being compelled to testify in formal legal proceedings about what they are told during negotiations.[18]

Mediators also work behind the scenes, in between negotiating sessions, using telephone contact or private meetings as a way of interacting with the parties. It is not at all unusual for significant negotiating to occur away from the bargaining table and mediators can be useful facilitators of that process.

Perhaps one of the most useful roles for a mediator is simply as a sounding board for proposals or strategies. A mediator who has been closely involved with both parties over an extended time has a unique perspective on what's doable and what isn't, and, most importantly, on what each side's priorities are. Without breaking either side's confidence, he can sometimes guide you in the most productive direction.

The Department does a pretty good job of selecting the mediators it hires. Without exception, they have worked in the labor relations field on one side or the other prior to becoming mediators,

---

[18] *See* 42 Pa. Cons. Stat. § 5949 (2012); 43 P.S. §211.34; Pa. R. Civ. P. 4011.

and often on both sides. Many have come from private industry and have that perspective as well. View them as a resource.

Mandatory v. Permissive Subjects of Bargaining; Impact Bargaining

Mandatory subjects of bargaining are those subjects that parties are legally obligated to negotiate over if requested to do so. A party can be relieved of the duty to bargain over such subjects under various circumstances, as for example when you have already done so and concluded a collective bargaining agreement, or when your contract has what is called a "waiver" clause through which the parties have agreed that during the term of their agreement they will not be required to bargain over any subject, regardless of whether it could have been brought up during contract negotiations (but wasn't).

What are the mandatory subjects? Generally, all aspects of wages, benefits, hours, and other "terms and conditions of employment" are covered. This stuff ends up being the meat of your contract. It is more enlightening to consider what is NOT a mandatory subject, a/k/a something that is a "permissive" subject, or, one you (or the union) cannot be compelled to bargain over. Permissive subjects include (surprisingly) most aspects of evaluation systems,[19] class size or caseload limits,[20] inclusion or exclusion of employees from a bargaining unit,[21] proposed settlement of outstanding unfair labor practice charges,[22] no smoking rules,[23] most aspects of dress codes,[24] whether employees are to be released from work for union business,[25] any contract provision that is contrary to law, who negotiates on behalf of a party,[26] the contents of job descriptions,[27] and the determination of the qualifications for a position.[28]

Section 702 of the PERA (discussed in more detail *infra*) defines several broad areas of managerial authority, with respect to which bargaining is permissive in nature:

> Public employers shall not be required to bargain over matters of inherent managerial
> policy, which shall include but shall not be limited to such areas of discretion or policy as

---

[19] *Crawford Cent. Educ. Support Pers. Ass'n v. Crawford Cent. Sch. Dist.,* 39 PPER ¶36 (H. Ex. 2008).

[20] *Pa. Labor Relations Bd. v. State Coll. Area Sch. Dist.,* 306 A.2d 404 (Pa. Commw. Ct. 1973); *Joint Bargaining Comm. of the Soc. Servs. Union v. Pa. Labor Relations Bd.,* 469 A.2d 150 (Pa. 1983).

[21] *Teamsters Local 430 v. Manchester Ambulance Club,* 32 PPER ¶32039 (Bd. 2001).

[22] *N. Wales Borough Police Dep't v. N. Wales Borough,* 37 PPER ¶176 (H. Ex. 2006).

[23] *Chambersburg Area Sch. Dist. v. Commonwealth,* 430 A.2d 740 (Pa. Commw. Ct. 1981).

[24] *PSSU, Local 668 v. Pa. Labor Relations Bd.,* 763 A.2d 560 (Pa. Commw. Ct. 2000); *Portage Area Educ. Ass'n v. Portage Area Sch. Dist.,* 29 PPER ¶29032 (H. Ex. 1998).

[25] *Temple Univ. Hosp. Nurses Ass'n v. Temple Univ. Health Sys.,* 41 PPER ¶51 (H. Ex. 2010).

[26] Public Employee Relations Act, 43 Pa. Stat. Ann. § 1101.1201(b)(2).

[27] *Service Employee International Union, Local 668 v. Commonwealth of Pennsylvania,* 40 PPER ¶88 (2009).

[28] *See Crawford,* 39 PPER ¶36.

the functions and programs of the public employer, standards of services, its overall budget, utilization of technology, the organizational structure and selection and direction of personnel. Public employers, however, shall be required to meet and discuss on policy matters affecting wages, hours and terms and conditions of employment as well as the impact thereon upon request by public employe representatives.[29]

Most of the cases holding that particular topics are permissive rely on one or more of these statutory categories.

Many districts, whether out of ignorance or by design, have chosen to bargain over permissive subjects, and once they are enshrined in a contract, the terms must be honored, at least until the contract expires. An employer can decline to continue past contractual terms relating to permissive subjects, but, as you might imagine, suddenly declaring a term of a collective bargaining agreement off limits after its inclusion in the contract for many years creates practical problems in terms of reaching agreement on a successor agreement.

An interesting example of the interplay between mandatory and permissive subjects can be found in the approach of teachers' unions to the subject of class size. It is rare these days to see a straightforward contract proposal that class sizes be limited to such and such numbers. However, you still see occasional proposals that say the district can have any class sizes it wants, but if the size gets over a certain number, the affected teachers will be paid extra. This approach, in the union's eyes, makes the proposal really a wage proposal. In my eyes, it doesn't, but often the most efficient way to turn aside a proposal on a permissive subject is simply to say NO, in emphatic terms, BOTH because you don't want to agree AND because it's unlawful for the union to demand that you bargain over it.

A party that insists to the point of an impasse[30] upon agreement on a permissive subject commits an unfair labor practice. A party confronted with a demand to bargain over a permissive subject can decline to discuss the subject. Insistence on those discussions occurring after the invitation is declined will also likely be found to be an unfair labor practice.

A distinction must be drawn between bargaining over a permissive subject, such as class size or job descriptions, and bargaining over the "impact" of changes the employer might make in the workplace related to such a subject. Thus, a union may claim that while it cannot insist on a contract provision establishing class sizes, it can propose that teachers be paid more if they teach very large classes, i.e., on account of the "impact" of the class sizes. Although you can argue this latter point with respect to class size, clearly there are some changes an employer can make in areas where it is free to act without consulting the union which nonetheless trigger some obligation to bargain over the "impact" or the "effects."

---

[29] 43 Pa. Stat. Ann. § 1101.702 (2012).

[30] The concept of "impasse" is discussed in detail in the next section.

A good example is the situation that exists when an employer materially changes the content of a job, i.e., the job description. If an employee's job is made materially more difficult, an employer may be required to bargain over an adjustment in the rate of pay for that job, even though its right to alter the job without first negotiating is beyond question. Similarly, if an employer creates a totally new job in the middle of a contract, its right to establish the new job is clear, but a rate of pay will have to be negotiated, even though the parties are not in the process of bargaining over an entire agreement at the time.

These are examples of "effects" or "impact" bargaining, which is a very real obligation. Of course, if such circumstances arise in the middle of a contract where a no strike pledge is in effect, the union may have very little bargaining power, but the exercise must still be undertaken in good faith.

Negotiating Contracting and Unilaterally Implementing Proposals

Elsewhere in this guide you will find comments about the importance and usefulness of having the topic of the district's right to outsource, or "subcontract" specifically addressed in contract language.[31] If you don't have the advantage of such language, unfortunately, you'll have to take your proposal to subcontract unit work to the bargaining table and deal with it like any other contract proposal you might make, i.e., you need to get the union to agree, or, if you want to press the point far enough, you must negotiate to the point of the exhaustion of all impasse procedures provided in Act 88. There is no question that subcontracting is a mandatory subject of bargaining.

Support unions are very sensitive to the threat of subcontracting, and view it as a real danger. The threat of subcontracting can be a very effective means of creating leverage at the bargaining table, as well it should if the threat is real.

Contracting with an outside provider sounds like a great idea to many boards as a quick way to control costs that may have gotten out of control. Boards should not move too quickly in this area and before a district goes down the road to subcontracting it should consider the full implications of what it is proposing and be prepared to accept them. First and foremost, it will likely stir up a political hornet's nest, as friends and family of the soon to be displaced workers show up at board meetings, make phone calls to board members they've known their whole lives, and bombard the newspaper with letters to the editor decrying the injustice of the proposal and predicting that somehow the kids will suffer. And make no mistake about it; you will be proposing the end of life as they know it, even if some or all of them are hired by the contractor. If a solid majority of the board is not willing to endure the controversy over many months, it shouldn't make the proposal.

---

[31] "Outsourcing" or "contracting" are more accurate terms, but the use of the term "subcontracting" appears to have become standard usage. The concept involves an agreement with a third party to provide services that formerly were provided by bargaining unit members.

The second reality a district has to consider is that getting from the initial proposal to the point where the district can lawfully implement a contracting plan without the actual consent of the union (and yes, contracts can be negotiated where that consent *is* obtained) is a project that will likely take many months. First, you must build a case for the proposal. That case usually revolves around cost savings, and demonstrating the savings requires that bid specifications be developed and advertised, and bids received from the potential contractors. You don't need to have any involvement with the union to develop specifications and obtain bids, although the act of doing these things will get the union's undivided attention. Be prepared for questions about what you're up to. The bids should be in hand before you even meet with the union to discuss the topic, so obtaining them should be part of the pre-negotiation planning. Otherwise you've just added more time to what may already be a long process.

When you meet with the union, have a written proposal prepared for them, along with all of the information on the bids and projected savings. In other words, make a real presentation. The union is entitled to this information, and if the presentation isn't convincing, you ought to rethink the whole idea. Expect the union to do its best to avoid dealing with the topic in a meaningful way for as long as possible. You may see lengthy pauses between meetings, and a long list of canned "information requests" prepared by the union's home office, intended in part to bog down the process. When you do have negotiating sessions, the union will want to talk about anything but your contracting proposal. They'll say they need lots of time to study the issue. You'll have to push to exert some pressure on the union to deal with the proposal. Expect the union to request that the PLRB order fact finding. It's also a good idea to make sure you have involved the state mediator early and often in the discussions, so that it is clear that this resource has been exhausted as well.

Why all the concern about the process?

"Impasse" is the key concept here. The law permits an employer to unilaterally (i.e., without the union's agreement) implement an offer on a mandatory subject of bargaining (like contracting) IF the parties are at impasse and have exhausted all of Act 88's relevant impasse procedures, such as mediation, fact-finding, and non-binding arbitration. Impasse is a slippery concept and whether one does, or does not, exist, is a very fact-specific determination. It is a judgment call to declare an impasse. Generally speaking, an impasse exists when you have made a good faith attempt to reach agreement and, despite your best efforts, the parties are simply intractably opposed to each other's positions with no realistic chance for an agreement in the foreseeable future. In short, they are dead locked. Impasses are usually characterized by a large number of fruitless negotiating sessions over an extended period. It is often characteristic of an impasse that the parties have gone an extended period with no meaningful movement on either side, and perhaps very few meetings as they stare at each other without budging. The district has usually made what it has described as its "final" offer on the subject and has stuck to it for a long time. The Supreme Court offered the following definition of "impasse" in *Norwin School District v. Belan,* 507 A.2d 373, 380 n.9 (Pa. 1986).:

The definition of an "impasse" is that point at which the parties have exhausted the prospects of concluding an agreement and further discussions would be fruitless – but its application can be difficult. Given the many factors commonly itemized by the [National Labor Relations] Board and courts in impasse cases, perhaps all that can be said with confidence is that an impasse is a "state of facts in which the parties, despite the best of faith, are simply deadlocked."

The "good faith" component is usually demonstrated by a history of flexibility in your position and offers prior to reaching the point of impasse. How can you show flexibility on a subject like this? There are a number of ways, centering around things you can offer to mitigate the effects on employees. You can propose severance packages, guarantees the contractor will offer jobs to displaced workers before hiring others, or even some type of guaranteed starting wage and benefit terms (if your contractor will accept that). You also can offer to accept revisions to your contract which will not save you as much as contracting will, but which will still be significant, even if unacceptable to the union.[32] All of those things will serve to demonstrate to the PLRB, when the inevitable unfair labor practice charges are filed, that you really did try to work the issue out before implementation.

You can see why this takes time.

You can expect the union to file an unfair labor practice charge if the district declares an "impasse" and implements a contracting arrangement unilaterally, i.e., without any agreement being reached in which the union consents to the arrangement. Because such litigation can take several years to run its course, the district runs the theoretical risk of hearing long after the decision is made that the requisite impasse didn't exist. There is no way to completely remove all risk of such a problem arising, and, consequently, the district needs to do everything it can to demonstrate the requisite good faith and the existence of an impasse. This is one reason that an adequate amount of time must be allowed for the process to unfold.

The potential financial consequences of unlawfully implementing a contracting proposal are quite significant. The PLRB can, in such circumstances, order a full back pay and reinstatement remedy, which may well affect a large number of employees. Contracting requires patience, resolve, and a steady hand. It is not for the faint hearted.

The good news is that the PLRB seems to have taken the position that in the unique case of subcontracting, out of all of the mandatory subjects of bargaining in the labor universe, the requirements that must be met before an employer can unilaterally implement a proposal are somewhat

---

[32] The Pennsylvania Labor Relations Board has expressed the view that an employer engages in unlawful "surface bargaining" if all it does at the bargaining table is calculate the savings that will result from subcontracting and tell the union it has to offer concessions of equal value. Some type of severance terms, or at least some willingness to accept less severe concessions, seems to be required under at least one decision. *See Upper Moreland School District*, 26 PPER ¶26010 (1994).

less than are required for other types of proposals. Nonetheless, the law is less than clear on the entire topic of unilateral implementation at "impasse."

In *Philadelphia Housing Authority v. Pa. Labor Relations Board,* 620 A.2d 594 (Pa. Commw. Ct. 1992), the Commonwealth Court found the employer to have unlawfully implemented a final offer that included changes to its health care plan. The employer maintained the parties were at impasse and that, as a result, implementation was permitted. Although the Court agreed an impasse existed, nonetheless the Court interpreted the PERA as requiring a strike occur before implementation in order for unilateral action to be lawful. Since the union hadn't struck, the employer committed an unfair practice by implementing. The Court's discussion sent a clear signal that it took a dim view of the practice of unilateral implementation. The practical effect of the Court's decision was to enable unions to prevent implementation by simply refraining from going on strike.

After the enactment of Act 88, *Philadelphia Housing Authority* was followed in 1996 by the Commonwealth Court's decision in *Burrell Education Association v. Burrell School District,* 674 A.2d 348 (Pa. Commw. Ct. 1996), in which, once again, an employer, believing it was at impasse, unilaterally implemented a contract proposal which altered an insurance benefit. In *Burrell,* the union had engaged in a strike. Although the procedural posture of the case was unusual (it involved an injunction action which had as its objective forcing the district to honor an interim agreement that did not actually resolve all of the outstanding issues between the parties), during the course of its decision, the Court signaled it would take a restrictive view of what constituted an impasse even when a strike had occurred. In *Burrell,* the union and the district had agreed to proceed with an Act 88 "non-binding arbitration" proceeding, even though the union's strike had apparently not been of sufficient duration to require that the arbitration occur. This fact, the Court noted, was inconsistent with the existence of an impasse. Among other things, the case stands for the proposition that impasses can be created and then broken, and lawful implementation absolutely requires that the impasse exist at the time implementation occurs.

As noted above, however, when the subject of unilateral implementation is subcontracting, as opposed to changes in insurance or other topics, the law appears to be somewhat more permissive. As recently as 2011, for example, the PLRB explicitly recognized a "distinction between subcontracting and wages, hours and working conditions" and acknowledged that subcontracting is unique because it implicates a fundamental level of "managerial decision-making" and "fundamental political decisions over the quality and quality of public services to be provided to … citizens."[33] Although there are surprisingly few reported appellate court decisions clarifying the fundamental rules applying in this area, it seems reasonably safe to say, with respect to subcontracting at least, that a strike is not a sine qua non to unilateral implementation.[34] It also seems reasonable to conclude that at

---

[33] *Ass'n of Pa. State Coll. & Univ. Facilities v. Pa. State Sys. of Higher Educ.,* 43 PPER ¶56 (PLRB 2011).

[34] *See Mars Area Ass'n of Sch. Serv. Pers. v. Pa. Labor Relations Bd.,* 538 A.2d 585 (Pa. Commw. Ct. 1987). Although *Mars* is a pre-Act 88 case, it has been favorably cited by the PLRB post Act 88. In *Mars,* the district subcontracted transportation after a "factual" impasse, in the absence of a strike.

least to the extent that circumstances make them available, Act 88's impasse resolution procedures should be invoked. This means an employer should be meticulous in complying with the statutory timetables, using the services of a state mediator, and probably availing itself of the right to insist on fact finding by April 12 of the bargaining year.[35] The situation with respect to topics other than subcontracting, however, is less clear and, as noted above, considerable troublesome and confusing authority exists.

There is one final aspect of subcontracting to consider. Subcontracting proposals are almost always made at the same time the entire collective bargaining agreement is being renegotiated, and there are good reasons for this. When the entire agreement is under discussion and the district is only proposing to subcontract a relatively small portion of a large unit (which is often the case) the district is in an inherently strong bargaining position. But what if the district is locked into a lengthy agreement and decides it would like to subcontract bargaining unit work in the middle of the contract's term? It may be possible to accomplish this, provided the contract does not contain problematic language.

Later in this guide, there is a discussion of waiver or integration clauses, sometimes referred to as "zipper" clauses, in connection with the subjects of whether past practices can be enforced as though they were written into a contract, and whether they can be unilaterally abolished. Such clauses can serve another purpose, however. They can effectively prevent an employer from subcontracting bargaining unit work during the fixed term of a contract. These clauses often say something like this:

> The parties agree that all negotiable items have been discussed during the negotiations leading to this agreement, and that no additional negotiations will be conducted on any item whether contained herein or not, during the life of this agreement.

An employer which proposes mid-term bargaining over subcontracting in the face of such language runs the very real risk that an arbitrator hearing a grievance challenging eventual implementation will rule that the integration clause effectively prohibits such action. To a lesser degree, there is some risk that even a standard recognition clause might be interpreted as having this effect if an arbitrator were sufficiently offended by the employer's action. Because may agreements contain waiver/integration clauses, most districts take the safe, and ultimately more effective, course of proposing subcontracting when the contract is up for complete renegotiation.

If, however, your contract does not contain such language, it is likely that subcontracting can be proposed lawfully in the middle of the contract term. Certainly there is no PLRB or court decision

---

[35] The PLRB has held that while unsuccessful fact finding is not absolutely required in order to establish an impasse on subcontracting (or any other issue), if it occurs, the employer must be prepared to show that it considered the results in some deliberate way and rejected them in good faith. See *Williamsport School District*, 41 PPER 46 (2010).

clearly holding that this cannot be done. There are several reported decisions where mid-term bargaining was part of the fact pattern and, while the district was ultimately unsuccessfully in the litigation for unrelated reasons, the PLRB said nothing to indicate that the timing of the proposal was of any significance.[36]

The Siege

Unfortunately, the negotiation of school labor contracts at times devolves into a siege-type situation where the actual expiration date of the contract seems to have little significance, yet the union shows no inclination to go on strike. Negotiations just seem to go on forever with little activity and no end in sight. Negotiations can extend for literally years after the expiration of the original agreement, and operating without a contract in place for a full school year, or more, isn't all that rare.

There is little a board can do in such situations except be patient and let things run their course. You can control some of the effects of the "siege," by avoiding fruitless meetings to the extent possible consistent with your obligation to bargain in good faith. And, if you truly lose patience with the process, you can make noises about withdrawing retroactivity from the offer which may get the union's attention if you have credibility at the table. Ultimately, a union that has no inclination to go on strike needs closure to the process much more than you do, because any improvements to wages or benefits must await the conclusion of negotiations. If, on the other hand, the proposals in dispute represent concessions on the part of the employees, that fact alone may well explain why you are negotiating a year after the contract expired, because the status quo may be better than the alternative.

There have even been occasions where it was perfectly obvious that a lengthy delay in resolving a contract was a conscious part of a "political" strategy by the union, intended to kill time while the union awaited the results of the next school board election. The thought was that a more union-friendly board would result from the election and be reflected in a change at the bargaining table in the union's favor. Once in a while, it works.

Early in my career as a labor lawyer, I had the privilege of practicing for a brief period with a wonderfully savvy senior attorney who told me that one of the qualities I would need to acquire to be an effective negotiator was a "cast iron ass." Over the years I have come to appreciate the advice. Patience is a virtue in labor negotiations and many mistakes have been borne of impatience with the process. Just remember that if the kids are still in school and the money is in the bank, you probably have no reason to be impatient. You have all the time in the world.

Communicating Directly with Employees

Although it should be sparingly done, under controlled circumstances, employers can lawfully communicate directly with the union's membership. It is usually done through personal letters. To have maximum effect, they can be sent to the employees' homes.

---

[36] *See, e.g., Easton Area Educational Support Personnel Association v. Easton Area School District,* 37 PPER 57 (2006).

A district should not take this step lightly because of the possible reaction of the union's leadership to what it may well perceive as either a nefarious attempt to bypass the union and negotiate directly with your employees, or an insulting implication that the union leadership is not being honest and forthright with the membership. Recall that some unions have an innate insecurity about their position and any perceived threat to their status as representative will likely be met with considerable hostility. Either way, they might get angry. In and of itself, this is not a reason to keep from communicating, but the situation is somewhat similar to that posed by sharing too many of the details of negotiations with the press. Remember that after the letters have gone out, you'll still be sitting down across the table from the union's leadership and its attitude may have a lot to do with whether any progress can be made.

If, however, things have gotten to the point where that is a secondary consideration and you feel that something significant can be gained by direct communication, it is lawful to do so provided you do not use the communication to argue in favor of your proposal, to attack the union leadership, or to reveal any proposal you have not already made to the union and given it a fair opportunity to accept. If you avoid those temptations, you can communicate the details of your offer and the union's response, provided you do so objectively and accurately. Sometimes such communications have a real effect if the union leadership has not done a good job of keeping its members accurately informed about what is going on, and the information the employees receive creates some real pressure on the union leadership. If the leadership is doing an effective job, however, the effort will likely yield nothing positive.

Sometimes during negotiations, school officials will be approached personally by individual employees seeking information about what's going on, or who want to try to influence you in some way. Often in the school setting, these are people the school official may have known for many years on a personal level. It is awkward to have to tell a longtime neighbor or childhood friend that you can't discuss something that is probably very important to both of you, but the same ground rules mentioned above should be followed when having such conversations. If you're asked for information, provide it as objectively and honestly as you can and try to avoid offering more than education about the circumstances. It's OK to explain there are certain rules that apply to what you are, and are not, allowed to say.

Union Information Requests

It is customary for a union entering into negotiations to submit a written request for various pieces of information about the bargaining unit, benefits, and the employer's finances. You may receive requests for a list of employees, their job titles, dates of hire, benefit enrollment categories and the like, as well as a request for copies of your last several budgets and various other publicly available financial records. If benefits are likely to be a big issue for either side, you may see a specific request for some highly detailed information on benefit costs and history. Although it may be annoying and take a bit of time to assemble some of the information, don't be offended and certainly don't make an issue out of providing it. The union has a right to information reasonably necessary to enable it to do its job of formulating proposals and responding to yours.

There is a distinction between information of a historical or factual nature and information which is clearly a part of the employer's internal planning and negotiations strategy. The former has to be shared; the latter does not (although it may be a good idea to share some of the information you have assembled specifically for negotiations if you are trying to persuade someone to see things your way).

The right is not unlimited. You don't have to invent information that isn't already assembled, nor do you have to respond to lengthy interrogatories clearly intended to annoy you. You don't have to provide information the union already has, and you don't have to drop everything to provide it by some arbitrary deadline the union may have unilaterally established.

Expect to receive some sort of request near the start of negotiations, and deal with it in a professional manner.

Act 93 Plans

Although, strictly speaking, not a part of the traditional labor relations environment within which school districts operate, compensation plans for administrators bear some superficial resemblance to union contracts, and are often formed and modified through a process which looks suspiciously like negotiations. They exist because of Section 1164 of the School Code, 24 Pa. Stat. Ann. § 11-1164 (2012), often referred to as "Act 93."

Act 93 is a very brief statutory provision which does nothing more than require that every school district have in effect at all times a written plan which adequately sets for the compensation and benefits to be received by those classified as "school administrators." The term "school administrator" is defined as anyone below the rank of superintendent who is not eligible for membership in a union bargaining unit by virtue of duties.[37] Business managers and personnel directors are specifically excluded. First-level supervisors, such as building principals, are not eligible to be included in union bargaining units under the PERA and are universally included in Act 93 plans as a result. In practice, many districts have included many non-union employees in their Act 93 plans who are not "supervisors" or "administrators" and who aren't necessarily required to be covered by the plan. There is nothing wrong with this practice. There also is no reason a district cannot have more than one Act 93 plan if it has a sufficiently complex group of non-union administrative personnel to justify having more than one plan with the accompanying systems of compensation and benefit packages. In

---

[37] Actually, Act 93 refers to the inclusion of employees who "by virtue of assigned duties [are] not in a bargaining unit of public employees." Clearly, those who are *ineligible* for inclusion in a bargaining unit because they have supervisory of policy-making responsibilities must be covered by an Act 93 plan. However, the employee involved in the *Curley* case, discussed *infra*, was actually a psychologist. Many bargaining units of professional employees include psychologists. The Commonwealth Court took an inclusive view of the coverage of Act 93 in its only reported decision.

fact, every employee of every school district must have his compensation and benefits authorized in some fashion by the board of school directors, whether through a collective bargaining agreement, an individual employment contract, an Act 93 plan, or other specific board action of some type.

An Act 93 plan can be for a term of several years or for a single year. Its required contents are nothing more than compensation and benefits for those covered. The Act specifically provides for the inclusion of evaluation programs if they directly relate to compensation decisions, as well as early retirement programs. "Fringe benefits" must be included, but the term is not defined.

Most districts prudently have adhered to the bare requirements of the Act, but some have strayed far beyond its mandates and have elected to include all sorts of things that aren't required. I've seen seniority language that controls appointments, transfers and promotions, as well as language that regulates furloughs and creates bumping rights. I've also seen language regulating disciplinary action, parent complaints, and a host of things that are typically found in union contracts. Such provisions fall under the category of self-inflicted wounds.

Act 93 does not require negotiations. It only requires that the district "meet and discuss in good faith" with "the administrators" prior to adopting a plan, and after being requested to do so by a majority of the administrative staff. There is a significant difference between "meeting and discussing" and negotiating. Following the discussion, which should be approached sincerely, the board is nonetheless free to adopt any plan it feels is appropriate. The plan does not have to contain any particular term that was in the prior plan, and can reflect the prevailing economic condition of the district, as many of them have. Agreement of the administrators or their committee of representatives is not required. Indeed, the Act only requires that the district meet with "the administrators" and does not require the district to restrict its discussion to any particular spokesmen or committee, self-appointed or otherwise.

As a practical matter, and to maintain morale among the administrative ranks, it is common practice to recognize a more or less official group of representatives as speaking for the administrative staff, and, in an ideal situation, everyone leaves the discussion satisfied that the result was fair. At the end of the day, however, the board has control of every aspect of the plan it adopts.

Even though a board is free to adopt any plan it chooses, that does not mean it can disregard or modify an Act 93 plan once it adopts one. In *Curley v. Board of School Directors of Greater Johnstown School District,* 641 A.2d 719 (Pa. Commw. Ct. 1994), the Commonwealth Court held that a school district could be compelled through legal action to pay an employee covered by an Act 93 plan in accordance with the plan, thus rendering the plan a binding commitment for all practical purposes. Although no reported decision has specifically addressed the subject of a district's attempt to formally *modify* a plan prospectively once it has been adopted, there are serious doubts that it would be successful in doing so. A district should expect to live with the plan once the terms are set, even if the board had a free hand in setting those terms in the first place.

As the result of potential problems should a district want to modify a multi-year Act 93 plan, consideration should be given to whether a multi-year plan is even advisable. They are sometimes entered into simply as matters of convenience but later determined to be inappropriate for various reasons. If a multi-year plan is going to be utilized, there seems to be nothing wrong with building in a provision that allows the district to terminate it early, or extend its terms, should circumstances warrant, as long as such provisions are clearly spelled out when the plan is initially adopted.

Concessionary Bargaining

The paradigm of bargaining changes somewhat when an employer engages in concessionary bargaining. Instead of defending its management rights against encroachment and trying to get through the process as inexpensively as possible, management in such circumstances has a more aggressive agenda, seeking reductions in benefits and costs. As insurance costs have skyrocketed and many districts have faced significant financial challenges, proposals for reductions in benefits, increased employee participation in benefit costs, and wage freezes have entered the picture. How does this change bargaining?

Faced with concessionary bargaining by a determined school board, many unions will simply dig in and resist bringing the process to a conclusion. After all, what is the incentive to settle when your primary objective is to maintain the status quo? Even the threat of withholding retroactivity, which a school board can sometimes use when it is offering at least some improvement in economic terms, is unavailable as a means of pressuring the union to reach an agreement. There is nothing positive to apply retroactively. On the plus side, a district that is proposing a wage freeze (as opposed to benefit concessions) can effectively achieve it without the agreement of the union if the union drags the negotiations out in the face of a concessionary or stand still proposal. When school starts without a contract, a freeze has been effectively implemented as long as the district holds its ground with respect to its basic bargaining position.

Just as in all bargaining, credibility is everything when a district engages in concessionary bargaining, or offers a freeze in pre-existing economic terms. The key to accomplishing these objectives is to convince the union that you are, indeed, serious about the position and are prepared to wait as long as it takes to address the concerns you have. Until and unless that happens, the process will simply not conclude.

Leverage

Ultimately, the outcome of negotiations is not dictated by reason, logic, or who has the best debating skills, although those things certainly help if they are in your favor. Most of the time, the outcome is determined by bargaining power, sometimes referred to as "leverage." Bargaining power can be lost, squandered, or wasted by a variety of factors or events, such as a failure to understand relevant legal principles, poor judgment, loss of patience or composure, or the like, but, without it, you aren't likely to have a satisfying outcome.

From a school board's perspective, where does bargaining power come from? It comes from the support of your community for your objectives, and the confidence the community has in its educational leadership. It comes from the discipline and solidarity of board members. It comes from patience on the part of board members, and a willingness to take the time necessary to accomplish your objectives. It comes from both the willingness and the capacity of the district to endure stress and inconvenience, and to tolerate a certain amount of risk. And, ultimately, it comes from having credibility in the eyes of the union – from being able to convince the union that these factors are present.

From the union's standpoint, bargaining power comes from the confidence of its membership in the union's leadership; the willingness of its members to act as the union's leadership directs, even if those actions cause discomfort; and a belief by management that the union is capable of pulling off a strike and willing to do so under the right circumstances, among other things.

An interesting aspect of bargaining power is that the absence of leverage by one party often translates into a corresponding relative *advantage* in the bargaining power of the other. Thus, if management commands few of the attributes that tend to give it leverage, the union, almost by default, gains the upper hand. The converse is also often true. And the one thing that will effectively *eliminate* leverage altogether is a realization by one party that the other is so in need of a settlement at a particular moment that it will simply take whatever deal it can get. A party in that unenviable position will always have an unhappy result, and it is one of the reasons it is always a good idea to guard against appearing too anxious to settle.

"Meet and Discuss"

The term "meet and discuss" appears in several places in the PERA and the School Code. In Code Section 1164, providing for Act 93 plans, a district is required to "meet and discuss" the terms of those plans, prior to adoption, upon request of a majority of administrators. In the PERA, although a district is not required to bargain over matters of inherent managerial policy, Section 702 requires an employer to "meet and discuss" them, upon request. Similarly, while first-level supervisors can't belong to a union bargaining unit under the PERA, Section 704 allows them to form a "meet and discuss" unit to talk about their terms of employment, even though any agreements subsequently reached are virtually unenforceable.[38]

The obligation to "meet and discuss," when it exists, is just that, and no district should feel pressured to make promises or concessions if it finds itself engaged in such discussions. It is little more than a formalized channel of communication, available to employees or their organizations, in very specific circumstances where bargaining simply is not required.

[38] *See Independent State Store Union v. PLRB*, 119 Pa. Commw. Ct. 286, 547 A.2d 465 (1988); *Curley, supra.*

CHAPTER 4

Specific Contract Terms

Union Security Clauses

Many laymen don't understand union security clauses and often don't understand the difference between being a union member, being a member of the bargaining unit represented by a union and being a "core" financial member/fair share fee-payer. These are distinct types of relationships that an employee can have with a union.

Most union contracts contain some form of union security provision. The only types permitted under the PERA are what is termed "maintenance of membership" and an agency shop. The first relates to requiring employees to be official "members" of the union and the second relates to requiring those who are not members to pay a fee to the union. Anything that purports to require more is invalid and unenforceable.

The permitted maintenance of membership provision requires that an employee, even though he never actually had to join the union in the first place, must maintain membership (i.e., cannot resign) during the life of the contract. Members, of course, are obligated to pay dues. An exception or an "escape period" must be allowed during a brief period before the contract expires. If an employee, once a member, does not resign during the escape period, when the successor agreement takes effect he's stuck for another contract term until the next escape period rolls around. The agency shop provision permitted by law, if it's included in your contract, requires any employee who is in the bargaining unit but is *not* a member must nonetheless pay what the union likes to call a "fair share" fee to the union. The fee is typically almost as much as the union dues charged to official members. If an employee disregards the obligations imposed by the agency shop, ultimately he can face discharge and/or a civil action by the union. There are still quite a few districts that have not surrendered agency shop and they employ many people who are not members. It drives the unions crazy. You may have both a maintenance of membership clause and an agency shop clause, or either, or neither.

The philosophical debate over compulsory union fees is an endless one. Unionists argue that it is only fair that those who receive the benefits of union representation ought to pay for that representation. Opponents argue it is fundamentally wrong to compel someone to financially support a purely private organization like a labor union, with which he may not agree. The unions' concerns about "freeload-ers" could be completely eliminated by changing the law to say that the union's duty (and right) of representation only extends to those who voluntarily chose to be members. Unions would oppose such a change to their dying breath, because they *want* to represent those people, whether they are members or not. They just want to be paid for it. And, indeed, all of their local bargaining units were originally organized with the union fully aware that it *had* to represent non-members after it was certified. Apparently the union felt it was worth it at the time.

Philosophy aside, it is important to understand how these clauses operate, and it is impossible to do so without an understanding of what it means to be a union member. A union member will have the right to vote in elections for union officers, and to ratify contracts. A "fair share" payer will not. A union member is subject to union rules and by-laws. A fair share payer is not. The last point can be a matter of some importance. Union membership is a form of legal contract that can be enforced by the union in court. And unions do indeed have rules against various things, like cross-ing a picket line, supporting or facilitating rival unions and the like. They can sanction a member for violating rules and can actually levy fines against offending members. It's happened. Not often, but it does happen.

Most laymen do not understand the difference between being a member of a bargaining unit and being a union member. If your district has employees in jobs covered by a union contract (i.e., the positions are covered by the union's PLRB certification) and those employees have chosen not to join the union, they are still covered by the contract to the same extent as union members. The union owes them a legal duty of representation. The union may demonstrate a marked lack of enthusiasm when called on to represent them, but the legal obligation is clear. Such employees may file grievances and most assuredly are not free to make their own deals with management on wages, hours, working conditions or any other negotiable topic. Union *members,* i.e., those employees who have officially joined the union, are not only covered by the contract, but also are obligated to pay 100% of all dues and fees charged by the union to its members and are subject to all lawful union rules and regulations, including such things as prohibitions on crossing a picket line, or supporting a rival union.

Deducting union dues from employees' pay and sending the money to the union is not required by law. Dues check off provisions must be negotiated into the contract and, while custom-ary, nonetheless represent a significant concession to the union.

Districts that are considering agreeing to such proposals should not discount the importance of these clauses to the union which is asking for them. Even though it costs the district nothing finan-cially to agree (you're spending your employees' personal freedom), it's a big deal to the union. You should get something very significant back for it if you are willing to give it away.

Recognition Clauses

Recognition clauses are found near the beginning of almost every labor contract. These clauses define which types of employees are covered by the contract and are an outgrowth of the union's "certification," a document akin to a birth certificate that is issued by the PLRB when a local union is created. Often, they parrot the language used in the original PLRB certification, which may, or may not, have been well drafted. Although not often of significance in disputes that find their way into the grievance procedure, occasionally such clauses assume importance.

Particular attention should be paid to how, and whether, the recognition clause deals with part-time or substitute employees, and how, precisely, the various types of employees are identified. Generally, specificity is in the employer's interest for several reasons. Obviously, it is useful for practical reasons to have a clear answer to the question of exactly who the contract applies to. You shouldn't have to waste time and energy fighting over that. Secondly, if the recognition clause goes into great detail about who is included in the unit, by implication, any position that is not mentioned is likely to be viewed as not being included. Disputes about unit coverage, while not common, do arise. A good, tightly worded recognition clause may provide some needed support when a new position is developed and the parties have a disagreement over whether it should be treated as such in the unit.

Recognition clauses also are sometimes used by unions to support grievances relating to subjects having nothing to do with which employees are, or are not, in the bargaining unit. For example, a recognition clause is often relied upon if a union decides to use the grievance procedure, rather than the unfair practice remedies of the PLRB, to enforce a claim that a district has improperly made a unilateral change in working conditions. As a matter of logic, such a use of the clause is of dubious merit, but it is commonly seen. Since recognition clauses don't seem to have a clear purpose, they tend to lend themselves to being used for any purpose. After all, they must mean "something."

Insurance

Insurance provisions are usually fairly straightforward and don't seem to lead to interpretation disputes very frequently. Their function is to specify clearly what benefits employees get, when they get them, and who gets them. If, upon reading your contract, the answers to these questions are *not* perfectly clear, your contract needs work. Promises about insurance do lead to a lot of expense, and difficult negotiations, but not many grievances.

Still, there are some typical provisions that require attention.

Eligibility questions usually are controlled by language which specifies how employees who work less than full time are treated, and how employees who are on leaves of absence are treated. Entitlement to benefits in these situations must be made crystal clear.

Often in employers with multiple bargaining units, there is some attempt to coordinate the benefit plans so that all eligible employees have the same plans, on the same terms, even if/when the plans or terms change. These attempts are often manifested in what are commonly referred to as "me too" clauses, the purpose being to make sure that if changes to the insurance provisions are negotiated in one bargaining unit, those changes automatically go into effect at the same time in other bargaining units, even if the contracts of those other units are not then being renegotiated. The changes, of course, can cut both ways, depending on how the negotiations go. Usually any changes are first negotiated with the professional unit, since it is the most numerous, and, typically, sets the tone for all of the district's other employees. It is difficult for the janitor to make a case for a better benefit package than the one given to teachers, or administrators, although the argument can be made that out-of-pocket costs like co-pays, deductibles, and premium shares should be less because support staff earn less. Incidentally, a desire to have one plan for all employees is a choice districts make. There is no reason that a district cannot have different benefit packages, including different plans, deductibles, co-pays, etc. for different groups. Benefits are, after all, nothing more than a form of compensation. We pay professional employees more salary than we do to support staff, and we pay administrators more salary than we do to teachers. Just as pay differs, so can benefits.

Your contract should give attention to the question of the district's right to make changes to the way benefits are provided. Ideally, you should have a clearly spelled out right to change carriers or benefit administrators, or to self insure if you are not doing so, all in order to take advantage of whatever savings might be available from shopping the benefits.[39] Often such provisions include some type of promise that if changes are made, the benefits themselves will not be less, or will at least be "substantially" the same.

It has become common for employers either to offer cash incentives to employees to decline some, or all, available coverage, or to require some type of coordination with plans that may be available to employees' spouses at their places of employment. The objective of such provisions is to try to shift some of the burden off of the typically very generous government employee health plans and onto other sources of coverage. In fact, reducing the number of people (employees and dependents) covered by your plan will have a much larger impact on your costs than will many other cost-saving measures. Unfortunately, insurance benefits for government employees tend to be much richer than those offered in the private sector, and, school employees, in particular, traditionally have not been required to subsidize much of their health care through either monthly payroll contributions or high deductibles as the plans are accessed. Schools, in particular, are often the insurer of choice in the community. Consequently, other employers reap the benefit of having their employees married to teachers and school support staff.

---

[39] The identity of the district's health insurance carrier, and the use of self-insurance systems are mandatory subjects of bargaining. The concept of "mandatory" subjects is discussed elsewhere in this guide.

Using positive incentives will obviously be more palatable to the union since it has the virtue of being voluntary. Requiring an employee whose spouse has insurance available to use that insurance, rather than yours, is a much tougher sell and carries with it a number of mechanical and administrative complications as well. If you utilize incentives, there are many details to consider apart from how much of an incentive you will provide. Consideration should be given to pro-rating the incentive to account for folks who leave at various times of the year, changed circumstances (e.g. death, divorce) of spouses, and the like. And of course, you should differentiate between single coverage employees and those eligible for full family benefits. If your incentive is a new feature of your contract, you also need to consider that you will likely now be paying something for employees who may *already* be off of your insurance for one reason or another.

Remember that requiring employees to pay a meaningful amount through monthly "premium" contributions has the benefit of discouraging unnecessary coverage and this is where any real savings will be achieved, not in the recovery of the contribution itself. When something is "free," or nearly so, people will simply take it without a second thought. The larger the amount the employee pays each month, the more likely it is that the employee may chose to insure his dependents on a spouse's plan, if one exists.

Early Retirement Incentives

Another fairly common feature of educational contracts is some provision for health insurance after an employee retires. The School Code requires that many PSERS annuitants be afforded the opportunity to maintain insurance at their own expense under the employer's group plan, and COBRA does the same thing for 18 months. But many districts either provide insurance for some period at the district's full or partial expense, or set up some type of post retirement subsidy based on an employee's years of service or unused sick leave at retirement, or both.

Many districts have bought into the concept of "early retirement incentives" and have offered benefits on a non-recurring basis to try to induce senior, high-paid staff to leave so they can be replaced with new, lower paid staff. The incentives typically offered are lump sum cash payments (sometimes quite large), or some continuation of health insurance after retirement. If your contract contains such provisions you should be careful to specify that any insurance which is provided is the prevailing insurance that active employees enjoy, as changed from time to time. You also should give consideration to ending it when the employee becomes eligible for Medicare, and to make sure the district requires an employee to pay at least an amount equal to the monthly subsidy the PSERS offers to retirees who maintain health insurance. In order to avoid age discrimination issues, eligibility for the incentive, as well as any reduction in its value if an employee delays taking advantage of it, should be expressed in terms of years of service and not age.

A healthy skepticism about the cost effectiveness of special "early retirement incentives" is justified. There is more than one point of view on whether they really save money, or at least as much as they claim to, and before adopting one you should at least consider that your "younger, lower paid teacher" is very likely to create greater dependent insurance costs for you, as well as significant expenses for post-graduate college credits that a more senior teacher won't incur. Further, you will only save money by the retirement of higher paid staff to the extent that such staff leaves sooner than they otherwise would have without the incentive. Everyone retires eventually. How much earlier did he really leave? That is the true measure of gross savings, from which you must subtract the newer, younger employees' offsetting expenses mentioned above, and the out-of-pocket cost of whatever you are giving as the incentive. If you are offering post-retirement insurance as part of the incentive, remember that this relatively older group tends to be populated with high consumers of covered health care services. This can be particularly significant if, like many districts, you are self-insured. The actual savings may be far less than you thought.

Many districts that have adopted early retirement incentives as a way to reduce costs have done so completely independently of their collective bargaining agreements. These districts have simply unilaterally adopted incentive plans and made them available to interested employees, sometimes without even talking to the union. Others have engaged the union in some type of discussion that can loosely be called "bargaining," then announced the incentive after it was clear the union was in favor of it, as it usually is. Technically, an early retirement incentive offered to current employees qualifies as a "term or condition of employment" which cannot be unilaterally implemented or changed, but, in the case of voluntary retirement incentives, few, if any, unions will ever object to them, as much as they'd like to take credit for getting the employer to offer them. If you do engage the union in a discussion about the incentive, you should feel no particular pressure to reach an "agreement," or to improve what you would like to offer as an incentive, simply to get the union's endorsement.

The usefulness of a retirement incentive is significantly enhanced if the incentive has a fixed life expectancy and the employees cannot be sure when it will be available again. If an employee always has the incentive available (even if it diminishes in value the longer the employee works, as they often do), some of the pressure to consider immediate retirement is lost. Incentives that are permanently enshrined in a contract with no specific sunset date occurring before the contract expires lack this important attribute.

Retirement incentives usually make little sense with respect to support staff. Unless your contract is very unusual, there will not be a very significant gap between newer, lower paid employees and senior staff, and certainly nothing like the tens of thousands of dollars per year differences that typically prevail for professional staff. Even if there is a meaningful gap between support staff start and top rates, the gap usually closes much quicker than the 15 to 20 years often provided for in professional salary schedules. Thus, the "savings" that provides the justification for the incentive is far less with support staff than what is usually projected for retiring top step teachers.

Probation and Trial Periods

Usually limited to support unit contracts, probation periods are best understood as creating an exception to the typical "just cause" clause, in so far as those clauses require the employer to have, and be able to prove, a very good reason to discharge an employee. A probationary employee can be dismissed safely, as far as the contract is concerned, if the employer is simply uneasy about his long-term prospects for success. Probationary status under a union contract does not immunize you from discrimination claims under the PHRA or federal employment discrimination statutes, nor does it prevent any legal claims based upon an allegation of an unlawful motive. It does, however, protect you from grievances claiming that your decision, even if lawful, was simply unfair or based on misperceived facts.

There are several ways to draft probation provisions. The best is simply to prohibit the union from filing grievances over the termination of a probationary employee, period. This will eliminate the possibility that a grievance can be processed not on the basis of the just-cause provision, but alleging a violation of some other provision of the contract, like the typical anti-discrimination provision, which mimics federal and state employment discrimination statutes. If the probation language only says that such an employee can be dismissed without regard to the just-cause clause, other theories for a grievance may still be available.

Probation language rarely appears in professional unit contracts. Professionals are required by law to work successfully for three school years as a temporary professional employee (TPE) before achieving tenure, and this apprenticeship period is generally accepted as the equivalent of a "probation" period. Unfortunately, it isn't, really. Many arbitrators have effectively obliterated the distinction between TPEs and tenured professionals, by holding that in the absence of contract language to the contrary, an employer must establish the same grounds for dismissing a TPE as it does for dismissing an employee with tenure. Some will apply some type of rather amorphous, but "lower" standard in cases involving TPEs, but don't count on it. There is a way to deal with this problem, however. A clear statement that TPEs cannot challenge dismissals through the grievance procedure, and are relegated to a legal challenge under the Local Agency Law, will suffice, but this is a rather uncommon provision.[40]

Distinguished from probation periods are trial, or "make out" periods, which are usually found in conjunction with language relating to transfers and bidding on vacant positions. Again found primarily in support contracts, they address the need for employees moving to new positions to receive training or familiarization, or, conversely, to demonstrate competence in order to remain in

---

[40] The Local Agency Law, 2 Pa. Cons. Stat. § 551 *et. seq.*, is a state law that requires a "due process" hearing before the school board if action is taken that deprives an employee of a property interest. Employment can be viewed as such an interest.

the new job. Sometimes they give the employee the option, during the trial period, to declare that he really doesn't want the new job and wants to return to his old one. Obviously, these clauses can be handled in a wide variety of ways and have many variations. From the employer's point of view, you will want to make sure that when an employee has been awarded a new position, there will be some period of time during which you can observe and evaluate performance to assure that the employee can, in fact, perform adequately. You also will want to be sure that you do not say anything in the contract that commits you to an obligation to train the employee if, in fact, you do not intend to assume such a responsibility. There is a distinction between training and orientation that has to be observed. Most contracts, in their transfer and bidding language, speak to a successful bidder/transferee having to be "qualified" in some sense, and most school employers are not equipped to train unqualified employees so that they can assume more specialized positions.

Employee Evaluation Clauses

Unions often try to regulate the manner and extent of employee evaluation through contract provisions. These provisions tend to take on more importance, and are typically more extensive in professional units. The reason for the unions' interest in the topic is obvious: poor evaluations can be job and career threatening. Unions seem by their nature to place great importance on making sure that management jumps through the appropriate hoops and has a very good, and most importantly, provable reason for concluding that an employee is doing an unsatisfactory job.

An unsatisfactory evaluation can be viewed as a form of disciplinary warning in and of itself, before an employee misses a day of pay. With respect to professional employees, a single (and first) unsatisfactory evaluation is almost universally viewed as punitive in nature and subject to review under a typical just cause clause. A second one, of course, is often fatal to a professional employee's career.

The School Code says virtually nothing about evaluation of non-professionals. Any restrictions that exist are solely created by a contract. By contrast, the School Code and Pennsylvania Department of Education (PDE) regulations contain very detailed mandates for the evaluation of professionals, and many court cases have served to apply and interpret those mandates over the years. If there were no union contracts to contend with, you'd still have to follow the rules. Almost certainly, an arbitrator will consider a district not to have acted with "just cause" if they're violated, or else he'll simply conclude that compliance with the law is an "implied" term of your contract and proceed to review the union's claim as though all of those School Code and regulatory provisions were printed within the pages of the contract.

In an ideal situation, your contract says nothing about the subject, and you simply (or not so simply) follow the law. Beyond such an ideal situation, be very careful what your language says.

One of the more typical provisions requires that an employee be given advance notice of a classroom observation, which assures that he'll be well prepared and on his game, if he's capable of it. An unannounced visit is, of course, far more likely to give a true picture of what goes on in the classroom. I've also seen whole blocks of days placed off limits for evaluation purposes, typically days just after school resumes, or right before holiday recess or summer. And then there is the old throwback to the days when principals allegedly listened in on class over the PA system which, I'm told, can work both ways in many schools. Concerns about such a practice lead to prohibitions against "secret" observations. I suppose the idea of the principal listening to a lesson being delivered without the teacher's knowledge violates someone's sense of fair play, but I confess I see nothing inherently wrong with it; indeed, I think the quality of teaching would likely improve if technology were developed which made it possible for every single lesson taught to be played back and thus observed at any time. That technology *is* available and I know of at least one progressive superintendent who intends to use it. Those charged with making sure that quality standards are met, and children thereby benefited, would be able to get a clear picture of what goes on at any time.

The state requires, through binding regulation, that teachers and other professionals be formally evaluated once, or, in the case of temporary professional employees, twice, each year. Districts are further required to use specific state-approved forms for doing so, unless the state pre-approves a home-grown evaluation form and criteria. For years the state mandated use of what is now universally viewed as a badly outdated and not very good form known colloquially as the "DEBE." In recent years, the state developed a more extensive and significantly altered document and in most situations permits, but does not require, that this modernized version be used. If your contract is silent on the subject of evaluation forms, congratulations. You may, without bargaining with your union, switch to the newer state forms, or develop your own and use it if you can get the PDE to approve it. Despite what union representatives would have you believe, the PLRB has fairly consistently held that employee evaluation constitutes an inherent managerial prerogative and therefore is not a mandatory subject of bargaining under the PERA.[41] Unfortunately, many contracts have gratuitously incorporated problematic language which requires union agreement before any changes are made to the evaluation documents used. I've even seen restrictions on changing not only the year-end evaluation form, but the documents which principals must use when they sit in class making an observation. If you've conceded such language, you must honor it at least until the 2013-14 school year, even though you probably could have refused even to discuss it at the bargaining table.

In 2013-14, the law changes this dramatically. In June 2012, as a part of the adoption of the state budget, the legislature for the first time took control of teacher evaluations in a meaningful way. Effective with the 2013-14 school year every district, intermediate unit and vocational-technical school is mandated by law to use an as yet (as of this writing) to be developed, new state evalu-

---

[41] *See, e.g., Crawford Cent. Educ. Support Pers. Ass'n v. Crawford Cent. Sch. Dist.,* 39 PPER ¶36 (H. Ex. 2008) and the many cases cited therein.

ation instrument for professional and temporary professional employees. From a labor relations standpoint, the most significant aspect of the 2012 School Code amendments is the following provision:

> No collective bargaining agreement negotiated by a school district and an exclusive representative of the employes in accordance with the Act … known as the "Public Employe Relations Act," … shall provide for a rating system other than as provided for in this section. A provision in any agreement or contract in effect on the effective date of this subsection that provides for a rating system in conflict with this section shall be discontinued in any new or renewed agreement or contract or during the period of status quo following an expired contract.

This provision appears to effectively nullify any inconsistent language in any collective bargaining agreement once that agreement expires. Districts will be required by law to use the new PDE form regardless of what their labor contracts say. As a practical matter, the legislature appears to have essentially rendered the evaluation instrument itself an unlawful bargaining subject, since districts have no choice but to use the state form. Other aspects of evaluation that may appear in a contract, such as days on which observations are restricted and similar purely procedural subjects are probably not affected by the 2012 Code revisions, but the central fixture of evaluations – what the evaluation criteria and standards are – has been removed from bargaining. As usual, the devil will be in the details, and, depending on exactly what the Department of Education comes up with, various elements of evaluation provisions may survive.

The entire concept of restricting or regulating the manner in which management forms its opinion of how well an employee is performing draws huge laughter when you explain it to people employed in the private sector. Try to tell a manager at General Electric that before he can observe the work of an engineer (also a type of professional employee), he has to give him several days advance notice of what work he's going to check, has to give him a written report of his conclusions within 48 hours of reaching them, when doing so can't use whatever checklist he thinks works best, and can't do it at all if the guy is about to go on vacation or just got back from one. He'll look at you like you're from Pluto. One of the reasons they build excellent locomotives is because they don't do silly things like that.

It's important to distinguish between how management forms its opinion of an employee's performance (i.e. makes an evaluation) *and what it does about it* if the opinion is negative. The procedural restrictions rankle. But it is a given in a union environment that the employee's representative has the option, and, in appropriate cases, the responsibility, to challenge *action* taken *based upon* that assessment.

Seniority Clauses

With the exception of the seniority rules found in the School Code for the protection of professional staff in layoff situations, seniority is totally a creature of contract. No law compels that it otherwise be given any weight, and an employee's seniority means only what the contract says it means, if anything.

Keep in mind that seniority is a zero sum game. If you advantage one employee because of his seniority, you necessarily disadvantage another in direct proportion.

Unions are devoted to the concept of seniority. They tend to see seniority as a "fair" way to decide all kinds of things, from how much money someone is paid (most contracts accept this concept, through the device of a salary schedule that increases pay in direct proportion to seniority) to who gets vacant positions, to who gets what grade assignments in an elementary school, etc., etc. Union folks will tell you they like seniority for two reasons. First, they just think it is inherently "fair," whatever that means. Second, they are skeptical of either the motives of management, or the wisdom of management, or both, if decisions are left up to management discretion. Seniority takes that discretion out of play.

As a result, unions try very hard to include in contracts various types of seniority provisions. The most common area where seniority plays a role is the filling of vacancies. The best situation for management, obviously, is to keep out of the contract any language restricting the district's right to choose who it thinks best to fill a vacancy. If that can't be done, the question becomes how to restrict the precise role seniority will play. In the worst case, seniority is the only factor, except for proper teaching certification in the case of professional vacancies (a legal requirement). A better, less troublesome provision would say something like seniority will control, provided the candidates are "equal"... meaning really equal and not just more or less, or substantially, "equal." And it would also define the qualifications to be considered as something more than just minimum qualifications. In the case of teaching positions, it would be clear that merely possessing the necessary certification is not enough to end the inquiry about whether someone is qualified at all, or is better qualified than someone else.

Many evenings have been spent arguing about the appropriateness of using seniority to make decisions about professional placements, in an attempt to convince teachers that as employees with jobs that are primarily intellectual and professional in nature, it doesn't make sense to fill teacher vacancies or make assignments in the same manner as is done for factory workers. Teachers are not interchangeable. They possess different skill sets, strengths and weaknesses, and personalities. Teaching is a very personal thing. Support contracts, too, can raise the same concerns. Is a custodian or a cafeteria worker who has long service really likely to be a good candidate for an aide position, or a building secretary's spot? Is a building secretary with long service in a job where typing and document preparation is much less important than people skills really likely to be a good candidate for a central office job which is very much like more of a traditional clerical position?

Related to seniority provisions is a type of language sometimes found in support contracts that allows for some type of "make out" or trial period after an employee has bid on another position. If the employee doesn't make it, he can return to his old job before some period of time. Sometimes the employee can choose to do this, or management can declare the experiment a failure and involuntarily move the employee back. At a minimum, it should be made clear the employer is not obligated to provide training (although you may choose to do so.) Orientation yes, but not training.

Transfers

Many contracts contain provisions dealing with the district's right to transfer employees (or a restriction against doing so). From management's perspective, restrictions against transfers should obviously be avoided if the district is to retain the ability to assign employees where they will be most effective. Many contracts make explicit reference to some right on the part of the district to make involuntary transfers and such provisions are to be encouraged.

Often such language is directly related to the contract's provisions dealing with posting and seniority. If a district is contractually required or, by practice, has historically posted openings by building and, in the case of elementary positions by grade level, the union has a good argument that an elementary grade four position at such and such a building is a discreet position which an employee "owns." In other districts where posting is for a generic "elementary" position, absent some specific contract language to the contrary, the district can probably reassign an elementary teacher to just about any elementary assignment it chooses from year to year. Language clarifying all of this with an express statement to the effect that the district can simply transfer employees to various assignments within their areas of certification obviously resolves any question.

Sick Leave Provisions

The Code mandates paid sick leave for professionals, and the original 10 day per year Code requirement, or more, is almost universally enshrined in collective bargaining agreements. Support contracts have typically recognized such a benefit on similar terms. Sick leave is not as simple as that, however, and it has evolved way past the original intention of the Code's authors that employees be protected against income loss if they are too ill to come to work.

A frequent subject of bargaining currently is allowing an employee's sick leave to be taken when someone in the family is ill *other* than the employee himself. Obviously, this will significantly increase the use, and consequent cost, of such leave. If you're inclined to allow this, and the trend seems to be to do so, you can negotiate any type of limits or controls you like, including the number of days that can be so used, which relatives' illnesses qualify, and the like.

Almost as common as paid sick leave itself is what is sometimes called "terminal leave pay," which doesn't sound like it has anything at all to do with sick leave unless the employee is terminally ill. This strangely worded benefit pays the employee at retirement for not using a lot of sick days during his career. It's usually not a full days' pay, but some fraction of that, and the total amount an employee can receive, or the total number of days that can "cashed in" is often capped. Sometimes different reimbursement rates apply depending on how many days are being cashed in. In some cases the employee is given the option of taking cash, or leaving the cash "on account" to be applied to post-retirement insurance coverage costs. Despite the almost universal nature of terminal leave pay, there is something discomforting about the usual argument advanced in support of proposals to create or improve the benefit, i.e., if you make this benefit valuable, employees will not use as many sick days. The inference of such an argument, of course, is that employees will call off sick on days when they really could come to work if they have "nothing to lose" by burning off the days. In other words, you are asked to give people an incentive not to steal from the district, which, presumably, they can be expected to do unless you reward them not to. Perhaps that's true, but, if it is, it's sad.

Sick leave "banks" appear now and then. Most work rather smoothly. The idea is that employees can sign up by donating sick days and thereby become eligible to use some other employee's sick leave in the event of a catastrophic illness which exhausts their own available leave. My only real caution concerning the operation of such provisions is that the district should have nothing to do with running it except for basic accounting of available leave and the obvious payroll consequences of extended paid leave. The union should take responsibility and an indemnification provision can be included so that it is clear the district has absolutely no liability for the actions of the committee or group that administers the system. Since it is a negotiated benefit system, you will have to make sure the system is rational and basically fair and sensibly explained, but after that it should be hands off. Apart from the operational details of sick leave banks, you should recognize that they have a cost, since an employee accessing the bank will be paid when otherwise he would not be. Simply stated, a sick leave bank will result in more usage of sick leave.

Finally, there is the issue of the coordination of FMLA leave and paid sick leave.[42] The PLRB has held that several important aspects of FMLA are subject to negotiation, even though FMLA leave itself is created by federal law and not collective bargaining. The district has an interest in requiring employees with paid sick leave available to use it during the 12-week FMLA leave period so that the maximum absence is not the sum of sick leave *and* FMLA leave. Requiring the *coincidental* use of the two types of leave must be either negotiated or established by a reliable, unobjected to, past practice. The other matter which may require negotiation is the method of accounting used for the 12-month entitlement period under the FMLA. The FMLA requires that an employer provide 12 weeks of leave per year, but it allows employers to use any of several methods of deter-

---

[42] The "FMLA" or Family and Medical Leave Act, is a federal law that, in general, requires an employer under certain circumstances to give an employee 12 weeks per year of unpaid leave in the event of a "serious" illness of the employee or an immediate family member, or the birth of a child. *See* 29 U.S.C. §§ 2601-54 (2012).

mining what a "year" is. You can use calendar years, anniversary date years, or a "rolling" 12-month period. Which one you use can have significant consequences. Generally, the "rolling" 12-month period is the most employer friendly and, once again, you must specify which one you will be using in collective bargaining or have an established practice you can confidently rely on.

Workers' Compensation Provider Panels

The Workers' Compensation Act allows employers to designate a list of health care providers that employees must visit for treatment of an occupational injury during the first 90 days following an accident. After that period, an employee is free to use other providers. If an employee does not use one of the designated providers during the initial period, he loses his eligibility for benefits. Unfortunately, the PLRB views the imposition of this list, and changes in it, as a mandatory subject of bargaining. Ideally, your contract should contain a provision which simply says the district can establish and, from time to time, alter the provider panel. In arguing that such language should be included in the contract, remember that after 90 days, an employee can see any health care provider he wishes. Absent such a provision, you will need to engage the union with respect to the posting of the list and the changes that will inevitably be made to it over time. In practice, many employers simply post it and either knowingly ignore their bargaining duty or are oblivious to it. Many unions have allowed districts to take that approach, either because they don't particularly care about the existence of the list, or are unaware of their ability to engage the employer in a discussion about it.

"For the Life of this Contract"

Sometimes negotiating parties decide to place something into their contract but one party or the other (usually the district) is uncomfortable with it, or unwilling to make an indefinite commitment to keep it there. The solution is sometimes found in language that says the provision in question is only effective "for the life of the contract," or "for the life of this contract." A special retirement incentive for teachers is an example of a type of provision that is sometimes qualified in this manner.

This is a common language trap. Districts which agree to this type of language often think the provision automatically expires at the scheduled end of the agreement in which it appeared. That's not how it works. In the next round of negotiations, the district will have to negotiate this language *out* of the contract, because if it doesn't, the same promise is made in the successor agreement. This is not simply a matter of semantics. Which party has the practical burden of asking for, and obtaining, consent to change often has a lot to do with what the final deal is. Additionally, it is not unusual for districts to experience long periods of time without a new contract if negotiations become protracted, which they frequently do. Should that happen, you will be advised by your lawyer at that time that you have important legal reasons to "maintain the status quo."

Think about it. Why would it be any easier to successfully negotiate out of a successor agreement language that said something was only good "for the life of this contract" than it would be simply to negotiate out of the contract *any* item you don't want to promise anymore? It won't be.

A better approach, and one that completely avoids this problem, is a *real* sunset provision that says the item in question expires, or is null and void, after what lawyers call a "date certain," i.e., a firm *calendar* date. Ideally, that date is the day before the contract term expires. Going into successor negotiations, the union must now obtain an affirmative commitment from the district to renew the item, and, if you have an extended period with no contract in effect, the "status quo" does not require that you continue to give the expired provision effect.

Statutory Savings Clauses

Unfortunately, most school contracts contain statutory savings clauses. These are probably the most misinterpreted and misused clauses found in these contracts. Such clauses usually say something innocent sounding, like, "Nothing contained in this agreement shall be construed as diminishing or relinquishing any rights an employee has by law." Sounds harmless enough. Unfortunately, in the interest of full employment, the vast majority of arbitrators have somehow interpreted such language as incorporating *into* the contract, as though it were printed there, any provision of law which benefits the employee. In most cases where this becomes a problem, it is the School Code which is relied upon, and every provision of the Code now becomes available to form the basis of a grievance. I've never read an arbitration decision that adequately explained why a statement that says a contract isn't intended to "diminish" an employee's legal rights really means that those rights are now an invisible part of the contract itself, yet that is the exact result in many significant reported decisions.

For example, arbitrators have almost uniformly assumed the authority to review whether professional employees were properly furloughed in accordance with the School Code's furlough and seniority rules even though the contract does not contain a single word regulating furlough decisions, and the district, correctly, believes it has never conceded any promises in that regard.

Why does it matter? Because if the union cannot access the grievance procedure to assert a purely legal (as opposed to contractual) right it will have to utilize either the court system, or, worse yet from the union's point of view, it will be relegated to a hearing in front of the school board to present its case. The court system will require effort, expense and time, and, the result likely will be determined by a judge whose income does not depend on being selected by the union in future cases. Arbitration is a much friendlier forum for the union. It also is one they can often "game." Many arbitrators are not lawyers, and they can be misled about exactly what the Code does, and does not, require. The current School Code is over 60 years old[43] and most of what it means is found not in the text of the Code itself, but in the hundreds of appellate court decisions interpreting

---

[43] A good deal of the archaic language still found in today's School Code was written before the Civil War.

it. There have been many misapplications of the Code by arbitrators, some frankly bordering on the bizarre.

Your contract probably has a statutory savings clause. If it does, you would be well advised to try to clarify it to make clear that it does not function as an "incorporation" clause. A less obvious way to accomplish the same thing is to develop language limiting an arbitrator's authority with respect to applying external law to contractual disputes. Such an approach would usually mean modifying the arbitration provisions of the grievance procedure rather than the savings clause itself.

Safe Conditions Clauses

Many contracts contain provisions either promising employees safe working conditions, or excusing them from working in unsafe conditions. Such clauses are difficult to justify opposing, since, after all, no employer wants to operate an unsafe workplace, for both moral and financial reasons. Unfortunately, much mischief can follow from such provisions, depending upon how they are worded.

What is essential is to craft the language so it is clear that neither the employee, nor an arbitrator, can make the determination that a condition is, in fact, both unsafe and something that can be corrected through reasonable measures. If such a provision is to be included in a contract at all, it should be little more than an expression of the employer's pre-existing philosophy, allowing little room for an effective challenge to the employer's judgment that no corrective action is justified. This can usually be accomplished by a straightforward statement that the final determination regarding the existence of an unsafe condition rests within the complete discretion of the employer.

Clauses of this type, which are not properly limited, can be used to support manifestly unreasonable requests for workplace modification, both for individuals and entire building faculties. Such provisions can form the basis for grievances seeking as a remedy the wholesale modification of buildings to deal with mold and asbestos; claims of compensation for slips and falls caused by snowy sidewalks; and a variety of grievances seeking actions benefiting individual employees ranging from air conditioners to special light bulbs. Indeed, in the case of an inner city high school with a high incidence of crime and assault, one could argue that extensive security and/or police presence is essential for a safe workplace, rendering the adequacy of the district's security efforts subject to supervision by an arbitrator.

Discipline Clauses

Most contracts contain what is typically referred to as a "just cause" clause. A union rep with a sense of humor once referred to one of my attempts to weaken such a clause as a desire to have the clause say we can discipline an employee "just cause" we feel like it. Life would be simpler indeed if management could correct errant employees without having to endure grievances, but such is not the environment we work in.

The typical discipline clause in an education contract provides that "no employee shall be disciplined, discharged, suspended, reprimanded, reduced in rank or compensation or denied any professional advantage without just cause," or words to that effect. In a support unit, the reference to "professional advantage" usually won't appear. A clause worded that broadly can cause problems. Although I've never reduced a teacher's "rank," whatever that is, many of the unions I've dealt with sure have believed that I've denied "professional advantages," whatever they are. The union will take the position that anything an employee views as an adverse consequence implicates the "professional advantage" provision, even if there was no punitive purpose. In the union's view the district has the burden of justifying, as "just," *anything* that an employee views as harmful. Some, but not all, arbitrators will buy the argument. The clause was obviously intended to protect employees from unjustified *punitive* action, and nothing more. Given its purpose, obviously the proscribed action should be limited to only punishments, or actions intended as such.

Issues also can arise regarding whether something is, in fact, discipline subject to the clause. Is an evaluation that contains significant negative material but which is overall satisfactory, "discipline?" Can it fairly be characterized as a reprimand or "corrective?" Is an unsatisfactory evaluation discipline, given that no money is lost and the employee's job is secure until/unless a second consecutive unsatisfactory is issued? Does a letter from the principal documenting some behavior the principal disapproves of and advising the employee if it persists there *might* be consequences count?

Even if you don't have a just cause clause, you might have one. How can that be? Simple. Most arbitrators will "imply" one into your contract, usually by making some unconvincing reference to the mere existence of an arbitration procedure as meaning the parties must have expected discipline grievances to be subject to arbitration.

Don't expect me to explain this logic. There isn't any, but regrettably, the courts have refused to vacate decisions based on this view. Let's just say that arbitrators almost uniformly come down on the side of rejecting claims that a dispute is not "arbitrable," which is the argument you'd make in a discipline case where there is no discipline language in the contract. Arbitrators seem loath to make decisions that tend to reduce the available work for arbitrators. Unless your union has asked for a just cause clause in negotiations and failed to get one (great evidence to avoid having one "implied"), you may have to act as though you have one, as many districts have learned through hard experience.

Maintenance of Standards/Past Practice and Zipper Clauses

Maintenance of standards clauses, sometimes styled past practice clauses, represent an attempt by the union to prevent an employer from changing things in ways that, strictly speaking, the contract does not address. Realistically, a labor contract cannot, and should not, attempt to describe every conceivable way of doing business that affects employees. To cover the innumerable unspoken matters, unions like to get a blanket guarantee that past practices, in general, will be maintained. Another common form of such a clause is a statement that all working conditions not specifically addressed in the contract will be maintained at not less than the highest standards in existence at the time the contract became effective.

Chances are you won't know what this type of language really means in practical terms until it's too late. In fairness, neither will the union, although the language will be a source of joy to the union rather than frustration when its usefulness becomes clear. If management's objective is to keep its managerial options open so that more efficient, effective, or innovative ways of doing things can be tried, it is in management's interest that the labor contract restrict change as little as possible. Unions, being conservative institutions, tend to be distrustful of change and uncomfortable with it. They certainly aren't sympathetic when the change is viewed as being harmful to employees' interests in some way. And they always want to be asked before anything important changes very much.

Past practices can be a problem even without a past practice clause in your contract. Virtually all arbitrators consider evidence of past practice to be a valid way of proving what an ambiguous contract term means. Many arbitrators will elevate past practices to status as an "implied" contract term, enforceable as though they were written into the document itself. This latter problem is more likely to arise if you change something that can be characterized as a "benefit" as opposed to something that just represents a change in managerial practice. The classic benefit change is an example from private industry. A company gives its employees a free turkey at Thanksgiving each year for many years. The union contract says nothing about turkeys, but the employees come to expect them each year. When the company falls on hard times and discontinues the turkeys, the union files a grievance based totally on the past practice. The union will very likely win such a case. The company can argue the circumstances underlying the practice have changed, and while that argument has some force, it probably won't carry the day.

On the other hand, consider the case of a school district that introduces computer grading in place of paper grade records. Or, for that matter, one that introduces computers at all. There was a time when computers did not exist in schools. A union trying to prevent the introduction of new technology based the argument that it creates new tasks for employees would very likely fail in the effort, just as it would if it tried to prevent a district from changing textbooks simply because that means that teachers will have to prepare new, or revised lesson plans.

The past practices in these latter examples are not "benefits," but, rather, matters of fundamental managerial concern. On the other hand, if a district for many years paid teachers a stipend for attending IEP meetings during their prep periods then suddenly stopped doing it, a grievance based on past practice would likely be successful, because an economic benefit is implicated.

The distinction can be tough to draw, but it is meaningful.

Fortunately, there is a way out of a troublesome practice, if you can identify and articulate it sufficiently. As noted in an earlier section, most arbitrators will consider a practice no longer binding if the employer informs the union during contract negotiations that it intends to discontinue it with the advent of the new agreement. The burden then shifts to the union to place the matter on the table and secure a commitment from the employer to continue the practice. If it fails to do so, the practice can be discontinued.[44]

Another type of contract clause related to past practices is sometimes termed a "zipper clause." Zipper clauses, also called "integration clauses," usually say something to the effect that the specific promises found in the contract constitute the complete agreement of the parties, or that the parties agree that each side waives any right to bargain over any matters not specifically discussed in the contract. Arbitrators have reacted to such clauses inconsistently. Some have taken them at face value and found them to be an effective way of preventing the creation of "implied" contractual promises based solely on past practice. Other arbitrators have dismissed them as unimportant "boilerplate" not to be given literal meaning. Few, if any, arbitrators have found them to be of any significance when past practice is used only as a means of clarifying ambiguous contract language as opposed to their being used to create substantive rights. Far better, of course, would be a clause which expressly provides that the employer is not bound to follow any practice not specifically guaranteed by some express provision of the agreement. Such clear assurances are rare.

Miscellaneous Monetary Provisions

All contracts contain a variety of benefits with relatively minor financial impact when viewed in isolation, or at least when compared to salary increases or health insurance benefits. In the aggregate, however, they can represent a considerable financial commitment.

One of the most common in professional unit contracts is some type of reimbursement for post-graduate education. Some even expressly provide reimbursement for Act 48 programs, which are mandated by the state if an employee is to retain his professional certificate. Most districts are philosophically committed to supporting the continuing education of teachers, and these provisions reflect that. Even so, a school district is legitimately concerned with getting some real value for what it is paying, and making sure it does not inadvertently pay more for such things than it planned on doing.

You may want to take care to define exactly what it is you are reimbursing for, particularly if accumulating credits also has the effect of moving the employee into a higher pay schedule, as many contracts with what is called "columnar movement" do. Credit reimbursement can be limited to a maximum number of total credits, a maximum number per year, only credits taken as part of an established masters' degree program, credits directly related to a teacher's existing area of certification or assignment, or those leading to an additional certification. Unfortunately, some language

---

[44] There are various arguments that an employer can use at arbitration to defeat a past practice claim, like, for example, the proposition that the underlying circumstances which gave rise to the practice have changed. Discussion of this, and other matters related to contract interpretation, is generally beyond the scope of this guide.

is so loosely worded that employees receive reimbursement for college credits totally unrelated to education. Of course, you should specify a maximum number of credits per year, and a cap on the amount you will pay per credit. You will also need to provide for the timing of payment, documentation of course completion, pre-approval procedures, and perhaps even a minimal grade achieved. If your obligation to reimburse is going to be subject to superintendent or board approval, the right to reject a course should be clearly defined.

Many districts have experienced problems with employees who receive a substantial reimbursement from the district, only to leave employment soon thereafter to work at another district. This is particularly offensive to districts that have paid to provide education intended to allow the employee to acquire administrative certification when administrators are in short supply. This situation can only be remedied through language which requires the employee to work for a specified length of time after the credits are reimbursed under penalty of having to pay it back. And even that has obvious practical problems associated with it.

Another common provision is some type of workers' compensation "make up pay." Such provisions provide an employee absent due to an on-the-job injury with the difference between workers' compensation disability benefits (typically around two-thirds of pay) and a full paycheck. Although this sounds compassionate, such a system gives an employee very little incentive to return to work very quickly, or even at all. There are even contracts that have such a benefit with no time limit on how long the employee can receive it. Fortunately, occupational injuries are relatively rare among teachers. Support employees, however, are a very different story and "make up pay" provisions can be a real problem in support contracts.

There seems to be no end to the inventiveness of unions when it comes to finding ways to get more money. One of the most devilish I've seen is a provision which rewards employees who do not use sick or personal days with salary increases which appear modest but which, over time, are far more valuable than the price that the employee paid, which often was really nothing more than coming to work when he was able to. And, of course, sick days have long since evolved past their original purpose, which was to protect the employee against loss of income when he is too ill to be at work. They have become entitlements and commodities which you are paid for even if you don't need them and which, in some places, employees can even donate to others or trade them in for something else.

Criticism of Employees, Disciplinary Records, and Disciplinary Meetings

Contracts often contain language regulating how employees are to be criticized and even investigated.

Most common is some restriction of "public" criticism, where the contact requires that corrective statements be made privately so as not to embarrass the employee. Violating this rule can invalidate what would otherwise be perfectly justifiable disciplinary action. It is prudent to negotiate qualifications to such language making clear there are some situations where immediate corrective action needs to be taken, and that in order for a violation to occur, the supervisor must intend to do what the contract prohibits. At least one grievance went to arbitration after a principal raised his voice in a meeting with an offending employee and the door was slightly ajar, resulting in the conversation being overheard unintentionally. Like all contract language, care must be taken to carefully circumscribe what you are promising. If the contract says that board members and administrators are not permitted to publicly criticize "teachers," are they allowed to discuss, generically, the perceived shortcomings of a high school guidance department at a board meeting, without ever naming specific employees? One arbitrator thought not.

Contracts also almost uniformly deal with disciplinary meetings. Many require advance written notice to the employee of the substance of the meeting and expressly guarantee a right to union representation. Under what the PLRB refers to as the Weingarten rule (named after an NLRB decision that first created the rule in the private sector), an employee has a right to the presence of a union representative at an "investigative" interview, which might reasonably be viewed as having the potential to lead to discipline of the employee being interviewed. Under the law, this right does not exist at a meeting held for the purpose of informing the employee of a disciplinary decision that has already been made, nor does it exist even for investigatory meetings where the employee being questioned is not the object of the investigation. Many contracts go beyond these minimal legal guarantees and you should be sensitive to whether yours does, and how. Incidentally, the PLRB has held that "Weingarten" rights do not apply to employees who are not in a union bargaining unit.[45]

When a contract provides for the presence of a union representative at a disciplinary or investigative conference, confusion sometimes exists over precisely what the role of the union representative is. Unless your contract very clearly provides for a different role, the representative's function should be limited to rendering advice to the employee and serving as a witness to what happens. He should not function as an advocate for the employee. That role comes later. Neither should he be permitted to disrupt the discussion with the employee in any way or interfere with the purpose of the interview. There have been instances where union representatives who have apparently watched entirely too much television have advised employees that they could, and should, simply refuse to answer any questions about an incident which was under investigation, thus exposing the employee to charges of insubordination, or to an inference that they were guilty as charged.

Occasionally an employee will try to bring private legal counsel to a disciplinary conference. No right to private counsel exists in such situations, and it would be a very undesirable practice to permit this. In fact, all discipline is arguably a legitimate labor management issue, regulated by the collective bargaining agreement, and, with respect to such matters, the employee's union is his *exclusive* representative. Technically, recognizing any other party as representative is an unfair labor practice.

---

[45] *See Fraternal Order of Police Christine Lodge No. 84 v. Freeland Borough*, 43 PPER ¶63 (H. Ex. 2011).

Finally, some agreements attempt to regulate the use or retention of information critical of an employee by requiring that files be "purged" after a specified time, that no negative information be retained or relied upon unless it is "validated" (whatever that means), or that an employee be promptly notified of any complaint from parents or community members. These types of provisions – which are to be avoided if at all possible – have the effect of creating significant obstacles to effective disciplinary action.

Clauses that require an employer to remove references to prior discipline after the passage of a certain period of time are particularly troublesome. These clauses are sold to employers in bargaining via the superficially appealing argument that it is "unfair" for an old disciplinary record to follow an employee throughout his entire career if he's behaved since. You can have some sympathy for this point of view if, along with it, the union would agree that lengthy seniority could not be considered by arbitrators as a mitigating factor on the reasonableness of a severe disciplinary penalty under "just cause" review. Of course, you never see union willingness to agree to that. They want to have it both ways so they retain the ability to use an employee's lengthy service to mitigate a severe penalty like discharge, yet the employer must pretend the same lengthy service was performed free of disciplinary incident. More than one employee has gamed the system created by such provisions, periodically incurring disciplinary penalties, then behaving just long enough to clear his record.

Unfortunately, many districts that have imprudently agreed to purge provisions have ended up regretting doing so. A single experience in which you have to pretend someone has been a good employee for a long period when, in fact, they've been abysmal, can be very upsetting. Lest you worry about the inherent fairness of using an old disciplinary incident against an employee, rest assured that if the prior incident is, indeed, so old as to be unfair to rely upon, most arbitrators will conclude just that, and give it appropriately little weight. The staleness of prior discipline speaks for itself.

If your contract has a provision requiring the removal of discipline after the passage of time, you may be able to limit its effect somewhat if you find yourself in a position to settle disciplinary cases through agreement rather than arbitration. Sometimes a union is willing to agree that a specific disciplinary record can remain in an employee's file indefinitely as an exception to the contract provision in exchange for a lesser penalty than the employer might otherwise have imposed.

Anti-Discrimination Clauses

It is fairly common to see contract clauses which appear simply to restate the law regarding employment discrimination. They usually consist of a fairly straightforward declaration that the employer will not discriminate on the basis of race, religion, age, gender, disability, national origin, or the like. These clauses seem harmless enough, since, after all, they merely restate what the law otherwise provides for. These provisions *are* significant, however, because they provide employees with the ability to raise such claims through the contract's grievance and arbitration procedures *in addition* to the procedures offered by the EEOC, the Human Relations Commission, and the courts. Absent such language in your contract, the employee can only utilize *those* agencies to redress a claim. This is a significant procedural option for an employee, which would not exist absent contract language. It's a lot harder, and more expensive, to pursue a lawsuit than it is to file and prosecute a grievance.

Class Size, Reduction in Force and Related Subjects

Although not so common as they once were, there are still occasional attempts by unions to include provisions regulating class size, or restricting the district's right to reduce the size of staff. Needless to say, a school district would be ill advised to go down those roads, for concessions in these areas relate to the very heart of the board's managerial authority and have significant budgetary implications. And the two topics are related. If the union can control class size through the contract, it can indirectly exert control over the number of employees you must employ and, perhaps, even the number of buildings you must operate. In a real sense, it will control your budget as well.

There are some aspects of force reduction that are frequently found in contracts, however, usually dealing with how seniority is employed in making decisions. The provisions of the School Code that control how layoffs of professional employees are to be executed specifically allow districts and unions to negotiate exactly how seniority will be utilized.[46] Some districts also have agreed to extend to temporary professional employees the same rights and protections the School Code provides to professional employees, either intentionally, or through inadvertence because of the careless way the contract was worded. Unfortunately, many arbitrators have "implied" into contracts that did not contain a word about furloughs a commitment by the district to follow the School Code, thus making the Code furlough provisions enforceable through a contract's grievance procedure rather than just the courts. Sometimes this "implied" contractual promise is rationalized as created by a statutory savings clause; at other times it is explained as being encompassed by a just cause clause which promises that no teacher will be deprived of any "professional advantage" without "just cause." The fact that the "just cause" clause was clearly intended to regulate disciplinary action (i.e., action taken with a punitive intent or effect) seems to have gotten lost along the way.

Merit Pay and Two Tiered Systems

Merit pay and bonuses are anathema to unions, even though they hurt no one and have the potential to benefit members of bargaining units. Unions view merit pay suspiciously and usually voice their objections in terms of fearing favoritism and the diversion of scarce resources that should, in "fairness," be spread out among all the troops. While the concern about not wanting to deplete scarce resources is touching and the union should be reminded of it at negotiations, the real reason

---

[46] *See* 24 Pa. Stat. Ann. § 11-1125.1(e) (2012).

unions hate the concept of merit pay has more to do with their own institutional interests and insecurity than anything else. Support for a union among the workforce depends in large measure on the employees fully appreciating that it is the union which is largely responsible for their pay and benefits, not the largesse of their employer or the inherent value of their labor. Merit pay is fundamentally inconsistent with this interest of the union, because, if an employee receives extra compensation beyond what the union contract requires the employer to pay, it is pretty clearly the result of something other than the union's efforts.

While there no doubt are districts that would poorly handle merit pay and bonus decisions if they had the latitude to make them, I doubt this would be the overarching problem unions predict it would be. In 2010, according to the United States Bureau of Labor Statistics, fully 93.1% of the private sector workforce was not unionized, which means that than nine out of 10 private sector workers in the United States worked in an environment where their employers were free to set compensation at levels they felt were appropriate and to reward special talent or outstanding accomplishment or effort without regard to any union contract. The vast majority of the private sector workforce in this country essentially operates on a merit pay, or, pay-for-performance basis, and the system works pretty well. It's not perfect and does not work perfectly in all organizations, but, then, the union's seniority-based, one-size-fits-all model of compensation has its drawbacks as well.

What is important for school boards and school administrators to realize is what a hot button issue any type of merit-based compensation is with unions.

A related concept that may someday take hold is the notion that some teaching credentials are more valuable than others. Let's face it, it is much more difficult to find and retain someone to teach AP physics than elementary education. Like it or not, there really are market forces to contend with in hiring professional staff in public schools. Ask any superintendent. It would make a lot of sense to recognize some of these realities in our pay systems. Unions don't like this concept, either, but it does have the virtue of taking the favoritism arguments off of the table. We are talking about an objective set of criteria as a basis for higher pay. Similar considerations could be given for teachers willing to take assignments in underperforming schools, or with underachieving students, for example.

More common are proposals for two-tiered pay systems, typically among support staff units. Two-tiered systems create two separate pay scales, with the second tier lower overall than the first, but only applicable to employees hired after a certain date. Existing employees are typically "grandfathered" under the former scale so no one loses anything. Predictably, unions aren't fond of these either, since the two-tiered approach has the inevitable effect of eroding, over time, the overall compensation levels of staff that have been fought for over time. Such systems, which are unusual but certainly not unheard of, are, however, the only really practical means of correcting a scale that has gotten out of control for one reason or another, or to help permanently control costs in a district that is experiencing structural financial difficulties. Arguments against such systems often take the form of a prediction that having employees working alongside one another performing the same work for significantly different rates of pay will create morale problems and is otherwise simply "unfair." Oddly, unions opposed to two-tier pay systems for these reasons see nothing unfair about a teacher with a few years of experience making tens of thousands of dollars less than a teacher with significantly more seniority doing exactly the same job.

Subcontracting Clauses

With support units, contracting is common and often makes good economic sense. In fact, over the years, student transportation has been transformed from a situation where almost every school district employed its own drivers to the current situation where hardly any of them do. Bus drivers literally priced themselves out of the market. In a few districts, custodial services have been contracted and, in others, food service. Countless districts have at least considered doing these things, because there is no shortage of private concerns willing to provide these services.

Language in your contract that contemplates contracting can go a long way toward streamlining this exercise should you decide to travel that road. There are a variety of ways to deal with the topic in advance in an agreement, ranging from providing specified amounts of advanced notice to pre-negotiating severance packages for affected employees and even requiring that potential contractors offer employment to displaced employees, or provide specified wages and benefits. Language on this topic is hard to achieve, but can be extremely useful if outsourcing becomes a serious consideration.

Although theoretically possible, subcontracting any significant portion of the work of teachers seems impractical. The only common subcontracting arrangements involving teachers are agreements with intermediate units to perform certain targeted services for contracting districts. The teachers' unions don't seem to mind, or indeed, even notice this work that would otherwise be "theirs" is being subcontracted, most likely because it's being done by other unionized teachers who are probably represented by the same parent union. Still, when professional services are performed in a local district by intermediate unit employees, there is no question that teaching is being done by a subcontractor, i.e., the intermediate unit. Virtually all professional contracts are silent on the subject.

Grievance and Arbitration Procedures

Virtually all contracts contain language describing a process under which the union can complain that the contract has been violated, culminating in binding arbitration. The functioning of a grievance procedure is discussed in a little more detail in a subsequent section.

There are several aspects of contractual language relating to grievance procedures that bear mentioning.

Your contract should define exactly what constitutes a "grievance" subject to the procedure, and most do. Ideally, a grievance should be defined as (only) an alleged violation of the contract, and nothing more. Unfortunately, there are grievance procedures that purport to make any "inequitable" application of any "district policy" subject to the grievance procedure, thus effectively incorporating all district policies into the contract and rendering them enforceable through the contractual procedure when they were never even discussed at negotiations. Other contracts make any violation of law subject to review through the procedure. Anything more expansive than a reference to violations of the contract is inviting a serious problem.

Your contract should require that a grievance must be submitted in writing, and that it clearly identify which sections of the contract are alleged to have been violated. Grievances can be amended and the union won't typically be held to a duty to identify its alleged violations with surgical precision at the outset of the procedure but, still, it is worthwhile to make them start thinking in very specific terms right at the outset.

The procedure should specify a firm time limit within which a grievance must be filed. The contract should also say if this time limit, or any time limit applicable to the union's processing of a grievance, is not met, the grievance is deemed abandoned and may not be advanced further. I've sometimes had spirited debates with union folks about whether there should be a parallel "default" provision that says if the management side fails to give an answer to the grievance within specified time limits, the union automatically wins. These arguments can be resisted on the ground that the union is the moving party in these matters, not the district, and it is the union's burden to decide whether the issue is worthy of being advanced to the next level.

No matter how clearly your contract specifies time limits for the initial filing of a grievance or for moving it through the procedure's steps, do not assume that you can win a grievance in arbitration on the basis of a procedural argument based upon a time limit. Arbitrators strongly disfavor deciding cases on the basis of what they view as "technicalities," and, while you should raise timeliness as an issue,[47] never assume it will be a winning argument. Before you allow a case to go to arbitration, make sure you are comfortable with the merits.

The Commonwealth Court has lately provided some real hope that timeliness arguments will be taken more seriously than they have been historically. In *Commonwealth of Pennsylvania v. Pennsylvania Corrections Officers Association,*[48] decided in late 2012, the full court unanimously vacated an arbitration award which had revised a disciplinary suspension. The grievance in question were filed several weeks late, but, because the employees remained on suspension for an extended time, the arbitrator had ruled that each new day was a "continuing violation," a theory often relied upon by

---

[47] If timeliness is to be raised as an issue, do not raise it for the first time at arbitration since raising the question that late in the process can be construed as a waiver. Mention the union's tardy filing or processing as soon as it becomes apparent and do it in writing, either in your written grievance response or in a separate communication.

[48] 44 PPER 47 (Commwlth. Ct., 2012).

arbitrators to avoid deciding cases on the basis of tardy grievance filing. If the view reflected in the *Correction Officers Association* decision is adhered to in later decisions, contractual language regarding time limits for processing grievances will take on new importance.

The contractual grievance procedure is the place where the contract addresses exactly how an arbitrator is to be selected. This topic is discussed in more detail elsewhere in this guide. There is some real merit in replacing the typical language on arbitrator selection with language that appoints a "permanent panel" of pre-selected arbitrators who will hear all cases arising during the life of the current agreement. This eliminates the random selection that sometimes occurs with panels provided by the Bureau of Mediation. This system is fairly common in private industry but has yet to make inroads into the public sector. In recent years, the panels provided by the Bureau of Mediation have become crowded with unknown and, in some cases relatively inexperienced arbitrators, making selection uncertain at best and difficult at worst.

Finally, you are free in the grievance and arbitration language to address a multitude of topics related to how arbitration hearings are to be conducted, ranging from whether the parties will share the cost of a transcript (something I highly recommend) to whether they have an absolute right to file a written post hearing brief (something I ordinarily do). Typically, costs of arbitration are equally divided, although I have seen provisions that say the "loser pays" the entire cost of the arbitrator's fees.

Management Rights Clauses

It is advisable, but not absolutely essential, to have some type of management rights clause in your contract. The principal benefit of including such a clause may be psychological, as it represents some degree of recognition by the union that there are at least some areas of decision making that are none of their business. There are relatively few arbitration cases where the outcome actually turned on the existence or specific terminology of such a clause, and in those cases where a management rights clause was referred to in support of a favorable decision, the district may have prevailed anyhow.

Many contracts contain a simple acknowledgement that the district has retained all of the normal and inherent rights of management, or, perhaps, that it retains the right to exercise discretion in the areas designated as inherent managerial prerogatives under Act 195, unless specifically restricted by some term in the agreement. A better approach is to actually list the items we're talking about, and some agreements contain reassuring lists of things that everyone agrees management ought to be allowed to do without any serious challenge. Included items may be things like determining the number and type of facilities, determining curriculum and programming, regulating the use of facilities, determining the amount and type of work performed, and a host of other topics.

Even in the absence of a management rights clause, almost all arbitrators recognize what they call the "reserved rights doctrine." This established arbitral principle holds that even in the absence of a specific statement of management rights, management is assumed to retain all of the "normal and inherent" rights of management, i.e., those prerogatives that are essential to the ability to manage the enterprise.

Reopener and Cost of Living Provisions

Normally, when parties agree upon a labor contract, the agreement and all of its sub-parts are in full effect for a fixed time, after which they all expire and need to be replaced with a new comprehensive agreement. Occasionally, a contract will contain language which identifies a particular part or parts of the agreement – typically wages and, lately, health insurance – that expire sooner than the agreement as a whole. The language will refer to these items as being "reopened" for negotiations limited to only the identified items. Usually, this language provides that if agreement is not reached within the allotted time, the no strike clause is cancelled and the union has the right to strike over the absence of agreement on the reopened terms. The addition to the bargaining agenda of any item not listed as reopened requires the consent of each party.

Protracted negotiations and strikes are relatively rare in negotiations over reopeners. This may be because with an agenda limited to at most one or two items, there often isn't enough at stake to justify going to extremes. There also is the question of leverage, which is often lacking on one side or the other when a reopener is in play. Leverage (defined as significant bargaining power due to circumstances) is almost never present when one side is satisfied with the status quo and the agenda is limited to one, or at most two, items.

Reopeners are neither good nor bad. Sometimes they are necessary to reach an agreement, or they just make sense to one or both parties. Uncertainty about the financial future in the short term can be a reason to consider one. They are somewhat more common in private industry contracts than in contracts governing public employees, and more common among support staff groups than they are with units of teachers. The important thing is to identify with precision what is being reopened so there is no room for disagreement on that score.

Even absent specific "reopener" provisions in a contract, there is nothing wrong with modifying a contract before it expires, if the parties can agree to the modification. For reasons that are not clear, some districts and unions seem convinced they either can't, or shouldn't, "reopen" their contracts in order to make some change in its pre-existing terms or to add an agreement on some item that wasn't included originally. It happens all of the time, is lawful, and is neither a good nor a bad practice inherently. If a mid-term modification, or addition, to the contract makes sense and the parties agree, executing a memorandum of agreement memorializing the understanding simply does not establish a precedent that should be of any concern, as long as the agreement is limited to the subject matter at hand and properly drafted.

Another way to reach an agreement that doesn't definitively settle everything at one time involves the inclusion of a cost of living provision, or, a "COLA" clause, in your contract. COLA is a concept that is limited to the salary or wage provisions of the contract. A clause of this nature lays out a formula by which the wage increase for a particular year is determined by the inflation experience during a period of time (almost always a year) immediately preceding the effective date of the increase. The United States Government publishes several different cost of living indices, using different samples of prices and measuring increases from different areas of the country and different sample communities. You can select an appropriate one and agree to adjust rates or salaries by a percentage equal to the percentage increase during the prior year in the COLA index you have selected, thus using the prior year's inflation experience to control the amount of the increase employees will receive. The indices are generally available with a two-month lag time.

Many COLA provisions incorporate the concept of either a "cap" or a "floor" or both. A cap is a maximum limit on the amount of increase that employees will receive, regardless of inflation during the measurement period. Thus, if inflation is 3% but the cap is only 2.5%, the employees will only receive 2.5%. Similarly, with a floor, the employees are guaranteed to receive some minimum increase regardless of how low inflation was during the measurement period.

Released Time and Leave for Union Business

Many contracts contain some provision for a set amount of time that the union president, or union officers collectively, can take off to attend to union business. A related provision might identify specific types of union activities, such as attendance at negotiations, grievance meetings or arbitration hearings, for which paid leave time is provided.

As in most areas of contract draftsmanship, it is important to be precise in describing what you are agreeing to. What exactly is "union business?" Everyone can probably agree that going to a regional meeting of union officials or attending some union training program qualifies. But what if a rank and file employee sues you, or files a discrimination charge and there is some proceeding relative to that matter? Does attendance at that qualify? For the employee himself? Or for a union officer who only comes to observe and to provide moral support? And if you have agreed to allow employees to have time off with pay to attend "grievance meetings," does this include arbitration hearings? If your custom is to have these hearings during the school day, as is often the case, have you considered that the union may decide it needs to have 10 employees testify? Questions such as these are best asked before the language is carved in stone, not afterward.

Leaves of Absence

School contracts universally provide for various types of paid and unpaid leaves of absence. Commonly seen are provisions for service on a jury, testifying pursuant to a subpoena, military service, child rearing, bereavement, service as a paid union officer, and extended disability leave after the exhaustion of paid sick leave. I've even seen one contract that granted an indefinite unpaid leave to serve in elected public office (not recommended). Most of these provisions are fairly straightforward, you've either agreed to provide the leave or you haven't, and there is little room for controversy. Still, a few cautions are in order.

If you grant leave for "legal" activities, be careful to properly define what you are agreeing to. It may sound innocent enough to allow for paid leave anytime an employee is subpoenaed to give testimony, but you probably won't like it when the union's attorney arranges subpoenas for a half dozen of your employees to testify against *you* in an unfair practice case, a lawsuit, or a grievance arbitration. You'll need to be sure your contract excludes from the coverage of such leave situations where the testimony is offered adverse to the district, or in connection with legal actions that are to the benefit of the employee.

Extended disability leave is another area where care must be exercised. Many contracts contain some type of assurance that a job will be held for an employee who has exhausted paid leave, but has not recovered from an illness or accidental injury sufficiently to return to work. Sometimes benefits are continued at district expense during this period. It is important to place some type of outside limit on such leave allowances even though they are unpaid. Holding a position and covering it with substitutes indefinitely can create real management headaches and can affect service. No one wants to be harsh in such situations, but at some point the district needs to be able to move on, and the employee has to realize that if he is not going to be able to return in any useful, foreseeable time frame, his relationship with the district is going to have to end. Your contract needs to deal with this hard reality.

Drug Testing

Drug testing of employees (as opposed to those not yet hired) is clearly a mandatory subject of bargaining. Consequently, an employer cannot simply announce that it is going to start doing drug testing of employees who are represented by a bargaining agent.

Agreements for drug testing are relatively rare in public education, but they are increasingly under consideration. There is no reason a collective bargaining agreement, or a separate memorandum of agreement, cannot address the topic.

Drug testing policies, and hence, agreements regarding what those policies can say, can deal with testing in a variety of contexts. Random testing is almost guaranteed to be quite controversial, and is viewed by many as an unwarranted invasion of employee's privacy interests. Whatever the merits of this view, random testing is likely to be a tough sell. Testing "for cause," while still resisted by many bargaining agents, is difficult to argue against rationally. "Cause" testing is usually described as testing after an accident, when aberrant or suspicious behavior is exhibited, or perhaps when an employee is returning for duty after an extended absence.

Those employers that have lawfully adopted testing policies after negotiating over the subject often include alcohol testing as well, when testing "for cause."

Although an extensive treatment of the subject is beyond the scope of this work, any school district considering the adoption of a random drug testing program for current employees, or even a universal pre-employment testing program for prospective employees, needs at least to be aware of the somewhat unsettled state of the law with respect to what the courts call "suspicion-less" testing. Even if a district has discharged its bargaining obligations under labor law, or otherwise obtained a waiver of interest in bargaining by a union, there are still significant constitutional considerations.

Generally, the courts have viewed most forms of drug and alcohol testing as "searches" within the meaning of the Fourth Amendment's prohibition on unreasonable searches and seizures. To render such a search "reasonable," courts have required a showing of individualized suspicion or some other specific basis for the test (such as typically exists in the case of "cause" testing under most policies). Suspicion-less tests have been held to be reasonable when they are applied to safety sensitive positions, including bus drivers, police and fire personnel, and even a sewage disposal plant operator. By contrast, they have been invalidated when applied to a position in a public library.

A strong case can be made that many school employees, including teachers and aides having direct responsibility for the safety of children, occupy safety sensitive positions, although there is as yet only sparse authority to establish this point. The law in this area is likely to develop further and, hopefully, a clearer view will emerge.

No Strike – No Lockout Clauses

Almost every contract contains some form of "No Strike – No Lockout" clause. These clauses represent the mutual pledges of the contracting parties that during the term of the contract there will be no forced interruption of either service (on the part of the employees) or the availability of work (on the part of the employer). Sometimes these clauses are as simple as that – a sentence or two saying there will be no strikes or lockouts during the term of the agreement. Sometimes the language goes a bit farther and expands on the meaning of the term "strike."

The PERA defines a "strike" in fairly expansive terms as any "concerted action in failing to report for duty, the willful absence from one's position, the stoppage of work, slowdown, or the abstinence in whole or in part from the full, faithful and proper performance of the duties of employment for the purpose of inducing, influencing, or coercing a change in the conditions or compensation or the rights, privileges or obligations of employment."[49] It is reasonable to assume that arbitrators, or courts, will interpret the term "strike" in the context of a labor contract to mean what the legislature declared it to mean when it drafted the PERA. Consequently, such things as an organized refusal to work overtime, or a concerted, union-orchestrated effort to induce teachers to

---

[49] *See* 43 Pa. Stat. Ann. § 1101.301(9).

refrain from activities they normally participate in, like open house or other after-school activities, arguably constitute a "strike" in the legal sense. If such activities occur during the effective term of a contract, they may constitute a violation of the contract's no strike clause, validly subject the participating employees to discipline, and expose the union to injunctive relief issued by a court. If they occur after a contract has expired but while mandatory impasse procedures are under way pursuant to Act 88, such behavior may likewise be unlawful. Even if lawful, they might constitute one of the two permitted strikes during a single school year. Unfortunately, there are no reported appellate cases addressing these issues, but they remain interesting possibilities for a willing school district to pursue.

Obviously, from a school district's perspective, the more expansive the definition of a strike the contract contains, the more protection the district has from any sort of "guerilla warfare" that a sufficiently irritated union may engage in. Even the most basic, simple no-strike pledge, however, is sufficient to provide the necessary protection.

In the unlikely event your contract does not contain a no-strike clause, most arbitrators will imply one into your contract by virtue of a binding arbitration provision, and, arguably, the PERA and Act 88 provisions relating to negotiations and strikes generally may be interpreted as making strikes during the term of an agreement unlawful even absent a specific contract clause so providing.

Long-Term Substitutes

A lot of confusion surrounds the concept of long-term substitutes, a term which is largely a creature of local practice and which is subject to wide variation. Long-term subs, or LTS's, are typically employees engaged to replace, on a temporary, but long-term basis, regular employees who are absent for one reason or another but who are expected to return. A typical example is an employee who is replacing a teacher on maternity leave. They may also be employed temporarily to fill a legitimate vacancy as, for example, when a teacher suddenly resigns or dies. They are to be contrasted with day-to-day substitutes who are viewed as casual employees. The PLRB and arbitrators have consistently ruled that LTS's are, or could be, members of a professional bargaining unit if they are employed for a "substantial" period of time and have some "expectancy of continued employment." The fact that they may be holding down a position that an absent employee may eventually reclaim does not negate bargaining unit status. Although there has been no definitive judicial declaration of what constitutes a "substantial" period, it seems as though a minimum of 45 days has become generally accepted.

This view has its genesis in a case that arose in my home district in Millcreek Township many years ago and the "test" for determining status as an LTS is sometimes referred to as the "Millcreek" test.[50] Simply stated, LTS's are full-fledged members of the bargaining unit, even though they are

---

[50] *See Sch. Dist. of the Township of Millcreek,* 10 PPER ¶10049 (Bd. 1979) *and Sch. Dist. of the Township of Millcreek v. Millcreek Educ. Ass'n,* 440 A.2d 673 (Pa. Commw. Ct. 1982).

engaged for a specific, time-limited period and can be freely released when the purpose of the assignment has been completed. While they are employed, however, they enjoy all of the benefits of membership in the union bargaining unit, including payment in accordance with the contract's salary schedule.

Because they are members of the bargaining unit, there is nothing prohibiting the district from negotiating special provisions relating to how aspects of the employment of LTS's are to be handled, and many districts have done so. There is no reason why a contract cannot establish special pay or benefit provisions relating to those engaged as LTS's. Absent such an agreement, however, LTS's must be accommodated in the same manner as regular employees.

An LTS is not the same thing as a temporary professional employee. Status as a temporary professional employee is significant under the Code for tenure purposes. The Code defines three significant categories of instructional employees, including professionals, temporary professionals, and substitutes. For labor relations purposes, however, LTS's are likely to be included, albeit temporarily, in your bargaining unit.

Automatic Renewal Clauses

Some contracts contain a provision, usually found near the end, that says that unless one party or the other gives a notice of an intention to "reopen" or renegotiate the contract by a certain date (usually January 10, to conform to the date by which negotiations must start by law), the contract automatically renews itself for a specific period of time (usually one year). Such clauses are lawful and should be treated as though they mean exactly what they say, although, as a practical matter, they rarely come into play. In fact, the only time an automatic renewal would work to the disadvantage of a school district is a situation where the district is proposing significant economic concessions and seems likely eventually to achieve them. Even in these circumstances, absent a lockout, the union can effectively accomplish an automatic renewal by simply not agreeing to a new contract, thus maintaining the status quo.

Union Access to School Facilities and Programs

Many agreements grant a union the ability to use school facilities to conduct after-hours meetings. Such provisions should be carefully worded to insure that such events do not interfere with school or community programs. The district usually does not have a reason to object to such use, provided it is properly scheduled and regulated.

Somewhat more problematic are provisions (or, in the absence of contract language, a past practice) which grant the bargaining agent access to intra-school mail systems, email networks, and bulletin boards. No one would likely have a problem with a union distributing meeting notices, formal notice of union business items or the like. But what if the union decides to use the school email system to advocate for the election of favored political candidates, perhaps in the next school board election? Or if it posts on the bulletin board in the facility lounge material related to a controversial public policy issue such as abortion or gun control legislation? Or material ridiculing the superintendent or school board president? Controversies such as these can be avoided by carefully delineating the conditions under which union access to internal communication is granted.

A few districts also have guaranteed a union representative the right to speak at in-service programs, usually at the start of the school year. Before agreeing to such a provision in your contract, consider carefully the message you are sending to faculty, particularly new faculty. Making the union look like management's partner in operating the system may, or may not, be an idea you want to project.

CHAPTER 5

Strikes

Pennsylvania has the dubious distinction of having had more school strikes than any other state in the nation. Fortunately, in recent years, there has been a significant decline in the number of strikes, but, unfortunately, we still have them. I've been involved in more than a dozen of them over the years and they were all trying experiences for my clients. The purpose of this chapter is to give you the basic information you'll need to understand how to respond to, and manage, a strike. I hope you never have to refer to it again.

Negotiating in the Context of a Strike

The possibility of a strike often affects bargaining before the strike actually occurs. A union really only has two weapons to enforce its bargaining demands – a strike and the threat of a strike. The union's bite is obviously worse than its bark, but the strike *threat* is a card that is often played. This usually takes the form of the "strike authorization vote," through which the union's leadership gets "permission" from the membership to order everyone out on strike at the leadership's discretion. It is questionable whether the "authorization" would be quite as easy to obtain if the question were put to the rank and file in the form of a decision to go on strike, say, next Monday, rather than as an abstract proposition, explained as just a way to give the union leadership the ability to bargain from a position of strength. An authorization vote really means nothing more than that the union leadership has gotten out of the way the democratic formality of a vote, clearing the way for a strike down the road.

There is no doubt that negotiations during a strike take on a different character than exists prior to the strike. The tension level rises considerably after the union raises the stakes and decides to inflict pain on parents and children as a means of enforcing its bargaining position. I often remind school boards that, prior to a strike, there are usually only two parties to the negotiations, the district and the union. After a strike begins, there are usually three parties, the district, the union, and the public. This may be one reason there are relatively fewer strikes these days. Educational unions have fallen on tough times when it comes to public sympathy, and going on strike can actually make it tougher for a union to achieve its objectives once John Q. Public takes a seat at the bargaining table, because once that happens, a board's position may harden. It plays out differently in different communities and at different times.

You can be certain, though, that the first thing a union will be looking for after it goes on strike is some sign that the board is panicking. Probably the worst thing you can do, unless the parties are very, very close to an agreement (in which case you are unlikely to have a strike in the first place) is to rush back to the bargaining table or appear to be anxious to do so. Hard though it may be, I often counsel just the opposite and suggest to boards that they remain calm, maintain their position at the table, and be in no particular hurry to resume having meetings. The worst thing you can do is make any type of immediate concession. If you do, you've just proven that going on strike was an effective move for the union. Once it becomes clear to the union that you aren't in panic mode and are prepared to wait them out despite the phone calls from parents whose lives the union has disrupted, the next thing the union likely will do is try to find an excuse to justify coming back to the table. When enough time has passed that it is clear that it is they who are anxious, and not you, it will be OK to talk about scheduling a meeting. Remember, the party which requests a meeting has at least a moral responsibility to have something new to say at the meeting, lest it look very foolish.

It can be difficult to follow this advice when the phone calls start, and when the local newspaper editor, who understands nothing about labor relations, is editorializing every day about how all of the "grown-ups" (meaning you) have to do what is right "for the children." Keep your eye on the ball, and remember that this too shall pass. If you have taken sound positions, in the long run, the district, and its students, will be better off if your positions substantially prevail.

Setting the School Calendar

In any school year in which a strike is a possibility, consideration should be given to the potential impact of official school holidays and the state's treatment of "Act 80" days. "Act 80" days are up to three days which the district may count toward the state-mandated 180 days of student attendance even though students aren't in attendance while other programming occurs. Basically, Act 80 days convert student days into extra in-service days.

For reasons that are difficult to understand, the Department of Education retroactively cancels any previously approved Act 80 days that have already occurred in any school year during which a strike occurs, regardless of when the strike occurs.[51] Consequently, if your union were to engage in a strike after Act 80 days have taken place, the district will have to make up those three student days, in addition to any student days lost as a result of the strike itself. This can have significant financial consequences, since the teachers will have already worked, and been paid for, the Act 80 days. After a strike occurs, they will have to work an additional three days beyond the normal contractual work

---

[51] *See* BEC 24 P.S. §15-1504 (2012), reproduced in the Appendix.

year in order to provide the three additional student make-up days required by the Department. The effect is that employees may actually make more money during a year when there is a strike than they would otherwise make.

The only way to avoid this possible scenario is to either (1) schedule your students for 180 days of actual instruction during any year when there is a realistic chance of a strike (i.e., have no Act 80 days), or (2) schedule the Act 80 days as late as possible in the school year, the theory being that a strike is much less likely in the late spring than it is at any other time of the year. If a strike occurs prior to late spring Act 80 days, you can simply cancel them as Act 80 days and the students can be required to attend in order to make up strike days.

With respect to official school holidays, the Public School Code authorizes a board to designate up to five days as "official school holidays." This must be done by official board action prior to the school year "within the resolution approving the school calendar."[52] Once designated, school cannot lawfully be held on such days. The existence of such holidays shortens the potential length of any strike, since they may not be used as "make-up days." To maximize usefulness in this regard, they should be designated as late in the school year as possible.

Although not normally an issue, care should be taken to make sure the district's first teacher workday falls *after* the official final day of the expiring contract. Otherwise, there is some arbitration authority to the effect that teachers have to be moved up the scale of the old contract even though the new scale for the about-to-begin school year has not been agreed upon. This may result in a temporary pay raise of 1.5 to 2% which the district would prefer not to give, and can be particularly problematic if the district's position on salary increases in the first year is a freeze or an offer of less than the average increase that is already built into the prior year's schedule.[53]

Finally, in order to minimize the available strike "make-up days," and thereby make any strike as short as possible, the start of the school year should be made as late as possible. The later the start, the shorter a strike can legally last.

Managing a Strike – Operational Concerns

There are a number of issues that need to be considered in connection with a strike. The Appendix contains a checklist which can be used to help make sure you are properly prepared, and most of the questions suggested by the checklist are addressed below. The Appendix also contains sample letters which can be sent to striking employees after the first day of the strike relating to the termination of insurance benefits and to any employee who elects to cross a picket line. This final letter accomplishes a resignation from the union and will serve to insulate the employee from internal union discipline which can include monetary fines for crossing a picket line.

---

[52] *See* BEC 15-1502, reproduced in the Appendix, and 24 Pa. Stat. Ann. § 15-1502.

[53] See the section on Retroactivity and Contract Extensions, *supra.*

1. Insurance Benefits

For any employee who is not on a sabbatical leave or off on a workers' compensation leave, insurance benefits should be terminated immediately. This can be accomplished by advanced arrangement with your insurance provider. A letter should be sent to all striking employees on the second day of the strike. You will need to attach to it a "COBRA Notice" indicating the amounts which the employee must remit to the district in order to maintain these benefits at his or her own expense. Whoever administers your insurance program can do this for you. These amounts may be 102% of the amount normally paid by the district for the premium. Note that employees have 60 days within which to elect COBRA coverage and an additional 45 days within which to make the actual payments should they elect to maintain the coverage. These timeframes are obviously far in excess of the maximum time permitted for the strike under Act 88, but the letter still has significant psychological value. An employee can simply wait during the 60 day period to determine if insurance was needed (i.e., if a claim would have been filed) before making the election. Experience shows that a number of employees will be sufficiently concerned to make the payment in any event. This device also serves to demonstrate to employees how much their benefits actually cost. Many employees are unaware of this cost.

2. Non-Union Employees

Consideration has to be given to handling other bargaining units and non-unionized staff. Employees in these capacities can be retained in employment or placed on layoff status during a strike, depending on the needs of the district. All staff should be reviewed to determine if there is useful work to be performed during the period of the strike and employees should be notified accordingly. Under normal circumstances, employees placed on layoff as a result of a strike will not be eligible for unemployment compensation during this period even though they are not part of the bargaining unit which is on strike. It is one of the unfortunate consequences of a strike by teachers that uninvolved support staff whose work is just not needed when students aren't in school will suffer loss of income as a result of a strike they have no direct interest in.[54]

Non-unionized staff and staff in other bargaining units should be advised that they have the right to report for work regardless of the presence of the picket line. Unionized staff with a contract in place cannot lawfully engage in a sympathy strike.[55] Obviously, if somebody is prevented from

---

[54] 43 Pa. Stat. Ann. § 802(d) (2012), which declares employees ineligible for unemployment compensation if unemployment is due to "a stoppage of work because of a labor dispute … at the … establishment … at which he is or was last employed." This broad statutory provision has been held to render ineligible employees who are unemployed because of a strike even if they are not members of the bargaining unit that called the strike. *See Unemployment Compensation Board of Review v. Tickle*, 339 A.2d 864 (Pa. Cmwlth. Ct., 1975). An exception exists, however, for non-striking employees for whom work is available despite the existence of a strike but who are prevented from working as a result of violence or threats.

[55] Section 1101 of the PERA, 43 Pa. Stat. Ann. § 1101.1101 (2012) provides that "public employees … who refuse to cross a picket line shall be deemed to be engaged in a prohibited strike …." Although not yet judicially interpreted, this provision seems to assure districts that all employees other than those engaged in a lawful strike can be required to work normally if the district wants them to.

crossing the picket line because of mass picketing or unlawful conduct on the part of the pickets, you do not wish anybody to place himself in jeopardy. Employees should be told that anybody that fails to report as a result of such conditions should promptly notify a designated individual and provide details concerning the reason they were unable to report for work.

3. Advance Notice of Strike

The law requires a 48-hour strike notice and you may plan in advance for an orderly shutdown of operations, notification to the community, etc. once the notice is received. Notice should also be promptly given to the Department of Education upon the actual commencement of the strike.

4. Other Organizations

Consideration should be given to the district's cooperative programs involving attendance of students at, and/or relationships with other organizations such as daycare operations, vocational technical schools or the intermediate unit. To the extent that such programs can be maintained in operational status, they should be. Similarly, the use of district's facilities by outside organizations should be permitted to continue if it can be done in a safe and orderly manner. Such activities have no real connection to the issues of concern to the striking employees or the labor relations problems of the district.

5. Security

Building security is sometimes a concern. Building principals should be informed clearly that this is their responsibility and appropriate steps should be taken to monitor the activities of pickets. Experience shows that unlike private sector employees, public employees tend to picket only during their normal working hours and it is unusual to encounter vandalism or after-hours activities that require monitoring. If problems of this nature develop, however, the district needs to be prepared to employ appropriate security measures to guarantee the safety of its facilities and after-hours employees.

6. Outside Contractors

If the district is employing any outside contractors to perform construction or other work, they should be notified of the situation and appropriate steps maintained so that access can be assured. Most building contractors are sensitive to labor relations problems and know how to deal with these issues. Transportation companies or others making deliveries to the district during the period of a strike should also be advised of the potential presence of pickets and access issues should be discussed with them.

7. Picketing

Questions often arise concerning the rights of picketing employees. Striking employees are entitled to picket any facility of the district provided they do so without blocking access or committing independent violations of the criminal law. Communication should be established with local law enforcement in the event that any problems develop, and you should determine how they wish you to provide notification of any incidents which you deem worthy of reporting. Should picketing activity occur which interferes with access to the premises by district employees or others having legitimate business, legal counsel should be notified so that consideration can be given to acquiring an appropriate injunction in the Court of Common Pleas. Typically in strikes by professional employees such action is not necessary, but in isolated cases problems can develop. In general, picketing tends to be most exuberant at the beginning of a strike. Pickets are permitted to stand in public access and public rights-of-way although not necessarily on all district-owned property. Sidewalks, road berms and the like are generally areas where picketing is a protected and permitted activity. The location of pickets farther up on the property and outside of areas customarily used for public access can normally be prohibited.

8. Employees Who Want to Work

From time to time, employees in the striking group may indicate a willingness to cross the picket line. Although this is unlikely due to the effects of peer pressure and the typical solidarity exhibited by striking employees, should an employee express a desire to come to work and should the district choose to allow such an employee to work, the employee should be advised that working behind a picket line can lead to internal union discipline if the employee is an official member of the union. This does not apply to "fair share" employees, only to full union members. An appropriate letter of resignation can be submitted to protect the employee from such discipline. Employees who are members of a striking union have a legally protected right to work. This right is enforceable through both a charge of unfair labor practices and civil (and perhaps criminal) action if they are threatened or coerced into honoring a picket line through any means other than the proper use of internal union disciplinary sanctions (which only apply to members of the union, not to all members of the bargaining unit) and peaceful persuasion. Unfortunately, these processes take too much time to be effective in most situations. There is simply no getting around the fact that crossing a picket line can be a difficult experience.

9. How Long Will the Strike Last?

Current law permits teachers to strike initially only for so long as the length of the strike, utilizing all available vacation and make-up days, does not jeopardize achieving 180 days of student instruction prior to June 15. Once a strike commences, a calculation can be made with confidence predicting the maximum length of time it can last. This computation should be made for everybody's information. The law permits a second strike later in the year, but only after certain procedures have been exhausted. The second strike must end in time for students to receive 180 days of instruction prior to June 30. Once a strike starts, you should calculate its maximum possible duration and communicate that information freely. People will want to know and it helps to see the light at the end of the tunnel.

10. Conducting Educational Activities

Consideration should be given to whether a partial program can or should be operated. This might involve educating only seniors, or teaching certain portions of the curriculum. Remember that in most cases substitutes may not be employed to do the work of striking teachers unless they have been employed by the district during the preceding school year. Experience generally shows that few, if any, substitutes are willing to serve under these conditions and, in any event, it often is not possible to operate a viable partial educational program.

11. Maintaining the "Status Quo"

Pennsylvania Unemployment Compensation Law converts a strike into a "lock-out," within the meaning of the unemployment compensation law if the strike follows unilateral action by an employer that alters working conditions or the "status quo." In such circumstances, strikers will be eligible for unemployment compensation benefits. Care should be taken during school operations prior to a strike to avoid taking any sort of action which is likely to be viewed as any type of change in working conditions. When in doubt, legal counsel should be consulted concerning the propriety of making particular changes in operations. A good rule of thumb is simply to try to do things as closely as you can to how they were done during the previous year in all respects. Obviously, even if the district has satisfied all impasse procedures and is in a position to unilaterally implement a contract proposal, such action, while not an unfair labor practice, may constitute a "lockout" for unemployment compensation purposes.

12. Communicating with Parents

In the stress of a strike it is easy to forget about the most important constituents a school board has – the parents. No one is impacted more by an interruption in school operation than students and parents. Expect them to be vocal and upset. It will go a long way toward calming the waters if you've kept them well informed about the negotiations as they neared a crisis point. It is important that parents (especially) understand that the issues creating the conflict are important ones and the district's positions are sound and justified. You are, in a real sense, asking parents and children to sacrifice as a result of the positions the district has taken. Parents should never be in the dark about any aspect of the situation.

Communication with parents can take several forms, including use of the media. Direct, written communications are a good idea because the message gets through. Expect telephone calls as well, and be prepared for them.

Considerations for Board Members

You can expect a number of tactics from the union, all intended to enhance its bargaining position and to weaken yours. The union will, of course, play to the public as best it can and try to identify its bargaining goals with "good education" and the interests of the students. In particular, if there are any language issues, the Association will try to characterize its positions on such issues as motivated by concern for students and may try to portray the strikers as representing the interests of students rather than their own narrow interests. For its part, the district should emphasize the importance of protecting its ability to manage the district and use its resources most effectively, and should stress the economic impact of the issues which are under negotiation. The larger public is most sensitive to financial and economic concerns, and can understand them most clearly.

You can expect some direct attacks on the board and its integrity. This can come in the form of references to the district's fund balance to try to portray it as easily having the ability to pay what the employees are asking, or reference to any controversial decisions in recent years on which the union believes the board may be vulnerable. Sometimes the union suggests that the full board is not being properly informed by its negotiating team and that this is contributing to the absence of a settlement.

Direct pressure and contacts with board members can be expected. This may come in the form of personal visits, telephone calls, letters, picketing at homes or businesses or the like. The union has a great interest in dividing the board and creating dissention among its members. Board members should avoid engaging in debates and individual conversations to the extent practical, and certainly public comment should be limited to the individual on the board who has been designated to act as spokesman. Although there is nothing wrong with board members having differences of opinion or internally debating the negotiating policies of the district, it is damaging to the district's bargaining position to have such differences debated publicly. Communication discipline is important to a successful outcome.

The union may try to negotiate with individual board members. Such approaches may come from employees or others who board members may have known for many years, and who they trust. Some approaches may be sincere. Some may be "set-ups." Avoid the temptation to try to be a "hero" by participating in such discussions. They will serve to divide the board and undermine the efforts of your negotiating team. You also may say something you will deeply regret.

It is important early in the strike that the district take an aggressive and visible role in explaining what the issues, its positions on the issues, and the reasons for those positions. The community will let you know how it feels once this information is presented. You can expect the union to be very aggressive in pushing its point of view, and there is no reason for the district to be shy about doing the same thing. A strike in a public school certainly affects the public welfare and the community deserves to know what the disagreements are about and the reasons for them.

A certain amount of posturing can be expected from the union. Appeals for "around the clock negotiations" or "binding arbitration" are common, as are requests that bargaining sessions be held with all board members attending personally. Occasionally, the union is bold enough to demand a public debate. These are all tactics designed to put you on the defensive. Frequently there are requests made to attack the district's professional negotiator or the superintendent. This is a ploy intended to isolate the board without professional advice so it can be dealt with in a more vulnerable posture. Be prepared to resist all of these common tactics. There are good responses which the district's spokesman can make in rejecting all of these approaches.

You can expect some erosion of public support over time. This is inevitable and understandable as parents and other members of the community become frustrated. In general, if your positions are sound and you understand the concerns of those who elected you, you will maintain a base of community support and your position will prevail.

Well-intentioned community leaders, with or without the instigation of the union, may attempt to get involved to mediate the dispute. Often appeals are made by the union or individual members to clergymen or political figures. Sometimes these leaders come forward of their own accord. Such individuals should be politely informed that their assistance is not necessary. The Commonwealth of Pennsylvania has provided a professional neutral labor mediator to facilitate discussions and the parties have their respective professional advisors. You should stress that the board is fully aware of the sensitivity of the issues and the impact on the community, and is doing its best to resolve things in a way consistent with the public interest. Individuals who are well intentioned and who try to involve themselves in the dispute are, when all is said and done, amateurs whose primary interest is in reaching an agreement without regard to, or a full understanding of, the importance that the settlement terms will have on the long-range operations of the district. Peace at any price has always been a bad idea, and you must remember the importance of the issues that brought you to this situation.

Sports and Activities During a Strike

There is often some sentiment on school boards to the effect that if the teachers provide the district with a strike notice, the board should either take formal action, or informally direct the superintendent to suspend sports and other extracurricular activities. I'm not sure what motivates such thinking, but I've heard the opinion expressed that it's just inappropriate to continue with sports if education isn't happening.

Such action seems inadvisable, particularly if, as often happens, athletic coaches indicate that if the strike occurs they will not coach. Obviously, sports programs cannot be safely or effectively run without the participation of coaches, many or most of whom are probably teachers.

If teachers strike and the coaches' view a refusal to perform their coaching duties as a part of strike activities, the athletic programs will, out of necessity, not operate. However, in that event, it is clear that the reason athletic opportunities are being denied to students is because of the *teachers' decision not to participate in them, and not any action of the district.* If the board takes the initiative to "cancel" athletic activities, then it is inevitable the parents and students who are adversely affected will view the board as being responsible for the fact that athletics are not being conducted. This will result in unnecessary criticism of the board for taking that action. Philosophically, some board members probably feel it is simply inappropriate for the district to be operating athletic activities when its educational program is interrupted. My advice is based on *practical* concerns about the consequences of such an action. The reality is that parents and student athletes who are affected will largely not share the view of those board members who believe it is simply inappropriate to conduct athletics. Their attitude will be that if athletics *can* be conducted, *why not* permit them to go on and why punish the student athletes unnecessarily? Such criticism is avoided, and the desired effect of not running athletics during a strike will still occur, if you simply let the teachers shut it down on their own.

CHAPTER 6

Grievances and Arbitration

The Nature of Grievances and Arbitration

The ideal contract defines a grievance as nothing more than a claim that a specific provision of the contract has been violated. Many, if not most, contracts follow this pattern. Here and there you will find districts that have imprudently agreed to more expansive definitions, ranging from an express recognition that amorphous "past practices" can be grieved, to wholesale incorporation of all of the school laws into the contract's ambit, to statements that any employee who has been treated "unfairly" or "inequitably" can process a grievance so claiming. More than a few contracts allow the procedure to be accessed to process a complaint that the district has not applied its own policies properly or equitably. This latter situation belongs in the category of self-inflicted wounds. The vast majority of grievances, however, really are nothing more than claims that some particular term of the contract has been violated.

Grievances are sometimes processed on behalf of employees who really don't want to pursue them. Indeed, unless your contract contains some rather unusual language, the union has the ability to press forward with a grievance even if one or more of the affected employees (usually referred to as "grievants" or "aggrieved" parties) isn't interested or supportive. There are situations where the union sees some larger purpose to be served that transcends the interests of individual members. There are practical limits in some cases to whether a union can pursue a grievance without the support of the individual(s) involved, particularly if there is a factual dispute and the union must rely on testimony from an unenthusiastic participant. A recalcitrant grievant simply may fail to appear, and it would be extremely rare, and highly embarrassing, for a union to have to subpoena its own grievant.

An aggrieved employee may approach his principal or the superintendent to express privately that he doesn't really want to go forward with a grievance but the union is "making" him do it, or doing it over his objection. That may or may not be true, as some people just want to curry favor and have the benefit of pressing their case without any risk of being thought less of by their professional colleagues. Take such private comments with a grain of salt.

Sometimes the motivation of the union in pursuing a particular grievance is difficult to understand, either because of the insubstantial nature of the issue or the small amount at stake (if the case has a monetary component). You scratch your head and wonder why the union would spend thousands of dollars over a case that may be worth a few hundred, or perhaps over an issue that is very unlikely ever to come up again. Indeed, I've had a case go to arbitration over less than $25.[56] I've given up trying to figure out this phenomenon, but it seems more common in districts that rarely have arbitration cases. Larger districts with a higher volume of labor management issues tend to concentrate on more consequential cases. Perhaps it is simply a matter of conservation of resources, but it may be that in quieter shops, sometimes the union feels it has to assert itself once in a while just to let everyone (and most especially its dues paying members) know it's still around and vibrant. Consider that the members in a district with 100 teachers paying approximately $550 per year each in union dues are paying a total of $55,000 per year for union representation. The staff representative might (or might not) be on the scene to negotiate a contract once every three years or so. If that same district goes three or four years without a single grievance going to arbitration, one could question whether people were getting their money's worth out of the system.

There are many other reasons why grievances are filed apart from their inherent merit in the union's eyes or a union's need to be active on behalf of employees. It is not uncommon for grievance activity to increase during, or just before contract negotiations as a means for the union to flex its muscles, or to retaliate against the district because of a tough district stand in bargaining. Sometimes union politics can play a role as well, if a member with influence has an axe to grind. Bad advice to the local union leadership from staff representatives also can play a role.

The law favors arbitration because it relieves the court system of the burden of deciding any case that manages to get resolved through arbitration. That's one of the reasons the law allows for so few reasons you can "appeal" an arbitration award. "Final and binding" arbitration usually means just that.

The PERA requires that arbitration provisions be bargained over and included in collective bargaining agreements.[57]

Were it not for the arbitration clause in your contract, the union would have to file a lawsuit in court every time it thought you violated the collective bargaining agreement. That, of course, is expensive and time consuming, and not a very practical way to enforce a collective bargaining agreement. The law provides that where the parties to a contract have agreed upon binding arbitration to

[56] The reader may note that it takes *two* parties to go to arbitration over a $25 case, and, at first blush, it looks just as unreasonable for a district to stand and fight over small matters as it does for a union to start the fight in the first place. However, the two parties have very different perspectives. A district that always capitulates when faced with "small" cases will get a lot of small cases. The only effective way to avoid what might be called death by a thousand cuts is to defend sound positions regardless of the amount in controversy. Remember that the *union* is the moving party and *it* decides whether a controversy is going to exist.

[57] *See* Section 903 of the PERA, 43 Pa. Stat. Ann. § 1101.903 (2012).

resolve disputes arising under their contract, that procedure must be followed and the result of the procedure must be honored, except in very rare circumstances. Indeed, once an arbitration clause is enshrined in a contract, the parties *can't* file a lawsuit to enforce contractual rights in most cases. They are *required* to use arbitration to resolve the dispute.

Arbitration results are enforceable in court, through what is called a "petition to confirm and enforce" an award. You cannot retry the merits of the case in defense of such a petition, and the sole function of the proceeding is to convert the private arbitration award into a court judgment enforceable, with some limitations, through the contempt powers of the court. A failure to comply with an arbitration award also has been found by the PLRB to constitute an unfair labor practice.

Unions worship at the altar of arbitration. They seem intuitively to view the contract's grievance and arbitration procedure as the "way to go" with virtually any type of dispute, even if it might make more sense tactically to file an unfair practice charge with the PLRB due to the nature of a particular dispute.

Although grievance arbitration has the virtues of efficiency, speed, and cost effectiveness (particularly from the union's point of view), it has some serious drawbacks. Principal among them is the inconsistent quality of the decision-making and its frequent unpredictability. You can expect arbitration to "malfunction" at least 25% of the time, meaning the result will simply be wrong. It may be "wrong" because the arbitrator misread the contract, or it may produce a result that is just inconsistent with good labor relations practice. The decision may be intellectually dishonest in the sense that it ignores arguments the arbitrator has no convincing way to reject. Incidentally, the 25% figure includes cases that districts have won that they should have lost. As noted elsewhere, an experienced practitioner who is fully informed about his case can almost always fit it into one of three categories: likely to win, likely to lose, and could go either way. My reference to arbitration "malfunctioning" refers to cases that fall into the first two categories, but didn't turn out as expected.

Why is this so? A lot of it has to do with the inconsistent quality of arbitrators, as well as an all too common lack of understanding by some arbitrators of how things work in schools on a practical level. Some of it is undoubtedly the result of bias, too. It's no mistake that on a typical panel of seven names, an experienced practitioner can usually predict who the union's first, and probably second strike will be, and the union advocate can usually do the same with the management choices. I see a distressing amount of this. Somewhere, somehow those same people are deciding cases for someone.

The point here is not to vent about arbitrators who have ruled against school districts. In fact, union advocates probably have a list of arbitrators they don't care for almost as long as mine. This subject is mentioned only so that arbitration can be put into perspective. It is an imperfect process, and along with it comes cost and some risk. Assess your situation objectively, weigh the costs and risks, and carefully decide whether to subject yourself to the process. Then do all you can to achieve a successful result, realizing that it is a system prone to "malfunction," and that over time, and despite your best efforts, you will lose some cases that were good ones.

Grievance Processing

Virtually every contract has a grievance procedure which describes how a dispute is processed prior to arbitration. There are usually a number of steps, typically consisting of the aggrieved employee's immediate supervisor, the superintendent, and then the school board. The final step of the procedure is arbitration. The preliminary processing of the grievance is absolutely critical to your counsel.

Arbitration has been referred to as "trial by ambush" because there is no formal pre-hearing discovery, so advocates have to guess at what the other side is going to present. The grievance procedure represents a very real opportunity for counsel to learn what the union intends to argue and what it intends to present by way of evidence. Your counsel needs to know those things in order to represent you effectively.

What types of questions should be asked of the union during grievance processing?

• What specific sections of the contract have been violated?

• What evidence does the union have to prove what it believes the facts to be?

• Have there been any prior cases of a similar type, involving similar principles?

• Is the grievance timely?

• Is there any claim of past practice? If so, what *exactly* is the practice? How many examples do they have? How old is the practice? Who in management do they think knew about it?

• What remedy do they seek?

• Do they have a compromise settlement to propose?

In some cases the district involves counsel quite early in the grievance process so he can help guide the "discovery" of important information. In others, he actually attends grievance meetings, usually when they are at the board level, so he can directly interrogate the union on the nature of its case. This helps immensely.

Keep in mind that during the grievance processing, the union also will have a great interest in learning information that may help, or hurt, its case if the grievance ends up in arbitration. In fact, many unions include a fairly aggressive request for information as a part of the written grievance itself. Often these written requests are too general or broad to be of much help to the union, and sometimes they are so poorly drawn as to be invalid. For example, I've seen a union request for "any and all evidence the employer has to support its position or which it intends to use in arbitration" or "all information used in any way to make the decision" which gave rise to the grievance. So stated, the employer probably has no obligation to provide anything because arbitration does not indulge the parties with pre-trial discovery akin to civil litigation. A union is not entitled to know exactly *how* you intend to present your case, nor can it dictate when you will prepare it. You should respond to such requests, but usually not with any information. Rather you should explain why you are not providing anything and suggest that a properly specific request would be considered.

More specific requests are obviously more problematic, and clearly a union evaluating a grievance or preparing for arbitration has some right to obtain information from an employer if that information is reasonably related to the union's ability to evaluate and present its case and is not otherwise available to it. But the employer does not have to respond to a set of homemade "interrogatories," conduct research expeditions for the union, or disclose who it will use as witnesses or exactly how its case will unfold at the hearing.

Many school administrators reflexively have witnesses, particularly students, write down what they saw or heard that might be relevant to a grievance, and sign the resulting document. Most often the temptation to do this arises in discipline cases. The thinking is that if the witness is unwilling or unable to make this affirmation of his recollection, he is not going to be very useful in proving what happened if it ultimately comes to that. Other administrators never think in such practical terms. I'm not critical of administrators in this regard since, after all, colleges of education typically don't offer Conducting Investigations 101.

The more astute union representatives will ask if any written statements were taken. You also may be asked simply to identify any witnesses who provided information on which the disciplinary action was based. Written witness statements should be taken with caution for several reasons. If the statement is written in the witnesses' own words, or written by a well-intentioned but unskilled building administrator, it may leave out things that are very important, or it may describe things in a way that can be used unfairly, but effectively, on cross examination of the witness. It is particularly dangerous to let children write out witness statements themselves. They typically have no idea what to say or not to say. It's not that they're not truthful. They just have no idea what they are doing. In fact, the only time written statements are really necessary is if there is a reason to think the witness may be prone to get cold feet, or may be particularly vulnerable to intimidation prior to being called to testify. In those cases, you might have to nail down the essentials of the story in order to make sure your case doesn't fall apart. Even then, I prefer to write the statement myself, after interviewing the witness, asking the witness to sign only after he is satisfied that what I have put down is accurate. Of course, if you have not taken a witness statement, then you can't be required to produce one for the union to use to plan its cross examination. And, as a practical matter, a witness statement is one of those things you will need to produce if requested. If that statement is obtained as a part of counsel's personal interviews, it represents attorney work product and is privileged from disclosure. Most (but not all) arbitrators will respect that position. Statements taken independent of hearing preparation likely must be produced if requested, although production can be delayed until fairly close to the date of the hearing to minimize the opportunity for witness influence or intimidation. If you are inclined to be uncooperative, remember that witness statements can be subpoenaed for an arbitration hearing.

When children are witnesses, you should be particularly guarded about when you identify them or produce any written statements they have given. Being a witness can be a difficult role for many people, and it is especially hard on children who, unfortunately, sometimes have to be involved. You should try to protect them from the pressure as much as you can for as long as you can, consistent with the district's legal obligations under the process.

Most grievance procedures require that the district make a written response to the grievance, on the same form that constitutes the grievance itself. The grievance response is not the place to issue a lengthy manifesto in defense of whatever action is being complained about. A simple "there is no violation of the contract and the grievance is denied" is technically sufficient and can't get you into trouble. It is often advisable to add just a bit more substance to the response, but in no event is it advisable to issue a lengthy rebuttal. For example, if you are denying a grievance that claims a job wasn't awarded to a person who had seniority and was qualified, and your defense is that the fellow really wasn't qualified, it is sufficient to say "The grievant was not qualified for the job." It is not necessary, or advisable, to get into lengthy detail about the individual's qualifications, or even what the job requires by way of qualifications.

One thing you absolutely should not do under any circumstances is make offers to settle grievances in your formal grievance answers. This mistake has been made too many times to count. Offers to settle are ordinarily not admissible at an arbitration hearing, and for good reason. If they were admissible, people would be reluctant to make them at all, which is generally viewed as a bad thing. However, if you place your offer onto the grievance form itself, *it will get into evidence* because that form is always going to be admissible. Thus, the arbitrator will see that you made an offer, albeit an unsuccessful one. Why is this undesirable? It is a subtle point, but most practitioners fear that an arbitrator who sees that a party was willing to compromise its position to resolve a case will perhaps conclude the party lacks confidence in the correctness of its position. As far as is visible to the arbitrator, you will want to project nothing but confidence in your position. Offers of compromise sometimes undermine that objective. You will want to make your offers, if they are in writing, in a completely separate letter or memorandum which speaks only to the idea of a settlement, and which will typically not be permitted into evidence.

As noted above, the final step of most grievance procedures is the presentation of the grievance to the board. Sometimes the procedure calls for an actual "hearing" or "meeting" between the board and the union, and sometimes this step is just a matter of paperwork. More typically, there is a meeting of some type, often with the entire board present. Many board members do not have a clear understanding of the nature of these meetings or what their role is, and unions sometimes try to exploit this. New board members, or board members in small districts that have few grievances, may never have attended one before. There are boards which think they are supposed to be impartial judges of the merit of a grievance and effectively put their own administration on trial in some sort of adversary environment at these meetings. I've even seen boards that have intentionally avoided knowing anything about the grievance in advance of the meeting, lest they bias themselves. They seem to confuse grievance meetings with the types of due process hearings they conduct for student expulsions and the like. The proper way to understand the board's role is as a level of management, not as judges.

Board members should be fully briefed on the grievance prior to the meeting with the union, and there is no excuse for them not to be. The purpose of the meeting is to give the union an opportunity to present its grievance to the board and for the board to consider what it has to say. When the presentation is over, board members should ask informational questions of the union, if something about the union's position, or what the union believes the facts to be, is not clear. Once that has been accomplished, though, the union should be invited to leave, as its portion of the meeting has ended. Afterward, in privacy, the board members and the administration and/or counsel can freely discuss any aspect of the grievance the board members wish to discuss, and determine what the board's response will be. While the board is certainly the last word on the grievance, in all but the rarest of cases, the board should be expected to back its administration's position. If it can't, something has gone wrong before the grievance meeting ever took place.

Winning Arbitration Cases

There are a number of factors that determine your chances of being successful in arbitration. At the risk of offending my professional colleagues, I would rank them in the following order:

- Selecting good cases to go to the mat over
- Carefully selecting the arbitrator who will hear your case
- Good advocacy, with an emphasis on good preparation

A good measure of luck also is helpful, because in the rent-a-judge world of labor arbitration, in the end, it's a roll of the dice.

As I've noted above, an experienced advocate who has studied his case thoroughly can easily place his case in one of three categories with regard to the likely outcome: favorable, unfavorable, or could go either way. He also has a good idea of what the most compelling rationale is for either favorable or unfavorable outcomes.

Selecting Cases

Too many employers seem to view arbitration as nothing more than an extension of the grievance procedure. It is that, of course, but it's also much more. Arbitration is a point of conflict in your labor relations culture, and the results can have consequences far beyond the specific outcome of the case. Arbitration results often set the tone of the relationship. For example, if a union continually succeeds at arbitration, you are much more likely to have future cases than if the experience leaves a bad taste in the union's mouth. Success at arbitration also sometimes makes a union feel empowered. And, of course, such success greatly enhances the political position of the incumbent union leadership. Although a grievance settlement may produce the same result (or nearly so) as an arbitration award, losing a contested issue is often much worse for the employer than making an agreed-upon concession. Knowing what cases should be *settled,* rather than taken to arbitration, is important. Cases that are weak on their merits are obviously candidates for settlement. So are some cases that do not involve issues that are likely to ever reoccur, provided you do not sense the union is simply pressing small cost cases hoping you aren't willing to spend the money necessary to defend a small matter. Settlements, when entered into, should be carefully documented through appropriate memoranda and, in many cases, language can be included declaring the settlement non-precedential and prohibiting the union from even referring to its existence in any future proceeding.

There are occasionally cases that *have* to be tried, even if the chances of success are small. There may be political purposes to be served, or the case might involve such significant consequences that settlement representing any sort of compromise is impossible. In general, though, it is better practice to avoid arbitration unless your counsel's assessment of your chances is at least 50-50. Pick your shots carefully, and then do your very best to win.

Once in a while, you will see a case that involves a very small amount of money, perhaps far less than the cost of the arbitration itself. I do not recommend giving in to such grievances simply because a small amount is in controversy. A policy like that is a slippery slope that will likely encourage more such disputes once the union realizes that management will not fight over trifles. You have no choice but to fight in such circumstances.

Selecting Your Arbitrator

Many cases are won or lost before the first word of testimony is offered, because the employer, or its counsel, was unsophisticated regarding the arbitrator selection process.

Most contracts provide for an arbitrator to be selected from a list of seven names provided by the Pennsylvania Bureau of Mediation. By statute, the employer strikes the first name, after which the parties alternate until one name is left. That's your arbitrator. There are other ways to do it which are preferable, and a few contracts provide for both a different source of arbitrators, a different selection process, or even a permanent panel where the names are pre-agreed during negotiations before anyone knows what the cases will be about or how many there will be. The most common alternative to the Bureau list involves obtaining names from the American Arbitration Association, a private dispute resolution organization. The AAA is more costly (you pay a fee of several hundred dollars, while the Bureau service is free), but I have found the quality of the panelists to be superior. You also are more likely with the AAA to get an arbitrator who hears private industry cases and who has more of a "real world" perspective. It is far harder for a prospective arbitrator to be listed with AAA than it is with the state Bureau. A proven track record of common acceptability and considerable experience is required.

Regardless of the source you use, or the particular selection procedure, in the end it is still important to know as much as possible about each potential arbitrator before making the selection. Your counsel's experience is critical here, because the same names tend to come up over and over again, particularly in the same geographic region, and the population of professional labor arbitrators is rather small. Unless someone is relatively new to the ranks of arbitrators, he's probably run into the fellow before, or at least heard of him or read a few of his published opinions. I have the good fortune to practice in a firm that does a great deal of labor arbitration. With six attorneys handling labor cases on a regular basis and over 35 years of personal experience, it is unusual to see a name that is completely foreign. With the hundreds and hundreds of cases in our firm's experience compiled into a computer database, a name, or type of issue, can be called up and history used to help rank a panel.

There also are several excellent (and expensive) commercial services that a labor counsel can subscribe to which provide valuable background material on arbitrators, including candid post-decision assessment by other management counsel who have used the particular candidate. Our firm has invested in these and has found them to be quite useful. Biographies of Bureau arbitrators also are available online from the Bureau of Mediation. If your counsel isn't taking advantage of all of these resources, he should be.

One of the best ways to research an arbitrator is to read his opinions, even if the cases are dissimilar to yours. You can get a feel for the person's analytical abilities and the quality of his judgment just by reading his cases. If you can find a case with a similar issue, you've really got your hands on useful information. Your adversary, the union, maintains a detailed data base of arbitration decisions and its local counsel benefits from centralized information sharing in this regard. So should you.

Arbitrators come in all shapes and sizes. There are a handful of full-time, professional arbitrators, whose entire livelihood depends on being acceptable to both sides on a regular basis. As a group, I favor them. The part-timers and the retired folks who are doing it as a source of retirement income are far more problematical. Most of those falling into this category are academics (at the college level), or retired union staffers or human resource managers. Many in both camps are, or were, practicing attorneys. I admit to certain biases regarding desired background, although there are many exceptions to my general preferences. I tend not to like academics, as I find many to be unrealistic and naive about the practicalities of labor relations. Some also are inclined to be sympathetic to professional educators because that's the environment they work in. They also tend to be politically liberal. With former HR managers and union staffers you have to be careful because some tend to bend over backward to favor unions or management, respectively, out of a concern that they appear to be "fair." I have a natural hesitation to select someone who made his living representing unions, and my union counterparts feel the same way about people who worked in management their whole lives. But you've got to be flexible. One of my favorite arbitrators was a PSEA representative in another life, and there are several former HR managers I avoid like the plague.

Experience with school law, or school labor relations, is helpful, but good judgment and common sense are more important. Attorneys are often good choices if your case has a legal component, or if you want your contract read in a literal manner. Lawyers tend to honor technicalities and also tend to give words their intended meaning rather than invent some purpose the parties never intended so that a "fair" result can be achieved.

Preparation

Arbitration is litigation. Consequently, as any trial lawyer will tell you, there is no substitute for thorough preparation. Unfortunately, and unlike the trial lawyer, the labor practitioner preparing for arbitration does not have the benefit of a book full of court rules providing for every imaginable type of pre-trial discovery. In a civil trial under the rules of court, only a poorly prepared lawyer is ever surprised by something said at trial. It's all been rehearsed beforehand, and stenographically recorded under oath. For all practical purposes, it's scripted. Documents and exhibits are exchanged beforehand, and witness lists are submitted. By contrast, the lack of such procedures in arbitration has been referred to as "trial by ambush."

To deal with this mess, it is imperative that the lawyer and client get their arms firmly around all of the facts and arguments the other side may make. One of the best ways to do this is through the grievance procedure of the contract, which may be utilized before the participants even realize there is going to be an arbitration hearing. District administrators ought to view grievance meetings as pre-trial discovery for their attorneys.

Before the Hearing

As noted above, a union has a statutory right to obtain information, including documents, when that information is reasonably necessary for either the evaluation of the merit of a grievance or the presentation of a grievance to arbitration. An employer's duty to provide such information is viewed as a manifestation of its duty to bargain in good faith. The union's right has its practical limits, however. The district is under no obligation to create information or documents that do not otherwise exist, to do investigative work for the union, to answer questions or interrogatories posed to it, to identify what witnesses it will call or what exhibits it will offer at arbitration, to disclose who it interviewed or what they said to the interviewers, or to produce the personal notes of its administrators regarding the matter at issue. In short, it is not the same as pre-trial discovery in a civil case. The union has a duty to provide information to the district as well, although there will not be many situations where the union will have information the district needs to evaluate and present its case.

Either side can use subpoenas in arbitration. Pennsylvania law gives arbitrators the authority to issue them and they are freely dispensed. Obviously, they have to be requested and served well before the hearing. Some arbitrators will notify the other side when one has been issued, but often you won't know if the other side has availed itself of a subpoena until the hearing, unless the person served with it tells you. They also can be used to compel the production of documents, but only at the hearing, not beforehand. As a matter of course, if a bargaining unit member is going to testify for the district, you should arrange a subpoena both to assure attendance and to provide some level of comfort to an employee who may well be uncomfortable testifying for the employer.

Many cases are won or lost on the basis of preparation, and no aspect of preparation is more critical than preparing the employer's direct evidence. Generally, there should be two meetings with all of the folks involved in an arbitration hearing. The first can be fairly called a brainstorming session, where you identify the issues, both factual and contractual, which are likely to be disputed, what you know of how the union will present its case, who is likely to testify for the union at the hearing, and how you will go about proving what you need to prove. Everyone who may be participating should have a thorough understanding of what the district's *theory* of the case is, both in terms of relevant contract terms and disputed facts. This is where any "discovery" that has been accomplished during the grievance processing becomes useful. You also should make sure that anyone who has never been involved in an arbitration hearing before understands what it looks and sounds like, and what the experience will be like for them. Most folks are somewhat apprehensive, and you should try to deal with that as well.

The second meeting is usually devoted to reviewing the precise questions and areas of questioning each witness will be responsible for, and what the union's counsel will likely ask about on cross examination. These discussions can be one-on-one, rather than with the full group, depending on logistics and the complexity of the testimony.

Do your best, as part of preparation, to anticipate who will be testifying for the union and about what. This is sometimes harder to do than it sounds. At the very least, you should inform your counsel about the identities of any staff who have requested time off to attend the hearing. If you haven't heard about any such requests from your facility administrators and it's only a few days until the hearing, by all means call the union president and ask him who will be attending. After all, unless it's an evening shift custodian, if the hearing is during the day, as most are, you'll have to arrange coverage and, therefore, you are entitled to know.

At the Hearing

Most arbitrators will grant a request that witnesses be sequestered. This means that no witness may be present in the hearing room while any other witness testifies, and witnesses are not permitted to discuss what was said when they were in the hearing with anyone outside of the hearing. Witnesses do tend to make sure their testimony is consistent with what others on their side of the case have said, if they know it, and sequestration can lead to some interesting results. Of course, if *you've* done thorough preparation of your group, everyone should have a pretty good idea of what the other witnesses will say. Even under a sequestration order, the grievant is entitled to be present throughout, and, in addition, each side can retain one representative for consultation with counsel and that person can still testify.

Some arbitrators will only administer oaths if requested, while others do it as a matter of course. I always ask for them. To me, they still mean something, and they add a modest measure of dignity to the process.

There should always be a court stenographer present, at the district's sole expense if necessary. A written brief should be filed after the hearing, and it is impossible to do a good job on a brief unless you can cite to the testimony. I'm amazed at how often a new line of argumentation occurs to me after I've had an opportunity to sit back and study what was actually said. In the distracting and stressful atmosphere of a hearing, it is easy to miss something of significance. Usually the cost of a transcript is divided between the parties, and my opponents always seem as interested in purchasing a copy of the transcript as I am.

Although there are some obvious superficial similarities between (for example) a jury trial and a labor arbitration hearing, the fundamental nature of what the advocates are doing is different. Although there is direct and cross examination of witnesses in an arbitration, the advocates are primarily concerned with making a record, rather than with being superficially or emotionally persuasive. Appearances and projecting a sympathetic position tend to be less important in arbitration, as the issues are viewed somewhat more dispassionately than they usually are in conventional litigation.

After the Hearing

Post-hearing briefs are extremely valuable. Feedback from arbitrators continually confirms this fact. Rarely should you agree to dispense with the brief, although in the simplest of cases sometimes I suggest what we call a "letter brief," which usually takes the form of a much shorter written summary of my argument. One way or another, it is important to organize your position and the supporting testimony and authority, in writing. It tends to keep the arbitrator intellectually honest, and occasionally wins the case for you. Preparing an effective post-hearing brief is where the record you made in black and white in the pages of a transcript pays off.

Counsel are frequently asked about taking an "appeal" from an adverse arbitration ruling. In all but the rarest of cases, forget it. The grounds for "vacating" an arbitration award (the technical term for it) are very narrow. Aside from proving the case was fixed, or the hearing was run in a fundamentally unfair manner, the only available grounds are that the award is in violation of law, or that it is so irrational it cannot be said to be rationally based on any viable reading of the contract. The fact that it's just plain wrong as a matter of contract interpretation (in the judge's eyes) is not enough. It has to be irrational.

Almost every arbitration case that is appealed to court through a petition to vacate ends up being reviewed under what the courts refer to as the "essence test." The "essence test" basically requires that the court uphold the award if it can be said under any view of the contract's terms that the decision at least "draws its essence" from the contract. This is an extremely deferential standard, and it clearly reflects the fact that the courts are typically hostile to requests to upset awards issued under a procedure the parties' contract mandates be used to resolve disputes. As noted above, the judge may disagree with an arbitrator's reading of a contract, even strenuously so, and yet be required to confirm his award. You should assume "final and binding" means just that.

Over the years, and particularly recently, courts have shown a tendency to reject arbitration awards as contrary to law in a variety of contexts, and awards that appear to be inconsistent with fundamental aspects of statutory law should, in such cases, be carefully reviewed for the viability of a petition to vacate. Even in these cases, courts will usually only vacate an award which requires a district to do something it is *prohibited* from doing by law. No school district should ever approach arbitration as simply the first stage of a protracted litigation process.

A FINAL NOTE

Labor relations are a fact of life in public education in Pennsylvania, and implementing a successful labor relations policy has become as important to school districts as hiring competent staff, raising adequate revenue or cultivating public support for education. Mishandled, labor relations can undo much that is good about our public schools and create a real impediment to the education of our communities' children.

The practice of labor relations is an eminently "practical" exercise, and there is little place in it for wishful thinking, naiveté or unrealistic objectives. It punishes those characteristics and rewards those who see things for what they are and who find ways to work with the tools at hand. Hopefully this guide will serve as one of those tools, and will help you to be a better superintendent, board member, or administrator.

APPENDICES

Glossary Of Common School Labor Relations Terms

Act 88 – Enacted in 1992, it establishes a revised process for negotiations by school employees. It establishes a mandatory timeline for bargaining; authorizes either party to initiate fact finding; prohibits selective strikes; requires a 48-hour advance notice of any legally authorized strike; establishes "nonbinding arbitration" as a new impasse procedure; and grants the Secretary of Education standing to seek injunctions whenever a strike threatens completion of the minimum 180-day school year.

Act 195 – Enacted in 1970, the Pennsylvania Public Employee Relations Act (PERA) governs collective bargaining between the Commonwealth's public employers and their employees.

American Federation of Teachers (AFT) – A national organization of public school teachers affiliated with the AFL-CIO. It is distinct from the NEA/PSEA.

Arbitration – A method of settling employment disputes through recourse to an impartial third party, whose decision is final and binding. It may be voluntary when both parties agree to submit disputed issues to arbitration or compulsory if required by law.

Bargaining Unit and Bargaining Agent – A bargaining unit is a group of employees with a community of interests that has been certified by the PLRB as an appropriate unit for bargaining purposes. All employees in the group are members of the bargaining unit, regardless of union membership. A bargaining agent is an organization selected by the members of a bargaining unit to represent them in bargaining with an employer. The recognized bargaining agent must be determined through procedures established by the PLRB and is the only agent with whom the employer may officially bargain with respect to employees in the bargaining unit.

Caucus – When the union or employer requests a recess to discuss, by itself, a proposal; or offer made by the other party or by a mediator during a negotiating session.

Certification – The formal determination by the PLRB that a particular union is the majority choice, and hence the exclusive bargaining agent, of all employees in a given bargaining unit.

Collective Bargaining – Collective bargaining is defined as the performance of the mutual obligation of a public employer and the representative of public employees to meet at reasonable times to confer in good faith with respect to wages, hours, and other terms and conditions of employment. This obligation does not compel either party to agree to a proposal or require the making of a concession.

Confidential Employee – An employee whose unrestricted access to confidential personnel files, or to knowledge or information pertinent to the labor relations activity of the employer, makes him/her inappropriate for membership in a labor organization. Confidential employees are excluded from the bargaining units.

Decertification – Removal by the PLRB of a union's certification as the exclusive bargaining representative.

Dues Deduction – The agreement of a public employer in a contract to deduct from the wages of a public employee, with his/her written consent, an amount for the payment of his/her membership dues in an employee organization, which deduction is then paid by the public employer to the employee organization.

Fact-finding – Identification of the major issues in a particular bargaining impasse dispute and recommended resolutions of differences by an impartial fact-finder. This process includes non-binding recommendations issued by the fact-finder in an attempt to resolve the impasse.

Fair Share Fee – A fee paid by non-members in lieu of union dues, but usually around 90% of what the dues are. Employees can be made to pay such fees only if the employer has agreed to a contract provision so providing.

Good Faith Bargaining – The requirement that the two parties to negotiations meet at reasonable times and confer in good faith with a willingness to reach an agreement on new contract terms. Good faith bargaining does not compel either party to make a concession or agree to any proposal, but it requires that negotiations be approached with a "sincere desire to reach agreement."

Grievance or Grievance Procedure – An alleged misinterpretation or misapplication of the provisions of the collective bargaining agreement. Grievance arbitration is the final step of grievance proceedings that attempt to settle disputes arising out of the interpretation of a collective bargaining agreement. The grievance procedure is a formal plan set forth in the collective agreement, which provides for the adjustment of alleged grievances through discussions at progressively higher levels of authority in management and the employer organization.

Impasse – That point in labor negotiations at which the parties are deadlocked and no further progress can be made toward reaching an agreement.

Injunction – A court order restraining one or more persons or the union from performing some act which the court believes is prohibited under Act 195. The order may be in the form of a temporary or permanent injunction.

Job Action – Any concerted effort by employees in the public sector to exert pressure on management during negotiations by using tactics which affect the quality and/or the quantity of their work performance.

Just Cause – A clause in a contract, which protects employees from employer action without reasonable cause. The term is ambiguous and is liberally applied by arbitrators.

Lockout – Shutdown of a place of work, or a change of the status quo, by the employer to discourage union strike activity or to enforce economic demands.

Maintenance of Membership – A union security system found in a contract under which an employee is not required to join a union, but if she/he does, or is already a member, binds him/herself to remain a member for the duration of the union contract. The procedure must contain an escape period during which the employee may resign from the union.

Management Prerogative – Employer function that is intrinsic to the ability to manage. These rights are often expressly reserved to management in the management rights clause of a bargaining agreement, and are provided for in Act 195. Employers do not have to bargain over them.

Managerial Rights – Acts 195 and 88 both identify as matters of inherent managerial policy such areas of discretion or policy addressing standards or services, the overall budget, use of technology, the organization structure, and selection and direction of personnel. The term can be viewed as synonymous with management prerogative.

Management Rights Clause – A provision in the collective bargaining agreement, which describes the scope of management rights, functions, and responsibilities.

Mandatory Bargaining Subject – Items that must be negotiated if demanded by either party.

Mediation – The attempt by a third party to assist in the settlement of an employment dispute through advice or suggestions. A mediator is an individual who acts as an impartial third party to help settle labor-management disputes.

Meet and Discuss – The obligation of a public employer upon request to meet at reasonable times to discuss recommendations submitted by representatives of public employees.

National Education Association (NEA) – A national employee union for teachers and educational support personnel. The PSEA is a state unit of the NEA.

No-Strike Clause – A provision in a collective agreement in which the employee organization agrees not to strike during the duration of the contract.

Pennsylvania Labor Relations Board (PLRB) – A specially appointed board that adjudicates legal issues relating to labor relations.

Pennsylvania State Education Association (PSEA) – A state employee union for teachers and educational support personnel.

Permissive Bargaining Subject – Subjects of bargaining which are neither illegal nor mandatory. If a party chooses not to negotiate upon such items, the other party cannot require that it be negotiated.

Picketing – The patrolling of the entrance to an establishment by union members, with the express purpose to persuade other workers to stop work; discourage people from entering the establishment; publicize the existence of a dispute, or prevent by force or persuasion the delivery of goods and services to the establishment.

Professional Employee – Any employee whose work: (i) is predominantly intellectual and varied in character; (ii) requires consistent exercise of discretion and judgment; (iii) requires knowledge of an advanced nature in the field of science or learning customarily acquired by specialized study in an institution of higher learning or its equivalent; and (iv) is of such character that the output or result accomplished cannot be standardized in relation to a given period of time. In the school context, the term has a special meaning, also signifying a teacher or administrator who has performed at least three years of satisfactory service and who has "tenure."

Ratification – The formal approval of a newly negotiated agreement by vote of the organization or members affected.

Recognition – Employer acceptance of a union organization as having authorization to negotiate for all members of a bargaining unit.

Reopener Clause – A provision in a collective bargaining agreement stating the time or the circumstances under which negotiations may be reopened, and which restricts bargaining to only certain provisions of the agreement but not to the agreement as a whole.

School Code – The Public School Code of 1949, as amended. The general body of laws governing operations of the public schools.

Seniority – An employee's status in relation to other employees established by his/her years of employment.

Strike – A strike is a concerted action in failing to report for duty; the willful absence from one's position; the stoppage of work, slow-down or the abstinence in whole or in part from the full, faithful and proper performance of the duties of employment for the purpose of inducing, influencing or coercing a change in the conditions or compensation or the rights, privileges, or obligations of employment. Act 88 imposed several restrictions upon the right to strike which did not exist under Act 195.

Strike Authorization – A vote taken among members of an employee organization to determine whether or not a strike should be authorized. Such a vote is usually taken during negotiations or near the expiration of the old contract.

Subcontracting – The subletting of certain parts of the operation to subcontractors frequently on the ground that the work can be performed more efficiently and with less expense through independent companies.

Unfair Labor Practice – Certain actions by an employer or union prohibited by Act 195.

Unilateral Action – Decisions made by only one of the parties involved in the collective bargaining process.

Uniserv Rep – A representative of NEA/PSEA who serves employee unions in all aspects of collective bargaining.

Waiver Clause – A provision in a collective bargaining agreement that specifically states that the written agreement is the complete agreement of the parties and anything not contained therein is not agreed to unless put into writing and signed by both parties following the date of the agreement. Sometimes called a "zipper clause," it is intended to stop either party from demanding renewed negotiations during the life of the contract.

Work Stoppage – A euphemistic term for a strike.

ADVICE OF COUNSEL

May 12, 2009

Christopher J. Hartman, Esquire
Hartman Shurr
1100 Berkshire Blvd.
Suite 301
P.O. Box 5828
Wyomissing, PA 19610

09-549

Dear Mr. Hartman:

This responds to your letters dated April 3, 2009, and April 13, 2009, by which you requested an advisory from the Pennsylvania State Ethics Commission.

Issue: Whether the Public Official and Employee Ethics Act ("Ethics Act"), 65 Pa.C.S. § 1101 et seq., would impose any prohibitions or restrictions upon either of two township commissioners with regard to participating in negotiations, meetings, discussions, and written and electronic communications pertaining to a contract with the bargaining unit for the township's employees or voting on a contract with such bargaining unit when: (1) the spouse of one township commissioner is a township employee and member of the bargaining unit; and (2) the other township commissioner is not employed by the township but is a member of the bargaining unit through a different employer.

Facts: As Solicitor for Muhlenberg Township ("the Township"), located in Berks County, Pennsylvania, you have been authorized by Township Commissioners Victoria S. Brown ("Mrs. Brown") and Randall Madara ("Mr. Madara") to request an advisory from the Pennsylvania State Ethics Commission on their behalf. You have submitted facts that may be fairly summarized as follows.

You state that the Township will be involved in negotiating a contract with Teamsters' Bargaining Unit 429 ("the Bargaining Unit"). You state that the negotiation process will include meetings, telephone conferences, and other communications among the Township Commissioners and with the Township Manager and the Township Solicitor.

Mrs. Brown's spouse is a Township employee and a member of the Bargaining Unit. Mr. Madara is not employed by the Township but is a member of the Bargaining Unit through a different employer.

Based upon the above submitted facts, you ask whether the Ethics Act would require Mr. Madara or Mrs. Brown: (1) to be excluded from negotiations, meetings, discussions, and written and electronic communications among the Township Commissioners and with the Township Manager and the Township Solicitor pertaining to the contract involving the Bargaining Unit; or (2) to abstain from any vote on the contract involving the Bargaining Unit.

Discussion: It is initially noted that pursuant to Sections 1107(10) and 1107(11) of the Ethics Act, 65 Pa.C.S. §§ 1107(10), (11), advisories are issued to the requester based upon the facts that the requester has submitted. In issuing the advisory based upon the facts that the requester has submitted, the Commission does not engage in an independent investigation of the facts, nor does it speculate as to facts that have not been submitted. It is the burden of the requester to truthfully disclose all of the material facts relevant to the inquiry. 65 Pa.C.S. §§ 1107(10), (11). An advisory only affords a defense to the extent the requester has truthfully disclosed all of the material facts.

As Township Commissioners, Mr. Madara and Mrs. Brown are public officials subject to the provisions of the Ethics Act.

Sections 1103(a) and 1103(j) of the Ethics Act provide:

§ 1103. Restricted activities

(a) **Conflict of interest.**--No public official or public employee shall engage in conduct that constitutes a conflict of interest.

(j) **Voting conflict.**--Where voting conflicts are not otherwise addressed by the Constitution of Pennsylvania or by any law, rule, regulation, order or ordinance, the following procedure shall be employed. Any public official or public employee who in the discharge of his official duties would be required to vote on a matter that would result in a conflict of interest shall abstain from voting and, prior to the vote being taken, publicly announce and disclose the nature of his interest as a public record in a written memorandum filed with the person responsible for recording the minutes of the meeting at which the vote is taken, provided that whenever a governing body would be unable to take any action on a matter before it because the number of members of the body required to abstain from voting under the provisions of this section makes the majority or other legally required vote of approval unattainable, then such members shall be permitted to vote if disclosures are made as otherwise provided herein. In the case of a three-member governing body of a political subdivision, where one member has abstained from voting as a result of a conflict of interest and the remaining two members of the governing body have cast opposing votes, the member who has abstained shall be permitted to vote to break the tie vote if disclosure is made as otherwise provided herein.

65 Pa.C.S. §§ 1103(a), (j).

Hartman, 09-549
May 12, 2009
Page 3

The following terms related to Section 1103(a) are defined in the Ethics Act as follows:

§ 1102. Definitions

"Conflict" or "conflict of interest." Use by a public official or public employee of the authority of his office or employment or any confidential information received through his holding public office or employment for the private pecuniary benefit of himself, a member of his immediate family or a business with which he or a member of his immediate family is associated. The term does not include an action having a de minimis economic impact or which affects to the same degree a class consisting of the general public or a subclass consisting of an industry, occupation or other group which includes the public official or public employee, a member of his immediate family or a business with which he or a member of his immediate family is associated.

"Authority of office or employment." The actual power provided by law, the exercise of which is necessary to the performance of duties and responsibilities unique to a particular public office or position of public employment.

"Immediate family." A parent, spouse, child, brother or sister.

"Business." Any corporation, partnership, sole proprietorship, firm, enterprise, franchise, association, organization, self-employed individual, holding company, joint stock company, receivership, trust or any legal entity organized for profit.

"Business with which he is associated." Any business in which the person or a member of the person's immediate family is a director, officer, owner, employee or has a financial interest.

"Financial interest." Any financial interest in a legal entity engaged in business for profit which comprises more than 5% of the equity of the business or more than 5% of the assets of the economic interest in indebtedness.

65 Pa.C.S. § 1102.

Pursuant to Section 1103(a) of the Ethics Act, a public official/public employee is prohibited from using the authority of public office/employment or confidential information received by holding such a public position for the private pecuniary benefit of the public official/public employee himself, any member of his immediate family, or a business with which he or a member of his immediate family is associated.

The above statutory definition of "conflict" or "conflict of interest" contains two exclusions, referred to herein as the "de minimis" exclusion and the "class/subclass exclusion."

The de minimis exclusion precludes a finding of conflict of interest as to an action having a de minimis (insignificant) economic impact. Thus, when a matter that would otherwise constitute a conflict of interest under the Ethics Act would have an insignificant economic impact, a conflict would not exist and Section 1103(a) of the Ethics Act would not be implicated. See, Kolb, Order 1322; Schweinsburg, Order 900.

In order for the class/subclass exclusion to apply, two criteria must be met: (1) the affected public official/public employee, immediate family member, or business with which the public official/public employee or immediate family member is associated must be a member of a class consisting of the general public or a true subclass consisting of more than one member; and (2) the public official/public employee, immediate family member, or business with which the public official/public employee or immediate family member is associated must be affected "to the same degree" (in no way differently) than the other members of the class/subclass. 65 Pa.C.S. § 1102; see, Kablack, Opinion 02-003; Rubenstein, Opinion 01-007. The first criterion of the exclusion is satisfied where the members of the proposed subclass are similarly situated as the result of relevant shared characteristics. The second criterion of the exclusion is satisfied where the individual/business in question and the other members of the class/subclass are reasonably affected to the same degree by the proposed action. Kablack, supra.

In Davison, Opinion 08-006, the Commission held that Section 1103(a) of the Ethics Act would allow a public official/public employee to participate in negotiations for a collective bargaining agreement covering or impacting an immediate family member subject to the condition that the class/subclass exclusion would be applicable. Id., at 5 (overruling Van Rensler, Opinion 90-017, to the limited extent it was inconsistent with the Commission's holding). The Commission noted that there may be uncertainty as to the direction negotiations will take during the process of negotiating a collective bargaining agreement, and the Commission generally advised that where the class/subclass exclusion initially would apply to permit a public official/public employee to participate in negotiations for a collective bargaining agreement covering or impacting an immediate family member, the public official/public employee would have to remain cognizant as to whether developments during the negotiating process would render the class/subclass exclusion no longer applicable, such that the public official/public employee would be required to abstain from further participation in the negotiations.

In applying the above provisions of the Ethics Act to the instant matter, you are advised that as to each Township Commissioner (that is, Mr. Madara or Mrs. Brown), pursuant to Section 1103(a) of the Ethics Act, the Township Commissioner generally would have a conflict of interest in matters before the Township Board of Commissioners that would financially impact him/her, a member of his/her immediate family, or a business with which he/she or a member of his/her immediate family is associated.

Having set forth the above principles, you are advised as follows.

With regard to Mr. Madara, in applying the statutory definition of the term "business with which he is associated" to the submitted facts, the necessary conclusion is that the Bargaining Unit is not a business with which he is associated because he is not a director, officer, owner, employee, or holder of a financial interest in the Bargaining Unit. The fact that he is a member of the Bargaining Unit is insufficient in and of itself to make the Bargaining Unit a business with which he is associated. Cf., Filbey, Advice 06-569. Therefore, Mr. Madara's membership in the Bargaining Unit would not in and of itself form the basis for a conflict of interest for him under the Ethics Act in matters pertaining to the Bargaining Unit.

Accordingly, you are advised that absent some basis for a conflict of interest such as a private pecuniary benefit to Mr. Madara, a member of his immediate family, or a business with which he or a member of his immediate family is associated, Section 1103(a) of the Ethics Act would not prohibit or restrict Mr. Madara from participating in negotiations, meetings, discussions, or written or electronic communications pertaining to the contract involving the Bargaining Unit or from voting on such contract.

With regard to Mrs. Brown, you are advised that Section 1103(a) of the Ethics Act would not prohibit Mrs. Brown from participating in the contract negotiations with the Bargaining Unit or from voting on the contract with the Bargaining Unit, subject to the condition that the class/subclass exclusion would be applicable as to any impact upon her spouse. You are further advised that Section 1103(a) of the Ethics Act would not restrict Mrs. Brown from participating in meetings, discussions, or written and electronic communications among the Township Commissioners and with the Township Manager and the Township Solicitor pertaining to the contract involving the Bargaining Unit, as long as the class/subclass exclusion would be applicable as to any impact upon her spouse.

It is parenthetically noted that the Public Employee Relations Act provides as follows:

§ 1101.1801. Conflict of interest

(a)   No person who is a member of the same local, State, national or international organization as the employe organization with which the public employer is bargaining or who has an interest in the outcome of such bargaining which interest is in conflict with the interest of the public employer, shall participate on behalf of the public employer in the collective bargaining processes with the proviso that such person may, where entitled, vote on the ratification of an agreement.

(b)   Any person who violates subsection (a) of this section shall be immediately removed by the public employer from his role, if any, in the collective bargaining negotiations or in any matter in connection with such negotiations.

43 P.S. § 1101.1801. Since the State Ethics Commission does not have the statutory jurisdiction to administer or interpret the Public Employee Relations Act, it is recommended that Mr. Madara and Mrs. Brown obtain legal advice as to any potential impact of that Act.

Lastly, the propriety of the proposed course of conduct has only been addressed under the Ethics Act. Specifically not addressed herein is the applicability of the First Class Township Code or the Public Employee Relations Act.

Conclusion: As Commissioners for Muhlenberg Township ("the Township"), located in Berks County, Pennsylvania, Randall Madara ("Mr. Madara") and Victoria S. Brown ("Mrs. Brown") are public officials subject to the provisions of the Public Official and Employee Ethics Act ("Ethics Act"), 65 Pa.C.S. § 1101 et seq. As to each Township Commissioner (that is, Mr. Madara or Mrs. Brown), pursuant to Section 1103(a) of the Ethics Act, the Township Commissioner generally would have a conflict of interest in matters before the Township Board of Commissioners that would financially impact him/her, a member of his/her immediate family, or a business with which he/she or a member of his/her immediate family is associated. Based upon the submitted facts that: (1) the Township will be involved in negotiating a contract with Teamsters' Bargaining Unit 429 ("the Bargaining Unit"); (2) the negotiation process will include meetings, telephone conferences, and other communications among the Township Commissioners and with the Township Manager and the Township Solicitor; (3) Mrs. Brown's spouse is a Township employee and a member of the Bargaining Unit; and (4) Mr. Madara is not employed by the Township but is a member of the Bargaining

Hartman, 09-549
May 12, 2009
Page 6

Unit through a different employer, you are advised as follows. With regard to Mr. Madara, the Bargaining Unit is not a business with which he is associated because he is not a director, officer, owner, employee, or holder of a financial interest in the Bargaining Unit. Therefore, Mr. Madara's membership in the Bargaining Unit would not in and of itself form the basis for a conflict of interest for him under the Ethics Act in matters pertaining to the Bargaining Unit. Absent some basis for a conflict of interest such as a private pecuniary benefit to Mr. Madara, a member of his immediate family, or a business with which he or a member of his immediate family is associated, Section 1103(a) of the Ethics Act would not prohibit or restrict Mr. Madara from participating in negotiations, meetings, discussions, or written or electronic communications pertaining to the contract involving the Bargaining Unit or from voting on such contract. With regard to Mrs. Brown, Section 1103(a) of the Ethics Act would not prohibit Mrs. Brown from participating in the contract negotiations with the Bargaining Unit or from voting on the contract with the Bargaining Unit, subject to the condition that the class/subclass exclusion would be applicable as to any impact upon her spouse. Section 1103(a) of the Ethics Act would not restrict Mrs. Brown from participating in meetings, discussions, or written and electronic communications among the Township Commissioners and with the Township Manager and the Township Solicitor pertaining to the contract involving the Bargaining Unit, as long as the class/subclass exclusion would be applicable as to any impact upon her spouse.

Lastly, the propriety of the proposed conduct has only been addressed under the Ethics Act. Specifically not addressed herein is the applicability of the First Class Township Code or the Public Employee Relations Act.

Pursuant to Section 1107(11) of the Ethics Act, an Advice is a complete defense in any enforcement proceeding initiated by the Commission, and evidence of good faith conduct in any other civil or criminal proceeding, provided the requester has disclosed truthfully all the material facts and committed the acts complained of in reliance on the Advice given.

This letter is a public record and will be made available as such.

Finally, if you disagree with this Advice or if you have any reason to challenge same, you may appeal the Advice to the full Commission. A personal appearance before the Commission will be scheduled and a formal Opinion will be issued by the Commission.

Any such appeal must be in writing and must be actually received at the Commission within thirty (30) days of the date of this Advice pursuant to 51 Pa. Code § 13.2(h). The appeal may be received at the Commission by hand delivery, United States mail, delivery service, or by FAX transmission (717-787-0806). Failure to file such an appeal at the Commission within thirty (30) days may result in the dismissal of the appeal.

Sincerely,

Robin M. Hittie
Chief Counsel

OPINION OF THE COMMISSION

Before: Louis W. Fryman, Chair
John J. Bolger, Vice Chair
Donald M. McCurdy
Paul M. Henry
Raquel K. Bergen
Nicholas A. Colafella

DATE DECIDED: 12/4/08
DATE MAILED: 12/12/08

08-006

Joseph R. Davison, Esquire
175 Strafford Avenue
Suite One
Wayne, PA 19087

Dear Mr. Davison:

This Opinion is issued in response to the appeal of Advice of Counsel, 08-566, which was issued on August 13, 2008.

I.   ISSUE:

Whether the Public Official and Employee Ethics Act ("Ethics Act"), 65 Pa.C.S. § 1101 et seq., would present any prohibition or restrictions upon a school director with regard to participating in contract negotiations with the bargaining unit for the school district's teachers where: (1) any collective bargaining agreement reached with the teachers' bargaining unit would serve as the framework for the benefit package negotiated with the other school district employee bargaining units; (2) if the school board would settle with the teachers' bargaining unit on an overall economic package resulting in a specific percentage increase for wages and benefits, the school board would seek to settle with the other bargaining units for an overall economic package increase of the same percentage; (3) the school director's spouse is employed by the school district as a secretary; and (4) the school director's spouse is not a member of the bargaining unit for the school district secretaries but would receive the wages and benefits negotiated by the school district secretaries' bargaining unit.

II.   FACTUAL BASIS FOR DETERMINATION:

As counsel for James B. Davison ("Mr. Davison"), an elected School Director for the West Chester Area School District ("School District"), you have appealed Unruh, Advice of Counsel 08-566, issued to Mr. Davison on August 13, 2008, through his former attorney, Ross A. Unruh, Esquire.

The initial advisory request submitted by Attorney Unruh on behalf of Mr. Davison presented facts that were summarized in the Advice of Counsel as follows:

> The Pennsylvania State Education Association ("PSEA") represents separate bargaining units for the School District's teachers and the School District's secretaries. A committee ("Negotiating Committee") of the School District School Board ("School Board") has commenced discussions with representatives of PSEA ("the Association Team") in an effort to reach an early agreement on the teachers' wages and benefits for the next collective bargaining agreement. The Negotiating Committee consists of Mr. Davison and two other School Board Members.
>
> You state that although the Negotiating Committee has commenced discussions with the Association Team, substantive discussions on wages and benefits have not yet occurred.
>
> You state that the School Board has an unwritten practice that whatever agreement is reached with the teachers' union as to benefits shall be the framework for the benefit package negotiated with the other employee bargaining units.
>
> As part of the negotiation process, the School Board is considering establishing an overall wage and benefits increase that would be the same percentage for all bargaining units. In particular, if the School Board would settle with the teachers' bargaining unit on an overall economic package (i.e., wages and benefits) resulting in a specific percentage increase, the Board would seek to settle with the other bargaining units for an overall economic package increase of the same percentage.
>
> Mr. Davison's spouse is employed by the School District as a secretary. Although Mr. Davison's spouse is not a member of PSEA, she receives the wages and benefits that PSEA negotiates in the collective bargaining agreement for the School District secretaries.
>
> Based upon the above submitted facts, you ask whether the Ethics Act would permit Mr. Davison to serve as one of three School Directors negotiating with the teachers' union representatives on the wage and benefit package for the next teachers' collective bargaining agreement.

Unruh, Advice of Counsel 08-566, at 1-2 (Emphasis added).

The facts as summarized by the Advice of Counsel were drawn from Attorney Unruh's advisory request, which stated, in part:

> The following facts have occasioned the request for an advisory opinion....The School Board has an unwritten practice that whatever agreement is reached with the teachers' union on benefits shall be the framework for the benefit package

Davison, 08-006
December 12, 2008
Page 3

          negotiated with the other employee bargaining units. In other words, the School Board wants to provide the same benefit package to all employees.

        ...

          Furthermore, the Board is considering establishing an overall wage and benefits percent increase which will be the same for all bargaining units. More particularly, if the School Board settles with the teachers on an overall economic package (that is, for wages and benefits) which results in a X% increase, the goal of the Board would be to settle with the other bargaining units for an overall economic package increase of X%.

Unruh letter of July 1, 2008, at 1-2.

Advice of Counsel 08-566 determined that as a School Director for the School District, Mr. Davison is a public official subject to the provisions of the Ethics Act. Based upon this Commission's holding in Van Rensler, Opinion 90-017, the Advice determined that pursuant to Section 1103(a) of the Ethics Act, Mr. Davison would be prohibited from serving as a negotiator for the School District with the teachers' union representatives on the teachers' wage and benefit package for the next teachers' collective bargaining agreement.

By letter dated September 11, 2008, you appealed Advice of Counsel 08-566. In your appeal letter, you contend that the Advice of Counsel is based upon "assumptions rather than actual facts." Davison letter of September 11, 2008, at paragraph 2. You further contend that the Advice of Counsel is inconsistent with prior Opinions of this Commission. Id.

By letter dated October 6, 2008, you were notified of the date, time and location of the public meeting at which your request would be considered.

On November 26, 2008, this Commission received your Brief, in which you contend that the School District does not have a policy--unstated, unwritten, or otherwise--that contact negotiations with any bargaining unit will influence, dictate, or be a framework/template for future contract negotiations with other bargaining units that negotiate with the School Board. You assert that Van Rensler should not be applied to exclude Mr. Davison from participating in contract negotiations with a bargaining unit of which his spouse is not a member.

On December 2, 2008, Mr. Davison submitted in support of his appeal a letter dated December 2, 2008, from James T. Smith, President of the School Board. Mr. Smith's letter states, in pertinent part, that "the West Chester Area School Board of Directors does not have a policy, unstated, unwritten, or otherwise that overall wage and benefits percent increases will be the same for all bargaining units."

At the public meeting on December 4, 2008, you appeared and offered commentary, which may be fairly summarized as follows. Although you acknowledged the existence of the factual recitation set forth in Attorney Unruh's advisory request letter, you asserted that based upon a resolution of the School Board passed by a 7-2 vote at a December 1, 2008, meeting, the School Board does not have a policy that the collective bargaining agreement reached with the teachers' bargaining unit would serve as the framework for contract negotiations with the other employee bargaining units. You reiterated your view that Van Rensler should be limited to situations where the immediate family member of the public official/public employee is a member of the bargaining unit. You proposed that this Commission decide the appeal based upon the submitted fact that Mr. Davison's spouse is not a member of the teachers' bargaining unit or, in the alternative, based upon your submission that the School Board does not have a policy that the collective bargaining agreement reached with the teachers' bargaining unit would serve as the framework for contract negotiations with the other employee bargaining units.

III.   DISCUSSION:

It is initially noted that pursuant to Sections 1107(10) and 1107(11) of the Ethics Act, 65 Pa.C.S. §§ 1107(10), (11), advisories are issued to the requester based upon the facts that the requester has submitted. In issuing the advisory based upon the facts that the requester has submitted, this Commission does not engage in an independent investigation of the facts, nor does it speculate as to facts that have not been submitted. It is the burden of the requester to truthfully disclose all of the material facts relevant to the inquiry. 65 Pa.C.S. §§ 1107(10), (11). An advisory only affords a defense to the extent the requester has truthfully disclosed all of the material facts.

It is clear that as a School Director for the School District, Mr. Davison is a public official subject to the provisions of the Ethics Act. Cf., Corcoran, Opinion 08-003; Quinn, Opinion 07-014; Confidential Opinion, 05-004; Means, Opinion 04-007.

We note that the relevant provisions of the Ethics Act were accurately set forth in Advice of Counsel 08-566, and they are incorporated herein by reference.

In applying the provisions of the Ethics Act to the instant matter, pursuant to Section 1103(a) of the Ethics Act, a public official/public employee is prohibited from using the authority of public office/employment or confidential information received by holding such a public position for the private pecuniary benefit of the public official/public employee himself, any member of his immediate family, or a business with which he or a member of his immediate family is associated. Mr. Davison's spouse is a member of his immediate family (see, 65 Pa.C.S. § 1102 (definition of "immediate family")). Subject to the "de minimis exclusion" and the "class/subclass exclusion" contained within the statutory definition of "conflict" or "conflict of interest" as set forth in the Ethics Act, 65 Pa.C.S. § 1102, pursuant to Section 1103(a) of the Ethics Act, Mr. Davison, in his public capacity as a School Director, would have a conflict of interest in matters that would financially impact him, his spouse, or a business with which he or his spouse is associated.

In order for the class/subclass exclusion to apply, two criteria must be met: (1) the affected public official/public employee, immediate family member, or business with which the public official/public employee or immediate family member is associated must be a member of a class consisting of the general public or a true subclass consisting of more than one member; and (2) the public official/public employee, immediate family member, or business with which the public official/public employee or immediate family member is associated must be affected "to the same degree" (in no way differently) than the other members of the class/subclass. 65 Pa.C.S. § 1102; see, Kablack, Opinion 02-003; Rubenstein, Opinion 01-007. The first criterion of the exclusion is satisfied where the members of the proposed subclass are similarly situated as the result of relevant shared characteristics. The second criterion of the exclusion is satisfied where the individual/business in question and the other members of the class/subclass are reasonably affected to the same degree by the proposed action. Kablack, supra.

We shall now address your contentions that Advice of Counsel 08-566 is based upon assumptions rather than actual facts and is inconsistent with prior Opinions of this Commission.

With regard to the contention that Advice of Counsel 08-566 is based upon assumptions rather than actual facts, we determine that the Advice of Counsel accurately summarized the facts submitted by Attorney Unruh in the advisory request. Furthermore, the Advice of Counsel rendered its determination based upon the submitted facts.

With respect to your remaining contention that Advice of Counsel 08-566 is inconsistent with prior Opinions of this Commission, we note the following.

In Van Rensler, supra, issued August 24, 1990, we considered whether the Ethics Act prohibited school directors from participating on a negotiating team and voting on a collective bargaining agreement when members of their immediate families were school district employees who were represented by the bargaining units. We held that school directors would not be prohibited from voting on a finalized collective bargaining agreement when members of their immediate families were school district employees represented by the bargaining unit, as long as the criteria for the class/subclass exclusion to the statutory definition of "conflict" or "conflict of interest" would be met. However, we further held that the school directors with affected immediate family members could not participate on the negotiating team. Our rationale for the latter conclusion was that the bargaining process would be free of any influence of such school directors and that the possibility of the use or transmission of confidential information would be minimized if not eliminated.

Subsequently, in Esposito, Order 832, issued February 27, 1992, we held that a borough business manager did not violate Section 3(a), now Section 1103(a), of the Ethics Act when he negotiated a contract with the borough union of which his brother was a member, because the borough manager's action in negotiating the contract affected to the same degree a subclass consisting of an occupation or other group that included a member of his immediate family.

In considering the above, it is our view that to the extent our rulings in Esposito and Van Rensler conflict, Esposito represents the proper application of Section 1103(a). We conclude that just as Section 1103(a) of the Ethics Act would allow a public official/public employee to vote on a collective bargaining agreement covering or impacting a member of the public official's/public employee's immediate family as long as the class/subclass exclusion would apply, Section 1103(a) of the Ethics Act would also allow the public official/public employee to participate on the negotiating team for such collective bargaining agreement as long as the class/subclass exclusion would apply. There is no basis in the Ethics Act for distinguishing between voting and participating in negotiations when the class/subclass exclusion is applicable.

Based upon the above analysis, we hold that Section 1103(a) of the Ethics Act would allow a public official/public employee to participate in negotiations for a collective bargaining agreement covering or impacting an immediate family member subject to the condition that the class/subclass exclusion would be applicable. Van Rensler, Opinion 90-017, is overruled to the limited extent it is inconsistent with our holding in this matter.

We would note that there may be uncertainty as to the direction negotiations will take during the process of negotiating a collective bargaining agreement. We would generally advise that where the class/subclass exclusion initially would apply to permit a public official/public employee to participate in negotiations for a collective bargaining agreement covering or impacting an immediate family member, the public official/public employee would have to remain cognizant as to whether developments during the negotiating process would render the class/subclass exclusion no longer applicable, such that the public official/public employee would be required to abstain from further participation in the negotiations.

Davison, 08-006
December 12, 2008
Page 6

In light of our holding above, we grant the appeal and reverse <u>Unruh</u>, Advice of Counsel 08-566. Based upon the submitted facts, you are advised that Section 1103(a) of the Ethics Act would not prohibit Mr. Davison from serving as a negotiator for the School District with the teachers' union representatives on the teachers' wage and benefit package for the next teachers' collective bargaining agreement, subject to the condition that the class/subclass exclusion would be applicable as to any impact upon Mr. Davison's spouse.

The propriety of the proposed course of conduct has only been addressed under the Ethics Act. Specifically not addressed herein is the applicability of the Public School Code or the Public Employee Relations Act. We note the following provision of the Public Employee Relations Act:

§ 1101.1801. Conflict of interest

(a)   No person who is a member of the same local, State, national or international organization as the employe organization with which the public employer is bargaining or who has an interest in the outcome of such bargaining which interest is in conflict with the interest of the public employer, shall participate on behalf of the public employer in the collective bargaining processes with the proviso that such person may, where entitled, vote on the ratification of an agreement.

(b)   Any person who violates subsection (a) of this section shall be immediately removed by the public employer from his role, if any, in the collective bargaining negations or in any matter in connection with such negotiations.

43 P.S. § 1101.1801. Since this Commission does not have the statutory jurisdiction to administer or interpret the Public Employee Relations Act, it is recommended that Mr. Davison obtain legal advice as to any potential impact of that Act.

IV.   CONCLUSION:

A School Director is a public official subject to the Public Official and Employee Ethics Act ("Ethics Act"), 65 Pa.C.S. § 1101 <u>et seq</u>. Section 1103(a) of the Ethics Act would allow a public official/public employee to participate in negotiations for a collective bargaining agreement covering or impacting an immediate family member subject to the condition that the "class/subclass exclusion" contained within the statutory definition of "conflict" or "conflict of interest" as set forth in the Ethics Act, 65 Pa.C.S. § 1102, would be applicable. <u>Van Rensler</u>, Opinion 90-017, is overruled to the limited extent it is inconsistent with our holding in this matter.

Under the submitted facts that: (1) James B. Davison ("Mr. Davison") is a School Director for the West Chester Area School District ("School District"); (2) Mr. Davison's spouse is employed by the School District as a secretary; (3) the School Board would use the collective bargaining agreement reached with the teachers' bargaining unit as the framework for the benefit package negotiated with the other School District employee bargaining units; (4) if the School Board would settle with the teachers' bargaining unit on an overall economic package resulting in a specific percentage increase for wages and benefits, the School Board would seek to settle with the other bargaining units for an overall economic package increase of the same percentage; and (5) Mr. Davison's spouse is not a member of the bargaining unit for the School District secretaries but would receive the wages and benefits negotiated by the School District secretaries' bargaining unit, you are advised as follows.   Section 1103(a) of the Ethics Act would not prohibit Mr. Davison

Davison, 08-006
December 12, 2008
Page 7

from serving as a negotiator for the School District with the teachers' union representatives on the teachers' wage and benefit package for the next teachers' collective bargaining agreement, subject to the condition that the class/subclass exclusion would be applicable as to any impact upon Mr. Davison's spouse. The appeal is granted, and Unruh, Advice of Counsel 08-566 is reversed.

The propriety of the proposed conduct has only been addressed under the Ethics Act.

Pursuant to Section 1107(10), the person who acts in good faith on this Opinion issued to him shall not be subject to criminal or civil penalties for so acting provided the material facts are as stated in the request.

This letter is a public record and will be made available as such.

Finally, a party may request the Commission to reconsider its Opinion. The reconsideration request must be received at this Commission within thirty days of the mailing date of this Opinion. The party requesting reconsideration must include a detailed explanation of the reasons as to why reconsideration should be granted in conformity with 51 Pa. Code § 21.29(b).

By the Commission,

Louis W. Fryman
Chair

Superintendent Interview Questions

1. What first-hand experience have you had with grievance handling, arbitration proceedings, and labor negotiations?

2. There are two general schools of thought on the proper role for a superintendent in labor negotiations. Some people feel the superintendent should be very involved personally because his/her work is affected so significantly by the results of the negotiations process. Others feel the superintendent needs to be isolated from the process, to the extent possible, so any animosity that occurs during negotiations does not interfere with the superintendent's ability to work with teachers or union officials after the negotiations are over. What are your thoughts on this and how would you resolve this conflict?

3. Some superintendents at times have difficulty in resolving the natural conflict that sometimes arises between wanting to be approved of and supported by teachers and union leaders on the one hand, and taking stands that may be unpopular with those same groups. This frequently, but not exclusively, occurs when controversial personnel issues arise such as disciplinary matters. What are your thoughts on this aspect of the position?

4. The district has historically relied heavily on outside labor counsel. Have you ever worked directly with specialized labor attorneys? What has been your experience and how, and when, would you make the judgment to involve such resources?

Basic Education Circulars (Purdon's Statutes)

Instructional Time and Act 80 Exceptions

24 P.S. §15-1504

DATE OF ISSUE: September 1, 1997

DATE OF REVIEW: March 19, 2009
                     January 2, 2008
                     July 1, 2001

PURPOSE

This BEC outlines requirements for instructional time and the process for requesting Act 80 exceptions.

BASIC REQUIREMENTS

All public schools are to be open each school year for at least one hundred eighty (180) days of instruction for pupils. The number of instructional hours in a school year is to be at least 450 for half-time pre-K and kindergarten, 900 for full-time pre-K and kindergarten and elementary, and 990 for secondary. Exceptions to the requirement for 180 days of instruction or to the daily school hours may be made based upon Section 1504, as amended by Act 80 of 1969.

No school shall be kept open on any Saturday for the purpose of ordinary instruction, except when Monday is fixed by the board of school directors as the weekly holiday (which would require that school be scheduled Tuesday through Saturday for the entire school term).

22 Pa. Code §11.27 provides pupils in graduating classes up to three days for graduation preparation under the supervision of certificated school employees. The Secretary of Education has determined that graduation practice days must be scheduled within 60 calendar days of the commencement ceremony and that graduation practice can be scheduled on a regular instruction day or on a Saturday. Since no other instructional activities can be conducted on Saturday, only the hours for the graduation practice can be counted as pupil instructional time.

State Board of Education Regulations, Chapter 11, Section 11.2 School day, defines instruction time for pupils as time in the school day devoted to instruction and instructional activities provided as an integral part of the school program under the direction of certified school employees. For the purposes of determining if an activity, other than instruction of curriculum, conducted during school hours can be counted as instructional hours in lieu of ordinary instruction, the Department has defined the following:

Activities which may be counted as pupil instruction time:

1. Pupil personnel services, such as guidance and counseling services, psychological services, speech pathology and audiology services, and pupil health services conducted during school hours,

2. Opening exercises, including circle time in pre-K and kindergarten, homeroom periods, supervised study halls and time when students are eating breakfast during the regularly scheduled homeroom periods or during classroom instruction,

3. Assemblies, clubs, student councils, and similar activities conducted during school hours,

4. School, group or class educational trips, to which admission is not charged to students or parents, if accompanied by a certificated school employee,

5. Civil defense, fire and other similar drills,

6. Pre-K and kindergarten orientation activities, snack-time and play-time if they are an integral part of the pre-K and kindergarten curriculum as long as they take place under the direction of a certified teacher and are used for students learning experiences. (Note: "Recess" time conducted with the same parameters as primary grade recess is not counted as instructional time),

7. For pupils in graduating classes, up to three days for graduation preparation within 60 days of the commencement ceremony under the supervision of certified school employees. Graduation preparation may be held on Saturdays, and

8. Early dismissal and delayed opening due to inclement weather.

Activities which may not be counted as pupil instruction time:

1. Lunch period. However, an exception is made for:
   a) special education students identified as moderately to severely handicapped if their Individualized Education Program (IEP) includes teaching social and motor skills related to meal-time activities such as the use of eating utensils; and,
   b) pre-K students if lunch is an integral part of the pre-K curriculum, takes place under the direction of a certified teacher and is used for student learning experiences,

2. Recess and time for passing from class to class,

3. Early dismissal or delayed opening for reasons other than inclement weather,

4. Teacher meetings dealing with routine matters, such as record keeping responsibilities, and other similar activities,

5. Transportation of pupils; for example, time spent transporting students to an area vocational-technical school,

6. Celebrating, picnicking, hunting, fishing, or harvesting crops,

7. Any activity for which admission is charged to students or parents, and

8. Viewing or reviewing material that has as its purpose the marketing of commercial products.

Section 1504, as amended by Act 80 of 1969, authorizes the Secretary of Education to grant an exception to the 180-day requirement or to the daily schedule "when in his opinion a meritorious educational program warrants." The requirement for minimum instructional hours for the school year must still be met. For purposes of granting approvals for Act 80 exceptions for a shortened school year or a shortened school day, the Department of Education has defined the following:

Activities which may be approved for an Act 80 exception:

1. Parent-teacher meetings,

2. Curriculum planning and development,

3. Strategic planning,

4. In-service programs dealing with new subjects or activities having an impact on the educational program,

5. Dismissal at the start of the school year of a partial group of kindergarten students while an orientation program is being conducted for another part of the group of current year kindergarten students,

6. Administration of the Professional Development Assistance Program assessment, and

7. Evaluation of graduation projects.

Requests for approval of an Act 80 exception should be made by completing the PDE-4085 "Request for Section 1504 (Act 80) Exception" form. Area vocational-technical schools should complete the PDE-4085A "Request for Section 1504 (Act 80) Exception-AVTS" form. Intermediate units should complete the PDE-4085I "Request for Section 1504 (Act 80) Exception-IU" form. Procedures for requesting approval are as follows:

1. The proposed request must be approved by the local school board. The form must be completed and submitted electronically in the Child Accounting Data Base System (CAD).

2. The request shall include the date of each requested exception.

3. The request shall include the reason for each requested exception.

There is no limit on the number of Act 80 exceptions that may be requested as long as the required minimum instructional hours for the school year are met. Requests for Act 80 approvals should be submitted prior to the date of the Act 80 activity; however, Act 80 approvals will be considered for approval if submitted before July 31 following the end of the school year.

The approval cannot be used for time lost due to inclement weather, mechanical or power failures, or other causes not provided for in the school laws. In the event that unforeseen circumstances warrant a rescheduling of the school year and a school district, area vocational- technical school or intermediate unit elects not to exercise its Act 80 approval, the number of instructional days required reverts to 180 days or 180 days minus the number of full-day Act 80 approvals used.

Approval will not be granted for Act 80 days where there has been a work stoppage by teachers. In addition, any Act 80 days approved by the department (except those approved as early dismissals), including those that have already occurred, will be rescinded upon initiation of a work stoppage.

REFERENCES:

Purdon's Statutes

24 P.S. §5-503
24 P.S. §15-1501
24 P.S. §15-1502
24 P.S. §15-1503
24 P.S. §15-1504

State Board of Education Regulations

22 Pa. Code § 11.1
22 Pa. Code § 11.2
22 Pa. Code § 11.3

CONTACT BUREAU/OFFICE:

Division of Subsidy Data and Administration
Bureau of Budget and Fiscal Management
Pennsylvania Department of Education
333 Market Street
Harrisburg, PA 17126-0333
Phone: 717.787.5423

Work Stoppage:

School Services Unit
Office of Elementary and Secondary Education
Pennsylvania Department of Education
333 Market Street
Harrisburg, PA 17126-0333
Phone: 717.787.4860

Basic Education Circulars (Purdon's Statutes)

Days Schools Not to be Kept Open

24 P.S. Section 15-1502

DATE OF ISSUE: March 1, 1999
DATE OF REVIEW: July 1, 2009
                              July 1, 2005

PURPOSE

This BEC identifies for the board of school directors when developing their school calendar which days may be used as instructional days and specific days of the week and holidays which may not be used for instruction under any circumstances. Also described is the process for establishing a board of school director's "local" holidays in the school calendar and restrictions related to those days.

School Calendar Development

Section 1502 states that "no school shall be kept open on any Saturday for the purpose of ordinary instruction, except when Monday is fixed by the board of school directors as the weekly holiday, or on Sunday, Memorial Day, Fourth of July, Christmas, Thanksgiving, the First of January, and up to five additional days designated as local holidays in the adopted school calendar by the board of school directors as official local school district holidays, nor shall any school be kept open in any district during the time of holding the teachers' institute for such district. The board of school directors may cancel any day designated as a local holiday in the event of a weather emergency or natural disaster."

No school shall be kept open on any Saturday for the purpose of ordinary instruction, except when Monday is fixed by the board of school directors as the weekly holiday (which would require that school be scheduled Tuesday through Saturday for the entire school term).

Official Local School District Holidays

If a board of school directors chooses to identify up to five "official local school district holidays" pursuant to Section 1502, these dates must be specifically designated as Section 1502 holidays within the resolution approving the school calendar (for example, Section 1502 holidays: November 14, 2003, January 20, 2004, February 14, 2004, etc.). This resolution must be passed by the school directors prior to the start of the school year. Once designated, Section 1502 "official local school district holidays" cannot be rescheduled and can only be canceled in the event of a weather emergency or natural disaster.

REFERENCES:
Purdon's Statutes
24 P.S. § 15-1502

CONTACT BUREAU/OFFICE:
Pennsylvania Department of Education
Office of Elementary and Secondary Education
School Services Unit
333 Market Street
Harrisburg, PA 17126-0333
Phone: 717.787.4860

Strike Action Checklist

1. Public Information/Media Relations
   Designate a spokesman for comment on operational issues and issues relating to negotiations. These may be different people, e.g., the superintendent for operational issues and the chief negotiator for matters related to bargaining.

2. Determine how to deal with non-striking employees, i.e., non-union staff and unionized employees in units not engaged in the strike or members of the striking unit who express a desire to come to work. Are they going to be furloughed? If so, when and who?

3. Communicate with insurance providers about terminating benefits.

4. Notify PDE of the existence of the strike.

5. Sports and Extracurricular Activities.
   Determine if any can be operated, and communicate with participants and then parents about status.

6. Special Education and Vocational Programs Provided by Non-District Sources (e.g. the IU or a regional technical school).
   Determine if these will continue and review the logistics. Communicate with providers, students, and parents.

7. Use of Schools for Miscellaneous Programs Not Staffed by Striking Employees. (e.g. day care programs).
   Determine if these will continue and notify participants.

8. Use of Facilities by Outside Organizations.
   Notify participating organizations regarding access and availability.

9. Building Security/Picketing Issues.
   Brief building administrators regarding access and picketing issues, and appropriate responses to any incidents. Notify local police of the existence of the strike.

10. Outside contractors and suppliers.
    Notify any outside contractors doing work at district facilities, and any outside parties expected to make deliveries or otherwise access district facilities.

11. Prepare letters to strike participants, as appropriate, regarding the strike, bargaining issues, and insurance.

Dear Employee:

    Pennsylvania law provides that striking public employees are not entitled to any form of compensation for any period of time they are engaged in a strike. Effective with the commencement of the strike, district-paid insurance benefits have been terminated. You may reinstate and maintain these benefits, or any portion of them, at your own expense by completing the enclosed form and returning it to the district administrative offices at any time within the next 60 days. The amounts you must pay for these benefits to be maintained also are enclosed. Checks should be made payable to the _____ School District.

    I hereby resign my membership in the National Education Association, Pennsylvania State Education Association, and the _____ Education Association, effective immediately. I also revoke any instruction or authorization I may have given to the _____ School District to withhold from my pay dues or fees to those organizations.

SESSION OF 1992   Act 1992-88
                            No. 1992-88

TABLE OF CONTENTS

ARTICLE XI-A. COLLECTIVE BARGAINING
    (a) General Provisions
    (b) Scope of Bargaining
    (c) Collective Bargaining Impasse
    (d) Strikes and Lockouts
    (e) Collective Bargaining Agreement
    (f) Secretary of Education
    (g) Prohibitions

The General Assembly of the Commonwealth of Pennsylvania hereby enacts as follows:

Section 1. The act of March 10, 1949 (P.L.30, No.14), known as the Public School Code of 1949, is amended by adding an article to read:

ARTICLE XI-A.

COLLECTIVE BARGAINING.

(a) General Provisions.

Section 1101-A. Definitions.-When used in this article, the following words and phrases shall have the following meanings:
    "Board" shall mean the Pennsylvania Labor Relations Board.
    "Employe" shall mean a public school employe who bargains collectively with a public school entity, but shall not include employes covered or presently subject to coverage under the act of June 1, 1937 (P.L.1168, No.294), known as the "Pennsylvania Labor Relations Act," or the National Labor Relations Act (61 Stat. 152, 29 U.S.C. Ch. 7 Subch. 11). The term does not include any management-level employe of any other school district.
    "Employe organization" shall mean a public school employe organization of any kind, or any agency or employe representation committee or plan in which membership is limited to public school employes, and which exists for the purpose, in whole or in part, of dealing with public school employers concerning grievances, public school employe-public school employer disputes, wages, rates of pay, hours of employment or conditions of work, but shall not include any organization which practices discrimination in membership because of race, color, creed, national

origin or political affiliation.

"Employer" shall mean a public school entity, but shall not include employers covered or presently subject to coverage under the act of June 1, 1937 (P.L.1168, No.294), known as the "Pennsylvania Labor Relations Act," or the National Labor Relations Act (61 Stat. 152, 29 U.S.C. Ch. 7 Subch. 11).

"Impasse" shall mean the failure of an employer and an employe organization to reach an agreement in the course of negotiations.

"Lockout" shall mean the cessation of furnishing of work to employes or withholding work from employes for the purpose of inducing, influencing or coercing a change in the conditions or compensation or the rights, privileges or obligations of employment.

"Representative" shall mean an individual acting for employers or employes and shall include employe organizations.

"School entity" shall mean a public school district, intermediate unit or area vocational-technical school.

"Strike" shall mean concerted action in failing to report for duty, the wilful absence from one's position, the stoppage of work, slowdown or the abstinence, in whole or in part, from the full, faithful and proper performance of the duties of employment for the purpose of inducing, influencing or coercing a change in the conditions or compensation or the rights, privileges or obligations of employment. The employe organization having called a strike once and unilaterally returned to work may only call a lawful strike once more during the school year. A written notice of the intent to strike shall be delivered by the employe organization to the superintendent, executive director or the director no later than forty-eight (48) hours prior to the commencement of any strike, and no strike may occur sooner than forty-eight (48) hours following the last notification of intent to strike. Upon receipt of the notification of intent to strike, the superintendent, executive director or the director may cancel school for the effective date of the strike.

A decision to cancel school may, however, be withdrawn by the superintendent, executive director or the director. Any subsequent change of intents to strike shall not affect the decision to cancel school on the day of the intended strike. For the purposes of this article, the decision to cancel school on the day of the intended strike shall not be considered a lockout.

(b) Scope of Bargaining.

Section 1111-A. Mutual Obligation.-Collective bargaining is the performance of the mutual obligation of the employer or his representative and the representative of the employes to meet at reasonable times and confer in good faith with respect to wages, hours and other terms and conditions of employment or the negotiation of an agreement or any question arising thereunder and the execution of a written contract incorporating any agreement reached, but such obligation does not compel either party to agree to a proposal or require the making of a concession.

Section 1112-A. Matters of Inherent Managerial Policy.-Employers shall not be required to bargain over matters of inherent managerial policy. Those matters shall include, but shall not be limited to, such areas of discretion or policy as the functions and programs of the employer, standards of services, its overall budget, utilization of technology, the organizational structure and selection and direction of personnel. Employers, however, shall be required to meet and discuss on policy matters affecting wages, hours and terms and conditions of employment as well as the impact thereon upon request by employe representatives.

(c) Collective Bargaining Impasse.

Section 1121-A. Submission to Mediation.-(a) If, after a reasonable period of negotiation, a dispute or impasse exists between the representatives of the employer and the employe organization, the parties may voluntarily submit to mediation, but, if no agreement is reached between the parties within forty-five (45) days after negotiations have commenced, but in no event later than one hundred twenty-six (126) days prior to June 30 or December 31, whichever is the end of the school entity's fiscal year, and mediation has not been utilized by the parties, both parties shall immediately in writing call on the service of the Pennsylvania Bureau of Mediation.

(b) The Pennsylvania Bureau of Mediation shall employ a complement of not less than twenty-five (25) mediators which shall be available to mediate according to the provisions of subsection(a).

Section 1122-A. Fact-finding Panels.-(a) (1) Once mediation has commenced, it shall continue for so long as the parties have not reached an agreement. If, however, an agreement has not been reached within forty-five (45) days after mediation has commenced or in no event later than eighty-one (81) days prior to June 30 or December 31, whichever is the end of the school entity's fiscal year, the Bureau of Mediation shall notify the board of the parties' failure to reach an agreement and of whether either party has requested the appointment of a fact-finding panel.

(2) No later than eighty-one (81) days prior to June 30 or December 31, whichever is the end of the school entity's fiscal year, either party may request the board to appoint a fact-finding panel. Upon receiving such request, the board shall appoint a fact-finding panel which may consist of either one (1) or three (3) members. The panel so designated or selected shall hold hearings and take oral or written testimony and shall have subpoena power. If, during this time, the parties have not reached an independent agreement, the panel shall make findings of fact and recommendations. The panel shall not find or recommend that the parties accept or adopt an impasse procedure.

(3) The parties may mutually agree to fact-finding, and the board shall appoint a fact-finding panel as provided for in clause (2) at any time except that the parties may not mutually agree to fact-finding during mandated final best-offer arbitration.

(4) The board may implement fact-finding and appoint a panel as provided for in clause (2) at a time other than that mandated in this section, except that fact-finding may not be implemented between the period of notice to strike and the conclusion of a strike or during final best-offer arbitration. If the board chooses not to implement fact-finding prior to a strike, the board shall issue a report to the parties listing the reasons for not implementing fact-finding if either party requests one.

(b) The findings of fact and recommendations shall be sent by registered mail to the board and to both parties not more than forty (40) days after the Bureau of Mediation has notified the board as provided in subsection (a).

(c) Not more than ten (10) days after the findings and recommendations shall have been sent, the parties shall notify the board and each other whether or not they accept the recommendations of the fact-finding panel, and, if they do not, the panel shall publicize its findings of fact and recommendations.

(d) Not less than five (5) days nor more than ten (10) days after the publication of the findings of fact and recommendations, the parties shall again inform the board and each other whether or not they will accept the recommendations of the fact-finding panel.

(e) The board shall establish, after consulting representatives of employe organizations and of employers, panels of qualified persons broadly representative of the public to serve as members of fact-finding panels. The board shall, within sixty (60) days of the effective date of this act, increase the number of available panels of qualified persons to serve as members of fact-finding panels to meet the expanded role of fact-finding as provided for in this act.

(f) The Commonwealth shall pay one-half of the cost of the fact-finding panel; the remaining one-half of the cost shall be divided equally between the parties. The board shall establish rules and regulations under which panels shall operate, including, but not limited to, compensation for panel members.

Section 1123-A.   Negotiated Final Best-Offer Arbitration.-(a) The parties to a collective bargaining agreement involving public school employes shall be required to bargain upon the issue of acceptance and adoption of one of the following approved impasse procedures, with the proviso that such an obligation does not compel either party to agree to a proposal or require making a concession:

(1) Arbitration under which the award is confined to a choice among one of the following single packages:

(i) the last offer of the representative of the employer;

(ii) the last offer of the representative of the employes; or

(iii) the fact-finder's recommendations, should there be a fact-finder's report.

(2) Arbitration under which the award is confined to a choice among one of the following on an issue-by-issue basis:

(i) the last offer of the representative of the employer;

(ii) the last offer of the representative of the employes; or

(iii) the fact-finder's recommendations, should there be a fact-finder's report.

(3) Arbitration under which the award is confined to a choice among one of the following on the basis of economic and noneconomic issues as separate units:

(i) the last offer of the representative of the employer;

(ii) the last offer of the representative of the employes; or

(iii) the fact-finder's recommendations, should there be a fact-finder's report.

(b) As used in this section, "economic issues" shall mean wages, hours, salary, fringe benefits or any form of monetary compensation for services rendered.

Section 1124-A.   Method of Selection of Arbitrators.-The board of arbitration shall be composed of three (3) members.   Arbitrators as referred to in this article shall be selected in the following manner:

(1) Each party shall select one (1) member of the panel within five (5) days of the parties' submission to final best-offer arbitration.   Each arbitrator shall be knowledgeable in the school-related fields of budget, finance, educational programs and taxation.

(2) The third arbitrator shall be selected from a list of seven (7) arbitrators furnished by the American Arbitration Association within five (5) days of the publication of the list.   Each of the seven (7) arbitrators shall be a resident of this Commonwealth and knowledgeable in the areas necessary to effectively make a determination.   Each party shall alternately strike one name until one shall remain.   The employer shall strike the first name.   The person so remaining shall be the third member and chairman.

(3) Payment of arbitrators shall be as follows:

(i) For voluntary arbitration, each party shall pay the cost of the arbitrator selected by it under clause (1) of this section.   The cost of the third arbitrator shall be divided equally between the parties.

(ii) For mandatory arbitration, the Commonwealth shall pay one-half of the cost of the arbitrators; the remaining one-half of the cost shall be divided equally between the parties.

Section 1125-A.   Final Best-Offer Arbitration.-(a) At any time prior to mandated final best-offer arbitration, either the employer or the employe organization may request final best-offer arbitration unless fact-finding has been initiated as provided in section 1122-A.   If fact-finding has been initiated, the parties shall complete fact-finding before requesting final best-offer arbitration. If either party requests final best-offer arbitration, the requesting party shall notify the Bureau of Mediation, the board and the opposing party in writing. The opposing party shall, within ten (10) days of the notification by the requesting party, notify the requesting party in writing of its agreement or refusal to submit to final best-offer arbitration. No strikes or lockouts shall occur during this ten (10) day period or until the requesting party is notified by the opposing party that they refuse to submit to final best-offer arbitration. Arbitration provided for in this subsection shall only occur if both parties agree to submit to final best-offer arbitration.

(b) If a strike by employes or a lockout by an employer will prevent the school entity from providing the period of instruction required by section 1501 by the later of.

(1) June 15; or

(2) the last day of the school entity's scheduled school year;
the parties shall submit to mandated final best-offer arbitration consistent with the arbitration option negotiated. A return to work for the purpose of submitting to final best-offer arbitration shall not be considered a unilateral return to work.

(c) If the parties are unable to agree on the adoption of one of the approved impasse procedures under section 1123-A, the mediator appointed pursuant to section 1121-A shall select the procedure.

(d) Within ten (10) days of submission to final best-offer arbitration, the parties shall submit to the arbitrators their final best contract offer with certification that the offer was delivered to the opposing party, together with documentation supporting the reasonableness of their offer. This documentation shall include, but not be limited to, the following:

(1) The public interest.

(2) The interest and welfare of the employe organization.

(3) The financial capability of the school entity.

(4) The results of negotiations between the parties prior to submission of last best contract offers.

(5) Changes in the cost of living.

(6) The existing terms and conditions of employment of the employe organization members and those of similar groups.

(7) Such other documentation as the arbitration panel shall deem relevant.

(e) Arbitration shall be limited to unresolved issues. Unresolved issues shall mean those issues not agreed to in writing prior to the start of arbitration.

(f) The parties may mutually agree to submit to final best-offer arbitration at any time except during fact-finding or during mandated final best offer arbitration.

(g) Upon submission to the arbitrator of both parties' final best offers under subsection (a) or (b), the employer shall post, within the time limits described in subsection (d), the final best contract offers in the school entity's main office for the purpose of soliciting public comments thereon. Copies of both parties' final best offers shall be available from the school entity's main office. The cost of copies shall be established by the school entity and shall be paid by the requestor.

(h) The public comment period shall close within ten (10) days of the first day of posting. All public comments shall be directed to the arbitrators for consideration who shall provide them on request to the employer and to the employes' organization.

(i) Within ten (10) days of the selection of the third arbitrator of the arbitration panel, the arbitrators shall begin hearings at which they will hear arguments from representatives of the employer and of the employes in support of their respective last best contract offers under subsection (a) or (b). At least five (5) days prior to the hearing, a written notice of the date, time and place of such hearing shall be sent to the representatives of both the employer and employes which are parties to the dispute. This written notice shall also be sent to the fiscal authority having budgetary responsibility or charged with making appropriations for the employer, and a representative designated by such body shall be heard at the hearing upon request of such body or of the employer as part of the presentation of the employer.

(j) Not later than twenty (20) days after the hearing pursuant to subsection (i), the arbitrators shall:

(1) examine each item of dispute;

(2) make a determination in writing consistent with the arbitration option agreed to by the parties; and

(3) forward a copy of the written determination to both parties involved in the dispute and to the board.

(k) The determination of the majority of the arbitrators reached as provided under either subsection (a) or (b) shall be final and binding upon the employer, employes and employe organization involved and constitutes a mandate to the school entity to take whatever action necessary to carry out the determination, provided that within ten (10) days of the receipt of the determination the employe organization or the employer does not consider and reject the determination at a properly convened special or regular meeting. This determination includes, but is not limited to, a determination which requires a legislative enactment by the employer prior to or as a condition for its implementation, including, without limitation, the levy and imposition of taxes.

(l) No appeal challenging the determination reached as provided under subsection (a) or (b) shall be allowed to any court unless the award resulted from fraud, corruption or wilful misconduct of the arbitrators. If a court determines that this has occurred, it shall declare the award null and void. An appeal of the award shall be made to the court of common pleas of the judicial district encompassing the respective school district.

(m) If the employer or the employe organization rejects the determination of the majority of the arbitrators:

(1) The employe organization may initiate a legal strike or resume a legal strike initiated prior to submission to final best-offer arbitration.

(2) The employer may hire substitutes as provided under subsection (b) of section 1172-A.

(3) The employer may initiate a legal lockout or resume a legal lockout initiated prior to submission to final best-offer arbitration.

Section 1126-A. Time Frame.-The time periods set forth in this article are mandatory and shall not be construed to be directory.

Section 1127-A. Exception. -Any school district of the first class with an appointed school board and the public employes of that school district as defined in the act of July 23, 1970 (P.L.563, No.195), known as the "Public Employe Relations Act," shall comply with and be subject to the binding arbitration provisions of the "Public Employe Relations Act" and shall not be subject to the provisions of section 1123-A, 1124-A or 1125-A.

(d) Strikes and Lockouts.

Section 1131-A. Strikes Prohibited in Certain Circumstances.-A strike must cease where the parties request fact-finding for the duration of the fact-finding. A strike must end where the parties agree to arbitration. Strikes are prohibited:

(1) During the period of up to ten (10) days provided for under section 1125-A(a).

(2) During final best-offer arbitration, including the period of up to ten (10) days after receipt of the determination of the arbitrators during which the

governing body of the school entity may consider the determination.

(3) When the arbitrators' determination becomes final and binding.

Section 1132-A.   Lockouts Prohibited in Certain Circumstances.-A lockout must cease where the parties request fact-finding for the duration of the fact-finding.   A lockout must end where the parties agree to arbitration.

Lockouts are prohibited:

(1) During the period of up to ten (10) days provided for under section 1125-A(a).

(2) During final best-offer arbitration, including the period of up to ten (10) days after receipt of the determination of the arbitrators during which the employer may consider the determination.

(3) When the arbitrators' determination becomes final and binding.

(e) Collective Bargaining Agreement.

Section 1151-A.   Agreement and Enforcement.-Any determination of the arbitrators to be implemented under this article shall be memorialized as a written agreement by and between the school entity and the employe organization to be signed and sealed by their duly appointed officers and agents as provided by law.   The executed agreement shall be enforceable by each party in the manner as provided by law, including without limitation and in derogation to the mandatory arbitration of disputes or grievances under the act of July 23, 1970 (P.L.563, No.195), known as the "Public Employe Relations Act."   In the event that a school entity or an employe organization refuses to execute a written agreement under this section, the employe organization or the school entity may institute a cause of action in the court of common pleas to compel compliance with the provision of this section requiring a written agreement and, in the appropriate case, specific performance of the determination.

Section 1152-A.   Existing Agreements; Provisions Inconsistent with Article.-Any provisions of any collective bargaining agreement in existence on the effective date of this article which are inconsistent with any provision of this article, but not otherwise illegal, shall continue valid until the expiration of such contract.   The procedure for entering into any new collective bargaining agreement, however, shall be governed by this article, where applicable, upon the effective date of this article.

(f) Secretary of Education.

Section 1161-A.   Injunctive Relief.-When an employe organization is on strike for an extended period that would not permit the school entity to provide the period of instruction required by section 1501 by June 30, the Secretary of Education may initiate, in the appropriate county court of common pleas, appropriate injunctive proceedings providing for the required period of instruction.

(g) Prohibitions.

Section 1171-A.   Selective Strikes.-The work stoppage practice known as "selective strikes" shall be considered an illegal strike.   Any strike which does not comply with the definition of "strike" contained in this article shall be considered a selective strike.

Section 1172-A.   Utilization of Strike Breakers.-(a) Except as provided in subsection (b), during a legal strike, as defined by this article, the school entity, as defined by this article, shall not utilize persons other than those employes who have been actively employed by the school entity at any time during the previous twelve (12) months.

(b) A school entity may utilize persons other than those employes who have been actively employed by the school entity at any time during the previous twelve

(12) months:

(1) when the employe organization or employer rejects the determination of the majority of the arbitrators, and

(2) when a legal strike will prevent the completion of the period of instruction required by section 1501 by the later of:

(i) June 15; or

(ii) the last day of the school district's scheduled school year.

PUBLIC EMPLOYE RELATIONS ACT

(Act of July 23, 1970, P.L. 563, No. 195, as amended) (43 P.S., Sections 1101.101 to 1101.2301 inclusive)

An Act establishing rights in public employes to organize and bargain collectively through selected representatives; defining public employes to include employes of nonprofit organizations and institutions; providing compulsory mediation and fact-finding, for collective bargaining impasses; providing arbitration for certain public employes for collective bargaining impasses; defining the scope of collective bargaining; establishing unfair employe and employer practices; prohibiting strikes for certain public employes; permitting strikes under limited conditions; providing penalties for violations; and establishing procedures for implementation.

TABLE OF CONTENTS

Article I.	Public Policy
Article II.	Short Title
Article III.	Definition
Article IV.	Employe Rights
Article V.	Pennsylvania Labor Relations Board
Article VI.	Representation
Article VII.	Scope of Bargaining
Article VIII.	Collective Bargaining Impasse
Article IX.	Collective Bargaining Agreement
Article X.	Strikes Article XI. Picketing
Article XII.	Unfair Practices
Article XIII.	Prevention of Unfair Practices
Article XIV.	Unfair Practices During
Article VIII	Procedures
Article XV.	Judicial Review
Article XVI.	Investigatory Powers
Article XVII.	Employe Organizations
Article XVIII.	Conflict of Interest
Article XIX.	Penalties
Article XX.	Savings Provisions
Article XXI.	Separability
Article XXII.	Repeals
Article XXIII.	Effective Date

ARTICLE I Public Policy

Section 101. The General Assembly of the Commonwealth of Pennsylvania declares that it is the public policy of this Commonwealth and the purpose of this act to promote orderly and constructive relationships between all public employers and their employes subject, however, to the paramount right of the citizens of this Commonwealth to keep inviolate the guarantees for their health, safety and welfare. Unresolved disputes between the public employer and its employes are injurious to the public and the General Assembly is therefore aware that adequate means must be established for minimizing them and providing for their resolution. Within the limitations imposed upon the governmental processes by these rights of the public at large and recognizing that harmonious relationships are required between the public employer and its employes, the General Assembly has determined that the overall policy may best be accomplished by (1) granting to public employes the right to organize and choose freely their representatives; (2) requiring public employers to negotiate and bargain with employe organizations representing public employes and to enter into written agreements evidencing the result of such bargaining; and (3) establishing procedures to provide for the protection of the rights of the public employe, the public employer and the public at large.

ARTICLE II Short Title

Section 201. This act shall be known and may be cited as the "Public Employe Relations Act."

ARTICLE III Definitions

Section 301. As used in this act:

(1)   "Public employer" means the Commonwealth of Pennsylvania, its political subdivisions including school districts and any officer, board, commission, agency, authority, or other instrumentality thereof and any nonprofit

organization or institution and any charitable, religious, scientific, literary, recreational, health, educational or welfare institution receiving grants or appropriations from local, State or Federal governments but shall not include employers covered or presently subject to coverage under the act of June 1, 1937 (P.L. 1168), as amended, known as the "Pennsylvania Labor Relations Act, the act of July 5, 1935, Public Law 198, 74th Congress, as amended, known as the "National Labor Relations Act."

(2)   "Public employe" or "employe" means any individual employed by a public employer but shall not include elected officials, appointees of the Governor with the advice and consent of the Senate as required by law, management level employes, confidential employes, clergymen or other persons in a religious profession, employes or personnel at church offices or facilities when utilized primarily for religious purposes and those employes covered under the act of June 24, 1968 (Act No. 111), entitled "An act specifically authorizing collective bargaining between policemen and firemen and their public employers; providing for arbitration in order to settle disputes, and requiring compliance with collective bargaining agreements and findings of arbitrators."

(3)   "Employe organization" means an organization of any kind, or any agency or employe representation committee or plan in which membership includes public employes, and which exists for the purpose, in whole or in part, of dealing with employers concerning grievances, employe-employer disputes, wages, rates of pay, hours of employment, or conditions of work but shall not include any organization which practices discrimination in membership because of race, color, creed, national origin or political affiliation.

(4)   "Representative" means any individuals acting for public employers or employes and shall include employe organizations.

(5)   "Board" means the Pennsylvania Labor Relations Board.

(6)   "Supervisor" means any individual having authority in the interests of the employer to hire, transfer, suspend, layoff, recall, promote, discharge, assign, reward or discipline other employes or responsibly to direct them or adjust their grievances; or to a substantial degree effectively recommend such action, if in connection with the foregoing, the exercise of such authority is not merely routine or clerical in nature but calls for the use of independent judgment.

(7)   "Professional employe" means any employe whose work: (i) is predominantly intellectual and varied in character; (ii) requires consistent exercise of discretion and judgment; (iii) requires knowledge of an advanced nature in the field of science or learning customarily acquired by specialized study in an institution of higher learning or its equivalent; and (iv) is of such character that the output or result accomplished cannot be standardized in relation to a given period of time.

(8)   "Unfair practice" means any practice prohibited by Article XII of this act.

(9)   "Strike" means concerted action in failing to report for duty, the willful absence from one's position, the stoppage of work, slowdown, or the abstinence in whole or in part from the full, faithful and proper performance of the duties of employment for the purpose of inducing, influencing or coercing a change in the conditions or compensation or the rights, privileges, or obligations of employment.

(10) "Person" includes an individual, public employer, public employe, authority, commission, legal representative, labor organization, employe organization, profit or nonprofit corporation, trustee, board or association.

(11) "Membership dues deduction" means the practice of a public employer to deduct from the wages of a public employe, with his written consent, an amount for the payment of his membership dues in an employe organization, which deduction is transmitted by the public employer to the employe organization.

(12) "Budget submission date" means the date by which under the law or practice a public employer's proposed budget, or budget containing proposed expenditures applicable to such public employer is submitted to the Legislature or other similar body for final action. For the purposes of this act, the budget submission date for the Commonwealth shall be February 1 of each year and for a nonprofit organization or institution, the last day of its fiscal year.

(13) "Confidential employe" shall mean any employe who works: (i) in the personnel offices of a public employer and has access to information subject to use by the public employer in collective bargaining; or (ii) in a close continuing relationship with public officers or representatives associated with collective bargaining on behalf of the employer.

(14) "Wages" means hourly rates of pay, salaries or other forms of compensation for services rendered.

(15) "Commonwealth employe" means a public employe employed by the Commonwealth or any board, commission, agency, authority, or any other instrumentality thereof.

(16) "Management level employe" means any individual who is involved directly in the determination of policy or who responsibly directs the implementation thereof and shall include all employes above the first level of supervision.

(17) "Meet and discuss" means the obligation of a public employer upon request to meet at reasonable times and discuss recommendations submitted by representatives of public employes: Provided, That any decisions or determinations on matters so discussed shall remain with the public employer and be deemed final on any issue or issues raised.

(18) "Maintenance of membership" means that all employes who have joined an employe organization or who join the employe organization in the future must remain members for the duration of a collective bargaining agreement so providing with the proviso that any such employe or employes may resign from such employe organization during a period of fifteen days prior to the expiration of any such agreement.

(19) "First level of supervision" and "first level supervisor" means the lowest level at which an employe functions as a supervisor.

ARTICLE IV Employe Rights

Section 401. It shall be lawful for public employes to organize, form, join or assist in employe organizations or to engage in lawful concerted activities for the purpose of collective bargaining or other mutual aid and protection or to bargain collectively through representatives of their own free choice and such employes shall also have the right to refrain from any or all such activities, except as may be required pursuant to a maintenance of membership provision in a collective bargaining agreement.

ARTICLE V Pennsylvania Labor Relations Board

Section 501. The board shall exercise those powers and perform those duties which are specifically provided for in this act. These powers and duties shall be in addition to and exercised completely independent of any powers and duties specifically granted to it by other statutory enactments.

Section 502. The board shall have authority from time to time to make, amend and rescind such rules and regulations as may be necessary to carry out the provisions of this act. (As amended by Act of July 9, 1976, P.L. 877, No. 160.)

Section 503. The board shall establish after consulting representatives of employe organizations and of public employers, panels of qualified persons broadly representative of the public to be available to serve as members of fact-finding boards.

ARTICLE VI Representation

Section 601. Public employers may select representatives to act in their interest in any collective bargaining with representatives of public employes.

Section 602. (a) A public employer may recognize employe representatives for collective bargaining purposes, provided the parties jointly request certification by the board which shall issue such certification if it finds the unit appropriate.

(b) Any employe representatives in existence on January 1, 1970, shall so continue without the requirement of an election and certification until such time as a question concerning representation is appropriately raised under this act; or until the board would find the unit not to be appropriate after challenge by the public employer, a member of the unit or an employe organization. The appropriateness of the unit shall not be challenged until the expiration of any collective bargaining agreement in effect on the date of the passage of this act.

Section 603. (a) A public employe, a group of public employes or an employe organization may notify the public employer that thirty per cent or more of the public employes in an appropriate unit desire to be exclusively represented for collective bargaining purposes by a designated representative and request the public employer to consent to an election.

(b) If the public employer consents, the public employe, group of public employes or employe organization whichever applicable may submit in a form and manner established by the board an election request. Such request shall include a description of the unit deemed to be appropriate, the basis upon which it was determined that thirty per cent or more of the employes desired to be represented and a joinder by the public employer. The board may on the basis of the submissions order an election to be held or it may at its discretion investigate or conduct hearings to determine the validity of the matters contained in such submissions before determining whether or not an order should issue.

(c) If a public employer refuses to consent to an election, the party making the request may file a petition with the board alleging that thirty per cent or more of the public employes in an appropriate unit wish to be exclusively represented for collective bargaining purposes by a designated representative. The board shall send a copy of the petition to the public employer and provide for an appropriate hearing upon due notice. If it deems the allegations in the petition to be valid and the unit to be appropriate it shall order an election. If it finds to the contrary it may dismiss the petition or permit its amendment in accordance with procedures established by the board.

(d) If a public employer receives notification that thirty per cent or more of the public employes desire to be exclusively represented for collective bargaining purposes by a designated representative and the party giving notice does not thereafter seek an election the public employer may file a petition for the same with the board. The board shall then follow the procedures as established for petitions filed under subsection (c) of this section.

Section 604. The board shall determine the appropriateness of a unit which shall be the public employer unit or a subdivision thereof. In determining the appropriateness of the unit, the board shall:

(1) Take into consideration but shall not be limited to the following:

  (i) public employes must have an identifiable community of interest, and (ii) the effects of over fragmentation.

(2) Not decide that any unit is appropriate if such unit includes both professional and nonprofessional employes, unless a majority of such professional employes vote for inclusion in such unit.

(3) Not permit guards at prisons and mental hospitals, employes directly involved with and necessary to the functioning of the courts of this Commonwealth, or any individual employed as a guard to enforce against employes and other persons, rules to protect property of the employer or to protect the safety of persons on the employer's premises to be included in any unit with other public employes, each may form separate homogenous employe organizations with the proviso that organizations of the latter designated employe group may not be affiliated with any other organization representing or including as members, persons outside of the organization's classification.

(4) Take into consideration that when the Commonwealth is the employer, it will be bargaining on a Statewide basis unless issues involve working conditions peculiar to a given governmental employment locale. This section, however, shall not be deemed to prohibit multi-unit bargaining.

(5) Not permit employes at the first level of supervision to be included with any other units of public employes but shall permit them to form their own separate homogenous units. In determining supervisory status the board may take into consideration the extent to which supervisory and nonsupervisory functions are performed.

Section 605. Representation elections shall be conducted by secret ballot at such times and places selected by the board subject to the following:

(1) The board shall give no less than ten days notice of the time and place of such election.

(2) The board shall establish rules and regulations concerning the conduct of any election including but not limited to regulations which would guarantee the secrecy of the ballot.

(3) A representative may not be certified unless it receives a majority of the valid ballots cast.

(4) The board shall include on the ballot a choice of "no representative."

(5) In an election where none of the choices on the ballot receives a majority, a run-off election shall be conducted, the ballot providing for a selection between the two choices or parties receiving the highest and the second highest number of ballots cast in the election.

(6) The board, shall certify the results of said election within five working days after the final tally of votes if no charge is filed by any person alleging that an "unfair practice" existed in connection with said election. If the board has reason to believe that such allegations are valid, it shall set a time for hearing on the matter after due notice. Any such hearing shall be conducted within two weeks of the date of receipt of such charge. If the board determines that the outcome of the election was affected by the "unfair practice" charged or for any other "unfair practice" it may deem existed, it shall require corrective action and order a new election. If the board determines that no unfair practice existed or if it existed, did not affect the outcome of the election, it shall immediately certify the election results.

(7) (i) No election shall be conducted pursuant to this section in any appropriate bargaining unit within which in the preceding twelve-month period an election shall have been held nor during the term of any lawful collective bargaining agreement between a public employer and an employe representative. This restriction shall not apply to that period of time covered by any collective bargaining agreement which exceeds three years. For the purposes of this section, extensions of agreements shall not affect the expiration date of the original agreement.

(ii) Petitions for elections may be filed with the board not sooner than ninety days nor later than sixty days before the expiration date of any collective bargaining agreement or after the expiration date until such time as a new written agreement has been entered into. For the purposes of this section, extensions of agreements shall not affect the expiration date of the original agreement.

Section 606. Representatives selected by public employes in a unit appropriate for collective bargaining purposes shall be the exclusive representative of all the employes in such unit to bargain on wages, hours, terms and conditions of employment: Provided, That any individual employe or a group of employes shall have the right at any time to present grievances to their employer and to have them adjusted without the intervention of the bargaining representative as long as the adjustment is not inconsistent with the terms of a collective bargaining contract then in effect: And, provided further, That the bargaining representative has been given an opportunity to be present at such adjustment.

Section 607. If there is a duly certified representative: (i) a public employe or a group of public employes may file a petition for decertification provided it is supported by a thirty per cent showing of interest, or (ii) a public employer alleging a good faith doubt of the majority status of said representative may file a petition in accordance with the rules and regulations established by the board, subject to the provisions of clause (7) of section 605.

ARTICLE VII Scope of Bargaining

Section 701. Collective bargaining is the performance of the mutual obligation of the public employer and the representative of the public employes to meet at reasonable times and confer in good faith with respect to wages, hours and other terms and conditions of employment, or the negotiation of an agreement or any question arising thereunder and the execution of a written contract incorporating any agreement reached but such obligation does not compel either party to agree to a proposal or require the making of a concession.

Section 702. Public employers shall not be required to bargain over matters of inherent managerial policy, which shall include but shall not be limited to such areas of discretion or policy as the functions and programs of the public employer, standards of services, its overall budget, utilization of technology, the organizational structure and selection and direction of personnel. Public employers, however, shall be required to meet and discuss on policy matters affecting wages, hours and terms and conditions of employment as well as the impact thereon upon request by public employe representatives.

Section 703. The parties to the collective bargaining process shall not effect or implement a provision in a collective bargaining agreement if the implementation of that provision would be in violation of, or inconsistent with, or in conflict with any statute or statutes enacted by the General Assembly of the Commonwealth of Pennsylvania or the provisions of municipal home rule charters.

Section 704. Public employers shall not be required to bargain with units of first level supervisors or their representatives but shall be required to meet and discuss with first level supervisors or their representatives, on matters deemed to be bargainable for other public employes covered by this act.

Section 705. Membership dues deductions and maintenance of membership are proper subjects of bargaining with the proviso that as to the latter, the payment of dues and assessments while members, may be the only requisite employment condition.

Section 706. Nothing contained in this act shall impair the employer's right to hire employes or to discharge employes for just cause consistent with existing legislation.

ARTICLE VIII Collective Bargaining Impasse

Section 801. If after a reasonable period of negotiation, a dispute or impasse exists between the representatives of the public employer and the public employes, the parties may voluntarily submit to mediation but if no agreement is reached between the parties within twenty-one days after negotiations have commenced, but in no event later than one hundred fifty days prior to the "budget submission date," and mediation has not been utilized by the parties, both parties shall immediately, in writing, call in the service of the Pennsylvania Bureau of Mediation.

Section 802. Once mediation has commenced, it shall continue for so long as the parties have not reached an agreement. If, however, an agreement has not been reached within twenty days after mediation has commenced or in no event later than one hundred thirty days prior to the "budget submission date," the Bureau of Mediation shall notify the board of this fact. Upon receiving such notice the board may in its discretion appoint a fact-finding panel which panel may consist of either one or three members. If a panel is so designated or selected it shall hold hearings and take oral or written testimony and shall have subpoena power. If during this time the parties have not reached an agreement, the panel shall make findings of fact and recommendations:

(1) The findings of fact and recommendations shall be sent by registered mail to the board and to both parties not more than forty days after the Bureau of Mediation has notified the board as provided in the preceding paragraph.

(2) Not more than ten days after the findings and recommendations shall have been sent, the parties shall notify the board and each other whether or not they accept the recommendations of the fact-finding panel and if they do not, the panel shall publicize its findings of fact and recommendations.

(3) Not less than five days nor more than ten days after the publication of the findings of fact and recommendations, the parties shall again inform the board and each other whether or not they will accept the recommendations of the fact-finding panel.

(4) The Commonwealth shall pay one-half the cost of the fact-finding panel; the remaining one-half of the cost shall be divided equally between the parties. The board shall establish rules and regulations under which panels shall operate, including, but not limited to, compensation for panel members.

Section 803. If the representatives of either or both the public employes and the public employer refuse to submit to the procedures set forth in sections 801 and 802 of this article, such refusal shall be deemed a refusal to bargain in good faith and unfair practice charges may be filed by the submitting party or the board may on its own, issue an unfair practice complaint and conduct such hearings and issue such orders as provided for in Article XIII.

Section 804. Nothing in this article shall prevent the parties from submitting impasses to voluntary binding arbitration with the proviso the decisions of the arbitrator which would require legislative enactment to the effective shall be considered advisory only.

Section 805. Notwithstanding any other provisions of this act where representatives of units of guards at prisons or mental hospitals or units of employes directly involved with and necessary to the functioning of the courts of this Commonwealth have reached an impasse in collective bargaining and mediation as required in section 801 of this article has not resolved the dispute, the impasse shall be submitted to a panel of arbitrators whose decision shall be final and binding upon both parties with the proviso that the decisions of the arbitrators which would require legislative enactment to be effective shall be considered advisory only.

Section 806. Panels of arbitrators for bargaining units referred to in section 805 of this article shall be selected in the following manner:

(1) Each party shall select one member of the panel, the two so selected shall choose the third member.

(2) If the members so selected are unable to agree upon the third member within ten days from the date of their selection, the board shall submit the names of seven persons, each party shall alternately strike one name until one shall remain. The public employer shall strike the first name. The person so remaining shall be the third member and chairman.

Section 806. (A) Whenever a panel of arbitrators is hereafter constituted pursuant to the provisions of section 806 of the act of July 23, 1970 (P.L. 563, No. 195), known as the "Public Employe Relations Act," the cost of the arbitrator selected by each party shall be paid by the respective party selecting the arbitrator. The cost of the impartial arbitrator selected by the arbitrators already selected or selected in accordance with the procedure set forth in section 806(2) of the act of July 23, 1970 (P.L. 563, No. 195), known as the "Public Employe Relations Act," shall be paid by the Pennsylvania Labor Relations Board. (As added by the Act of May 20, 1976, P. L. 142, No. 67.)

Section 807. Repealed. Act of May 20, 1976, P.L. 142, No. 67.

ARTICLE IX Collective Bargaining Agreement

Section 901. Once an agreement is reached between the representatives of the public employes and the public employer, the agreement shall be reduced to writing and signed by the parties. Any provisions of the contract requiring legislative action will only be effective if such legislation is enacted.

Section 902. If the provisions of the constitution or bylaws of an employe organization requires ratification of a collective bargaining agreement by its membership, only those members who belong to the bargaining unit involved shall be entitled to vote on such ratification notwithstanding such provisions.

Section 903. Arbitration of disputes or grievances arising out of the interpretation of the provisions of a collective bargaining agreement is mandatory. The procedure to be adopted is a proper subject of bargaining with the proviso that the final step shall provide for a binding decision by an arbitrator or a tripartite board of arbitrators as the parties may agree. Any decisions of the arbitrators or arbitrators requiring legislation will only be effective if such legislation is enacted:

(1)   If the parties cannot voluntarily agree upon the selection of an arbitrator, the parties shall notify the Bureau of Mediation of their inability to do so. The Bureau of Mediation shall then submit to the parties the names of seven arbitrators. Each party shad alternately strike a name until one name remains. The public employer shall strike the first name. The person remaining shall be the arbitrator.

(2)   The costs of arbitration shall be shared equally by the parties. Fees paid to arbitrators shall be based on a schedule established by the Bureau of Mediation.

Section 904. Any provision of any collective bargaining agreement in existence on January 1, 1970 which is inconsistent with any provision of this act but not otherwise illegal shall continue valid until the expiration of such contract. The parties to such agreements may continue voluntarily to bargain on any such items after the expiration date of any such agreement and for so long as these items remain in any future agreement.

ARTICLE X Strikes

Section 1001. Strikes by guards at prisons or mental hospitals, or employes directly involved with and necessary to the functioning of the courts of this Commonwealth are prohibited at any time. If a strike occurs the public employer shall forthwith initiate in the court of common pleas of the jurisdiction where the strike occurs, an action for appropriate equitable relief including but not limited to injunctions. If the strike involves Commonwealth employes, the chief legal officer of the public employer or the Attorney General where required by law shall institute an action for equitable relief, either in the court of common pleas of the jurisdiction where the strike has occurred or the Commonwealth Court.

Section 1002. Strikes by public employes during the pendency of collective bargaining procedures set forth in sections 801 and 802 of Article VIII are prohibited. In the event of a strike during this period the public employer shall forthwith initiate an action for the same relief and utilizing the same procedures required for prohibited strikes under section 1001.

Section 1003. If a strike by public employes occurs after the collective bargaining processes set forth in sections 801 and 802 of Article VIII of this act have been completely utilized and exhausted, it shall not be prohibited unless or until such a strike creates a clear and present danger or threat to the health, safety or welfare of the public. In such cases the public employer shall initiate, in the court of common pleas of the jurisdiction where such strike occurs, an action for equitable relief including but not limited to appropriate injunctions and shall be entitled to such relief if the court finds that the strike creates a clear and present danger or threat to the health, safety or welfare of the public. If the strike involves Commonwealth employes, the chief legal officer of the public employer or the Attorney General where required by law shall institute an action for equitable relief in the court of common pleas of the jurisdiction where the strike has occurred or the Commonwealth Court. Prior to the filing of any complaint in equity under the provisions of this section the moving party shall serve upon the defendant a copy of said complaint as provided for in the Pennsylvania Rules of Civil Procedure applicable to such actions. Hearings shall be required before relief is granted under this section and notices of the same shall be served in the manner required for the original process with a duty imposed upon the court to hold such hearings forthwith.

Section 1004. An unfair practice by a public employer shall not be a defense to a prohibited strike. Unfair practices by the employer during the collective bargaining processes shall receive priority by the board as set forth in Article XIV.

Section 1005. If a public employe refuses to comply with a lawful order of a court of competent jurisdiction issued for a violation of any of the provisions of this article the public employer shall initiate an action for contempt and if the public employe is adjudged guilty of such contempt, he shall be subject to suspension, demotion or discharge at the discretion of the public employer, provided the public employer has not exercised that discretion in violation of clauses (1), (2), (3) and (4) of subsection (a) of section 1201, Article XII.

Section 1006. No public employe shall be entitled to pay or compensation from the public employer for the period engaged in any strike.

Section 1007. In the event any public employe refuses to obey an order issued by a court of competent jurisdiction for a violation of the provisions of this article, the punishment for such contempt may be by fine or by imprisonment in the prison of the county where the court is sitting or both in the discretion of the court.

Section 1008. Where an employe organization wilfully disobeys a lawful order of a court of competent jurisdiction issued for a violation of the provisions of this article, the punishment for each day that such contempt persists may be by a fine fixed in the discretion of the court.

Section 1009. In fixing the amount of the fine or imprisonment for contempt, the court shall consider all the facts and circumstances directly related to the contempt including but not limited to:

(i) any unfair practices conducted by the public employer during the collective bargaining processes;

(ii) the extent of the willful defiance or resistance to the court's order;

(iii) the impact of the strike on the health, safety or welfare of the public, and (iv) the ability of the employe organization or the employe to pay the fine imposed.

Section 1010. Nothing in this article shall prevent the parties from voluntarily requesting the court for a diminution or suspension of any fines or penalties imposed. Any requests by employe representatives for such participation by the public employer shall be subject to the requirements of "meet and discuss."

ARTICLE XI Picketing

Section 1101. Public employes other than those engaged in a nonprohibited strike who refuse to cross a picket line shall be deemed to be engaged in a prohibited strike and shall be subject to the terms and conditions of Article X pertaining to prohibited strikes.

ARTICLE XII Unfair Practices

Section 1201. (a) Public employers, their agents or representatives are prohibited from:

(1) Interfering, restraining or coercing employes in the exercise of the rights guaranteed in Article IV of this act.

(2) Dominating or interfering with the formation, existence or administration of any employe organization.

(3) Discriminating in regard to hire or tenure of employment or any term or condition of employment to encourage or discourage membership in any employe organization.

(4) Discharging or otherwise discriminating against an employe because he has signed or filed an affidavit, petition or complaint or given any information or testimony under this act.

(5) Refusing to bargain collectively in good faith with an employe representative which is the exclusive representative of employes in an appropriate unit, including but not limited to the discussing of grievances with the exclusive representative.

(6) Refusing to reduce a collective bargaining agreement to writing and sign such agreement.

(7) Violating any of the rules and regulations established by the board regulating the conduct of representation elections.

(8) Refusing to comply with the provisions of an arbitration award deemed binding under section 903 of Article IX.

(9) Refusing to comply with the requirements of "meet and discuss."

(b) Employe organizations, their agents, or representatives, or public employes are prohibited from:

(1) Restraining or coercing employes in the exercise of the rights guaranteed in Article IV of this act.

(2) Restraining or coercing a public employer in the selection of his representative for the purposes of collective bargaining or the adjustment of grievances.

(3) Refusing to bargain collectively in good faith with a public employer, if they have been designated in accordance with the provisions of this act as the exclusive representative of employes in an appropriate unit.

(4) Violating any of the rules and regulations established by the board regulating the conduct of representation elections.

(5) Refusing to reduce a collective bargaining agreement to writing and sign such agreement.

(6) Calling, instituting, maintaining or conducting a strike or boycott against any public employer or picketing any place of business of a public employer on account of any jurisdictional controversy.

(7) Engaging in, or inducing or encouraging any individual employed by any person to engage in a strike or refusal to handle goods or perform services; or threatening, coercing or restraining any person where an object thereof is to

    i. force or require any public employer to cease dealing or doing business with any other person or (ii) force or require a public employer to recognize for representation purposes an employe organization not certified by the board.

(8) Refusing to comply with the provisions of an arbitration award deemed binding under section 903 of Article IX.

(9) Refusing to comply with the requirements of "meet and discuss."

ARTICLE XIII Prevention of Unfair Practices

Section 1301. The board is empowered, as hereinafter provided, to prevent any person from engaging in any unfair practice listed in Article XII of this act. This power shall be exclusive and shall not be affected by any other means of adjustment or prevention that have been or may be established by agreement, law, or otherwise.

Section 1302. Whenever it is charged by any interested party that any person has engaged in or is engaging in any such unfair practice, the board, or any member or designated agent thereof, shall have authority to issue and cause to be served upon such person a complaint, stating the charges in the respect, and containing a notice of hearing before the board, or any member or designated agent thereof, at a place therein fixed not less than five days after the serving of said complaint. Any such complaint may be amended by the board, member or agent conducting the hearing at any time prior to the issuance of an order based thereon. The person so complained of shall have the right to file an answer to the original or amended complaint and to appear in person, or otherwise, to give testimony at the place and time set in the complaint. In the discretion of a member or agent conducting the hearing or of the board, any other person may be allowed to intervene in the said proceeding and to present testimony. In any such proceeding, the rules of evidence prevailing in courts of law or equity shall be followed but shall not be controlling.

Section 1303. Testimony shall be taken at the hearing and filed with the board. The board upon notice may take further testimony or hear argument. If, upon all the testimony taken, the board shall determine that any person named in the complaint has engaged in or is engaging in any such unfair practice, the board shall state its findings of fact, and issue and cause to be served on such person an order requiring such person to cease and desist from such unfair practice, and to take such reasonable affirmative action, including reinstatement of employes discharged in violation of Article XII of this act, with or without back pay, as will effectuate the policies of this act. Such order may further require such person to make reasonable reports, from time to time, showing the extent to which the order has been complied with. If, upon all the testimony, the board shall be of the opinion that the person or persons named in the complaint has not engaged in or is not engaging in any such unfair practice, then the board shall make its findings of fact and shall issue an order dismissing the complaint. A copy of such findings of fact, conclusions of law, and order shall be mailed to all parties to the proceedings.

Section 1304. Until a transcript of the record in a case shall have been filed in a court as hereinafter provided, the board may at any time, upon reasonable notice, and in such manner as it shall deem proper, modify or set aside, in whole or in part, any finding or order made or issued by it: Provided, That any agreement made between an employer and a bona fide employe organization, and all the provisions thereof, shall be entitled to full force and effect unless the board specifically finds that these provisions involve the commission of an unfair practice within the meaning of Article XII of this act.

Section 1305. The proceedings before the board or before any of its examiners shall be conducted with speed and dispatch. No findings shall be made on the basis of evidence relating to acts which occurred prior to the original passage of this act.

Section 1306. All cases in which complaints are actually issued by the board, shall be prosecuted before the board or its examiner, or both, by the representatives of the employe organization or party filing the charge, and, in addition thereto or in lieu thereof if the Department of Justice sees fit, by a deputy attorney general especially assigned to this type of case. No examiner shall have any other position with the government of this State or of the United States or with the Pennsylvania Labor Relations Board while in the employ of the board.

ARTICLE XIV Unfair Practices During Article VIII Procedures

Section 1401. Notwithstanding any of the provisions of Article XIII, the board upon the filing of a charge alleging the commission of an unfair labor practice committed during, or arising out of the collective bargaining procedures set forth in sections 801 and 802 of Article VIII of this act, shall be empowered to petition the court of competent jurisdiction for appropriate relief or restraining order. Upon filing of any such petition the board shall cause notice thereof to be served upon such person and thereupon the court shall have jurisdiction to grant to the board such temporary relief or restraining order as it deems just and proper.

ARTICLE XV Judicial Review

Section 1501. The board shall except where an employe of the Commonwealth is involved have power to petition the court of common pleas of any county wherein the unfair practice in question occurred, or wherein any person charged with the commission of any unfair practice resides or transacts business, for the enforcement of such order and for appropriate temporary relief or restraining order, and shall certify and file in the court a transcript of the entire record in the proceeding, including the pleadings and testimony upon which such order was entered and the findings and order of the board. In the instance of the exception involving the said Commonwealth employes, the board shall file its petition in the Commonwealth Court. Upon such filing, the court shall cause notice thereof to be served upon such person, and thereupon shall have jurisdiction of the proceeding and of the question determined therein, and shall have power to grant such temporary relief, restraining or mandamus order as it deems just and proper or requisite to effectuate the policies of this act and to make and enter upon the pleadings, testimony, and proceedings set forth in such transcript a decree enforcing, modifying and enforcing as so modified, or setting aside, in whole or in part, the order of the board. The parties before the court shall be the board, the person charged with the commission of any unfair labor practice, and may include the charging party. No objection that has not been urged before the board, its members or agents shall be considered by the court unless the failure or neglect to urge such objection shall be excused because of extraordinary circumstances. The findings of the board as to the facts, if supported by substantial and legally credible evidence, shall be conclusive. If either party shall apply to the court for leave to adduce additional evidence, and shall show to the satisfaction of the court, that such additional evidence is material, and that there were reasonable grounds for the failure to adduce such evidence at the hearing before the board, its members or agent, the court may order such additional evidence to be taken before the board, its members or agent, and to be made a part of the transcript. The board may modify its findings as to the facts or make new findings by reason of additional evidence so taken and filed, and it shall file such modified or new findings which, if supported by substantial and legally credible evidence, shall be conclusive, and shall file its recommendations, if any, for the modification or setting aside of its original order. (As amended by Act of June 3, 1971, P.L. 146, No. 6.)

Section 1502. Repealed. Act of April 28, 1978, P.L. 202, No. 53. (For disposition of repealed subject matter, relating to review in court of common pleas and Supreme Court, see Disposition Table preceding Title 42, Judiciary and Judicial Procedures, of the Pennsylvania Consolidated Statutes Annotated.)

Section 1503. The commencement of proceedings under sections 1501 or 1502 of this article shall not, unless specifically ordered by the court, operate as a stay of the board's order.

Section 1504. When granting appropriate temporary relief, a restraining or mandamus order or making and entering a decree enforcing, modifying, or enforcing as so modified, or setting aside in whole or in part an order of the board, as provided in this section, the jurisdiction of courts sitting in equity shall not be limited by acts pertaining to equity jurisdiction of courts. The act of June 2, 1937 (P.L. 1198), known as the "Labor Anti-Injunction Act," shall not be applicable to orders of the board, or to court orders enforcing orders of the board, or any provision of this act, or to violations of any order of the board, or of court orders enforcing orders of the board, or any provisions of this act.

Section 1505. No petitions or charges involving questions arising under clause (2) of subsection (a) of section 1201 of Article XII shall relieve the board of determining any questions arising under sections 603, 604 and 605 of Article VI immediately, and in their regular and normal order, and the making of a certification thereon if such is warranted. No petition or charge shall be entertained which relates to acts which occurred or statements which were made more than four months prior to the filing of the petition or charge. (As affected by Act of April 28, 1978, P.L. 202, No. 53.)

ARTICLE XVI Investigatory Powers

Section 1601. For the purpose of all hearings and investigations which, in the opinion of the board, are necessary and proper for the exercise of the powers vested in it by Article VI and Article XIII, and for the purpose of investigating and considering disputes, other than a question concerning the representation of employes, which it shall be the duty of the board to undertake whenever petitioned so to do by either an employe organization, an employer, or the representative of any unit of employes, the board shall have the Investigatory powers granted in this article.

Section 1602. The board or its duly authorized agents shall at all reasonable times have access to, for the purpose of examination and the right to copy, any evidence of any person being investigated or proceeded against that relates to any matter under investigation or in question. Any member of the board shall have the power to issue subpoenas requiring the attendance and testimony of witnesses and the production of any evidence that relates to any matter under investigation or in question before the board, its members or agent conducting the hearing or investigation. Such subpoenas shall be issued as a matter of right upon the request of either party at any time during the pendency of a proceeding. Any member of the board, or any agent designated by the board for such purposes, may administer oaths and affirmations, examine witnesses, and receive evidence.

Section 1603. If any witness resides outside of the Commonwealth or through illness or other cause is unable to testify before the board or its members or agent conducting the hearing or investigation, his or her testimony or deposition may be taken within or without this Commonwealth, in such manner and in such forms as the board or its members or agent conducting the hearing, may by special or general rule prescribe.

Section 1604. In case of contumacy or refusal to obey a subpoena issued to any person the court, upon application by the board, shall have jurisdiction to issue to such person an order requiring such person to appear before the board, its members or agents, there to produce evidence if so ordered, or there to give testimony touching the matter under investigation or in question, and any failure to obey such order of the courts may be punished by said court as a contempt thereof. (As affected by Act of April 28, 1978, P.L. 202, No. 53.)

Section 1605. No person shall be excused from attending and testifying or from producing books, records, correspondence, documents or other evidence in obedience to the subpoena of the board on the ground that the testimony or evidence required of him may tend to incriminate him or subject him to a penalty or forfeiture, but no individual shall be prosecuted or subjected to any penalty or forfeiture for, or on account of, any transaction, matter or thing concerning which he is compelled, after having claimed his privilege against self-incrimination, to testify or produce evidence, except that such individual so testifying shall not be exempt from prosecution and punishment for perjury committed in so testifying.

Section 1606. Complaints, orders and other process and papers of the board, its members or agent may be served, either personally or by registered mail or by telegraph or by leaving a copy thereof at the principal office or place of business of the person required to be served. The verified return by the individual so serving the same, setting forth the manner of such service, shall be proof of the same and the return post office receipt or telegraph receipt thereof when registered and mailed or telegraphed as aforesaid, shall be proof of service of the same. Witnesses summoned before the board, its members or agent shall be paid the same fees and mileage that are paid witnesses in the courts of this Commonwealth, and witnesses whose depositions are taken and the person taking the same shall severally be entitled to the same fees as are paid for like services in the courts of this Commonwealth.

Section 1607. Repealed. Act of April 28, 1978, P.L. 202, No. 53. (For disposition of repealed subject matter, relating to place of service, see Disposition Table preceding Title 42, Judiciary and Judicial Procedures, of the Pennsylvania Consolidated Statutes Annotated.)

ARTICLE XVII Employe Organizations

Section 1701. No employe organization shall make any contribution out of the funds of the employe organization either directly or indirectly to any political party or organization or in support of any political candidate for public office. The board shall establish such rules and regulations as it may find necessary to prevent the circumvention or evasion of the provisions of this section. If an employe organization has made contributions in violation of this section it shall file with the board a report or affidavit evidencing such contributions within ninety days of the end of its fiscal year. Such report or affidavit shall be signed by its president and treasurer or corresponding principals. Any employe organization which violates the provisions of this section or fails to file any required report or affidavit or files a false report or affidavit shall be subject to a fine of not more than two thousand dollars ($2,000). Any person who wilfully violates this section, or who makes a false statement knowing it to be false, or who knowingly fails to disclose a material fact shall be fined not more than one thousand dollars ($1,000) or imprisoned for not more than thirty days or both. Each individual required to sign affidavits or reports under this section shall be personally responsible for filing such report or affidavit and for any statement contained therein he knows to be false. Nothing herein shall be deemed to prohibit voluntary contributions by individuals to political parties or candidates.

ARTICLE XVIII Conflict of Interest

Section 1801. (a) No person who is a member of the same local, State, national or international organization as the employe organization with which the public employer is bargaining or who has an interest in the outcome of such bargaining which interest is in conflict with the interest of the public employer, shall participate on behalf of the public employer in the collective bargaining processes with the proviso that such person may, where entitled, vote on the ratification of an agreement.

(b) Any person who violates subsection (a) of this section shall be immediately removed by the public employer from his role, if any, in the collective bargaining negotiations or in any matter in connection with such negotiations.

ARTICLE XIX Penalties

Section 1901. Any person who shall wilfully resist, prevent, impede or interfere with any member of the board, or any of its agents, in the performance of duties pursuant to this act, shall be guilty of a misdemeanor, and, upon conviction thereof, shall be sentenced to pay a fine of not more than five thousand dollars ($5,000), or by imprisonment for not more than one year, or both.

ARTICLE XX Savings Provisions

Section 2001. The rights granted to certain public employes by the following acts or parts thereof shall not be repealed or diminished by this act:

(1) Section 24 of the act of August 14, 1963 (P.L. 984), known as the "Metropolitan Transportation Authorities Act of 1963."

(2) The act of November 27, 1967 (P.L. 628), entitled "An Act protecting the rights of employes of existing transportation systems which are acquired by cities of the third class or any authority thereof or certain joint authorities; requiring cities of the third class or any authority thereof or any such joint authority to enter into contracts with labor organizations acting for such employes, and providing for arbitration in case of disputes."

(3) Section 13.2 of the act of April 6, 1956 (P.L. 1414), known as the "Second Class County Port Authority Act."

Section 2002. This act shall not be construed to repeal the act of June 24, 1968 (Act No. 111), entitled "An act specifically authorizing collective bargaining between policemen and firemen and their public employers; providing for arbitration in order to settle disputes, and requiring compliance with collective bargaining agreements and findings of arbitrators."

Section 2003. Present provisions of an ordinance of the City of Philadelphia approved April 4, 1961, entitled "An Ordinance to authorize the Mayor to enter into an agreement with District Council 33, American Federation of State, County and Municipal Employes, A.F.L.-C.I.O., Philadelphia and vicinity regrading its representation of certain City Employes," which are inconsistent with the provisions of this act shall remain in full force and effect so long as the present provisions of that ordinance are valid and operative.

ARTICLE XXI Separability

Section 2101. If any clause, sentence, paragraph or part of this act, or the application thereof to any person or circumstances, shall, for any reason, be adjudged by a court of competent jurisdiction to be invalid, such judgment shall not affect, impair or invalidate the remainder of this act and the application of such provision to other persons or circumstances, but shall be confined in its operation to the clause, sentence, paragraph, or part thereof, directly involved in the controversy in which such judgment shall have been rendered and to the person or circumstances involved. It is hereby declared to be the legislative intent that this act would have been adopted had such invalid provisions not been included.

ARTICLE XXII Repeals

Section 2201. The act of June 30, 1947 (P.L. 1183), entitled "An act relation to strikes by public employes; prohibiting such strikes; providing that such employes by striking terminate their employment; providing for reinstatement under certain conditions; providing for a grievance procedure; and providing for hearings before civil service and tenure authorities, and in certain cases before the Pennsylvania Labor Relations Board," is hereby repealed as to those public employes covered by the provisions of this act, and any penalties or other limitations currently in force or presently pending against any public employes, shall be deemed null and void.

ARTICLE XXIII Effective Date

Section 2301. This act shall take effect in ninety days, except that provisions of Article V and the amnesty provisions of the repeater shall take effect immediately.

About the Author

Richard W. Perhacs was born in Pittsburgh in 1949. He was educated in the public schools in the City of Pittsburgh, Baldwin Whitehall and West Mifflin Area districts. He graduated from high school in the West Mifflin Area School District in 1967 and attended Saint Vincent College in Latrobe, where he graduated with honors in 1971 with a degree in political science. He received his law degree with honors from Duquesne University in 1974. Following law school, Mr. Perhacs served as a law clerk to the Honorable Harry A. Kramer of the Commonwealth Court of Pennsylvania from 1974 until 1976.

After completing his service to the Court, Mr. Perhacs began private practice in Erie with Richard H. Zamboldi, an experienced labor and employment attorney. In 1990, Mr. Perhacs and Mr. Zamboldi relocated their practice to Knox McLaughlin Gornall and Sennett where they established the firm's Labor and Employment Group, which now numbers seven attorneys. Mr. Perhacs has served as Chairman of the Group and is a member of the firm's Board of Directors.

During the course of his career, spanning more than 35 years of private practice, Mr. Perhacs has represented the management of more than 25 different school districts, including the School District of the City of Erie, and his home district in Millcreek Township. His practice also has involved the representation of numerous municipalities and municipal authorities, non-profit organizations, and private companies. He has twice been appointed by the County Executive as Solicitor for Labor Relations for the County of Erie and serves as special counsel to the Mayor of the City of Erie. He is a frequent lecturer on educational labor relations and served as an Adjunct Professor at Gannon University where he developed and taught a course in practical labor relations for MBA candidates.

Mr. Perhacs' personal interests include a lifelong interest in aviation. A former commercial pilot, he was an active flight instructor for many years, and holds both instrument and multi-engine ratings on his commercial certificate. A passionate hockey fan, he holds a USA Hockey Level IV advanced coaching certificate and coached youth travel hockey for 10 years. He also serves as a test proctor for American MENSA. In recent years, he has devoted much of his free time to traveling in Central America and learning to speak Spanish. His long-range plans include becoming an ESL teacher and performing volunteer work with the Latino immigrant community.

Mr. Perhacs lives with his wife, Grace, and sons, Doug and Sean, in Millcreek Township, Erie County. Both of his sons attended school in the Millcreek Township School District. You can read more about his practice at www.kmgslaw.com . Comments and inquiries can be directed to rperhacs@kmgslaw.com.